COLLABORATIVE FEDERALISM
Economic Reform in Australia in the 1990s

This original and provocative study of federalism identifies a new pattern of intergovernmental relations in Australia. Through his general discussion of the nature of the Australian federal system, and close analysis of recent developments in Australian politics and policy-making, Painter argues that our federal system is being fundamentally reshaped as state and Commonwealth governments cooperate more closely than ever before on joint policy-making schemes. Much of this collaboration has been prompted by the need for micro-economic reform in the 1990s, and increasing concern about the degree of overlap, inefficiency and duplication across the federal system. The book includes a narrative account of the often fraught progress of the Special Premiers' Conferences and the Council of Australian Governments. It also includes detailed discussion of a number of key examples.

Martin Painter is Head of the Department of Government and Public Administration at the University of Sydney. He is a National Fellow of the Institute of Public Administration Australia, and has been co-editor of the *Australian Journal of Public Administration* and president of the Australasian Political Studies Association. He has published widely on public policy, public management, microeconomic reform and public sector restructuring and is the author of *Steering the Modern State* (1987) and editor of *Managerialism: The Great Debate* (1997).

RESHAPING AUSTRALIAN INSTITUTIONS

Series editors: Geoffrey Brennan and Francis G. Castles, Research School of Social Sciences, Australian National University.

Published in association with the Research School of Social Sciences, Australian National University.

This program of publications arises from the School's initiative in sponsoring a fundamental rethinking of Australia's key institutions before the centenary of Federation in 2001.

Published in this program will be the work of scholars from the Australian National University and elsewhere who are researching and writing on the institutions of the nation. The scope of the program includes the institutions of public governance, intergovernmental relations, Aboriginal Australia, gender, population, the environment, the economy, business, the labour market, the welfare state, the city, education, the media, criminal justice and the Constitution.

Brian Galligan *A Federal Republic*
    0 521 37354 9 hardback 0 521 37746 3 paperback
Patrick Troy (ed.) *Australian Cities*
    0 521 48197 X hardback 0 521 48437 5 paperback
Ian Marsh *Beyond the Two Party System*
    0 521 46223 1 hardback 0 521 46779 9 paperback
Elim Papadakis *Environmental Politics and*
    Institutional Change
    0 521 55407 1 hardback 0 521 55631 7 paperback
Chilla Bulbeck *Living Feminism*
    0 521 46042 5 hardback 0 521 46596 6 paperback
John Uhr *Deliberative Democracy in Australia*
    0 521 62458 4 hardback 0 521 62465 7 paperback
Mitchell Dean and Barry Hindess (eds)
    Governing Australia
    0 521 58357 8 hardback 0 521 58671 2 paperback
Nicolas Peterson and Will Sanders (eds) *Citizenship*
    and Indigenous Australians
    0 521 62195 X hardback 0 521 62736 2 paperback

COLLABORATIVE FEDERALISM

Economic Reform in Australia in the 1990s

MARTIN PAINTER

CAMBRIDGE UNIVERSITY PRESS
Cambridge, New York, Melbourne, Madrid, Cape Town,
Singapore, São Paulo, Delhi, Mexico City

Cambridge University Press
The Edinburgh Building, Cambridge CB2 8RU, UK

Published in the United States of America by Cambridge University Press, New York

www.cambridge.org
Information on this title: www.cambridge.org/9780521590716

© Martin Painter 1998

This publication is in copyright. Subject to statutory exception
and to the provisions of relevant collective licensing agreements,
no reproduction of any part may take place without the written
permission of Cambridge University Press.

First published 1998

A catalogue record for this publication is available from the British Library

Library of Congress Cataloguing in Publication Data
Painter, Martin, 1947– .
Collaborative federalism: economic reform in Australia in the
1990s/Martin Painter.
p.   cm. – (Reshaping Australian institutions)
Includes bibliographical references and index.
ISBN 0-521-59071-X (alk. paper)
1. Federal government – Australia. 2. Australia – Politics and
government – 1945– . 3. Australia – Economic policy. I. Title.
II. Series.
JQ4020.S8P35   1998
320.8´3´0994–dc21   96-13520

ISBN 978-0-521-59071-6 Hardback
ISBN 978-0-521-12056-2 Paperback

Cambridge University Press has no responsibility for the persistence or
accuracy of URLs for external or third-party internet websites referred to in
this publication, and does not guarantee that any content on such websites is,
or will remain, accurate or appropriate. Information regarding prices, travel
timetables, and other factual information given in this work is correct at
the time of first printing but Cambridge University Press does not guarantee
the accuracy of such information thereafter.

Contents

List of Abbreviations		viii
Acknowledgements		ix
1	National Problems, Federal Solutions	1
2	The Theory and Practice of Cooperative Federalism	10
3	SPC, COAG and the Politics of Reform	32
4	Achieving Cooperation: Players and Processes	61
5	The Machinery of Intergovernmental Relations: An Institutional Analysis	92
6	The Institutions of Collaborative Federalism	121
7	Duplication and Overlap: New Roles, Old Battles	153
8	The Future of Collaborative Federalism	181
List of References		191
Index		199

Abbreviations

ACTU	Australian Council of Trade Unions
AFR	*Australian Financial Review*
ANTA	Australian National Training Authority
ASC	Australian Securities Commission
ATAC	Australian Transport Advisory Council
CEO	chief executive officer
COAG	Council of Australian Governments
DEET(YA)	Department of Employment, Education and Training (and Youth Affairs)
NCOA	National Commission of Audit
NCSC	National Companies and Securities Commission
NRTC	National Road Transport Commission
PD	*Parliamentary Debates*
SPC	Special Premiers' Conference
TAFE	Technical and Further Education

Acknowledgements

I began the research for this book in 1994, while attached as a Sabbatical Fellow and Visiting Fellow in the Reshaping Australian Institutions Project at the Research School of Social Sciences, Australian National University. At the time I was undertaking a Special Studies Program granted by my home institution, the University of Sydney. I later returned to the ANU as a Visiting Fellow for shorter periods while writing the book. My interest in investigating the topic of federal reform and the Council of Australian Governments was sparked by a coming together of two separate research agendas with which I was then concerned, one on economic reform and public sector restructuring and the other on the politics of Australian federalism. In the second half of 1994 I spent six very fruitful months at the Federalism Research Centre, now sadly no longer extant as an active research centre. Its then Director, Brian Galligan, provided a very congenial environment, and provided much personal support and encouragement. The centre's library and the Department of Political Science's newspaper clippings were an invaluable resource.

While at the Federalism Research Centre, I took the opportunity, in collaboration with fellow Visitor Peter Carroll from the Queensland University of Technology, to organise a Conference on Microeconomic Reform and Federalism in Australia, whose proceedings were subsequently published by the centre. This conference, funded and supported by the centre, allowed me to bring together a number of the key actors involved in the processes of federal reform that are the subject of this book, and afforded many valuable contacts, as well as source material in the form of the proceedings themselves. Stephanie Hancock was the conference organiser, just as she was my personal organiser while I was a Visitor at the centre.

ACKNOWLEDGEMENTS

Discussions with state and Commonwealth officials involved in the events described in this book provided a major part of the source material. I talked to officials in Perth, Adelaide, Sydney, Canberra, Melbourne and Brisbane. I was also fortunate to gain access to a small amount of central agency file material from the two years of the Special Premiers' Conference. But the bulk of the material that has been drawn on for this book is on the public record in some form, for example as submissions to public inquiries. To all those who provided personal assistance in the gathering of information I extend my thanks and appreciation. For her superb research assistance at various points in the project, particularly in tracking down obscure public documents and harassing patient public officials to post material out to us, I give special thanks to Liz Clegg. Alan Walker did a fine job with the index. Finally, among many colleagues with whom I have discussed federalism and related topics during the writing of this book I would like to make special mention, for their guidance and stimulation, of Campbell Sharman, Christine Fletcher, Cliff Walsh, Janice Caulfield, Peter Carroll, Helen Nelson and Brian Galligan.

MARTIN PAINTER

CHAPTER 1

National Problems, Federal Solutions

Australia's federal system has undergone a fundamental reshaping in recent years. State and Commonwealth governments have found themselves, often against their immediate wishes, cooperating ever more closely on joint schemes of policy and administration. As a consequence there has been a shift in the rules of the game of federal politics towards collaborative, as distinct from arm's-length, patterns of intergovernmental relations. While conflict and political sparring remain commonplace, state and Commonwealth ministers and officials are more and more to be observed sitting around the table and devising joint schemes of policy and administration that emphasise national uniformity and the removal of interstate barriers and differences. While the history of such collaboration goes back a long way, the advent of Bob Hawke's New Federalism in 1990, and the work of the Special Premiers' Conferences (SPC) and the Council of Australian Governments (COAG) that resulted from this initiative, greatly accelerated the trend. Just to give a few examples, state and Commonwealth governments since 1990 have agreed on a national competition policy; established a scheme of mutual recognition that sweeps away many barriers to interstate trade that formerly existed due to differing systems of state regulation; set up a National Road Transport Commission to devise new, uniform schemes of road vehicle regulation to be implemented by state governments; and introduced uniform gun laws. These and many other examples are discussed in this book. State and Commonwealth ministers and officials are not only cooperating more on joint schemes, they are doing so in new ways that blur their distinctiveness as separate political actors in a federal system. They are collaborating in new institutional arrangements that further entangle them in webs of financial and bureaucratic relations.

This process of change is evolutionary rather than revolutionary, and as such it is not a simple matter to judge when a new set of rules, structures and habits of mind might have supplanted the old. Indeed, there is a chance that the process will be halted as the changing shape of federal institutions becomes clearer, prompting alternative models and interests to be advanced. As the end of the century approaches, the future contours of the federal system remain uncertain and contested. The new collaborative institutional forms and patterns may or may not take a lasting grip on Australian federal government. This uncertainty about future directions is an opportunity to reflect and choose. Which way do we want the federal system to develop? Should Australia seek to revive the traditions of arm's-length, coordinate federalism, or should it embrace the possibilities of a much more closely and systematically managed, collaborative system of intergovernmental cooperation in which the separate political status of distinct governments, particularly state governments, is increasingly submerged?

These questions are not the product of armchair musings, but have been posed by recent events. In particular, the federal system in Australia has been put to the test by the urgencies and necessities of economic reform and restructuring. A paradox of modern government in a globalising economy is that economic policies which give pride of place to the market are frequently accompanied by the need for fundamental state restructuring, requiring a concerted and determined application of state power. Australian advocates of economic reform espousing or implementing 'more market' policies in reaction to a decaying tradition of big government have found themselves bewailing the incapacities of governments and bemoaning the frailties of state and Commonwealth politicians. In Australia, where fundamental economic restructuring began in the mid-1980s and is proceeding apace in the 1990s, much of this criticism has been directed at the federal system itself. Some argue that we have too many governments, and most would agree with the claim that they are very bad at cooperating in the face of urgent common problems; rather, they are more likely to be noticed squabbling over money, turf and power. 'Never stand between a state premier and a bucket of money,' as former Prime Minister Paul Keating once remarked, while berating the premiers for protesting over the latest cut in Commonwealth grants to the states.

It is nothing new for federalism to be under sceptical and critical scrutiny like this. Galligan (1989) has charted the preference for a unitary system of government in Australian political thinking. In Rufus Davis's words, denigrating federalism in 'a language of disparagement and denial' seems part of Australia's political traditions:

NATIONAL PROBLEMS, FEDERAL SOLUTIONS

> The constitution was the 'worst' in the world; it was a 'misfit', a 'failure', it was 'impractical', 'unworkable', 'inefficient', ... 'undemocratic' ... it was incapable of coping with 'outstanding problems' of the 'new technological age'; it was incapable of satisfying 'living demands' or 'keeping pace with the tempo of the life of giant capitalism'; it was ill-designed; it promoted irresponsible government; it was wasteful; it was excessively costly ... [1995, 5]

Criticisms similar to these have been commonplace in recent years as Australian state and Commonwealth governments have struggled to cope with an agenda of economic reform. Does divided government prove an impediment or an encouragement to major economic and social transformations? What actions in fulfilling the economic reform agenda might either be facilitated or constricted by the particular institutional forms of the Australian federal system? Business groups, echoing the fashionable neo-liberal critique of 'government failure', have asked: Does federalism impose costs and burdens that harm Australia's 'international competitiveness'? Is federalism itself an obsolete hangover from the nineteenth century? (See, for example, comments by the Business Council of Australia, *Australian*, 10 July 1991.)

On 19 July 1990, Prime Minister Bob Hawke gave a speech about federalism at the National Press Club titled 'Towards a Closer Partnership'. As is often the case when Australians talk of their federal system, Bob Hawke's speech turned to the topic of railways:

> our railways remain burdened with the legacy of differences between our colonial engineers. A cargo container being sent by rail between Sydney and Perth may be subjected to: three non-integrated rail systems; four changes of locomotives; five different safe working systems; six different sizes of loading gauge; ten different engineering standards of the basic standard gauge track; twelve or more hours at sidings or junctions for crew changes, refuelling, inspections.

The prime minister gave other examples of problems of lack of coordination: schools in different states had different minimum starting ages and curricula; lawyers and doctors needed to apply for licences to work interstate; one state demanded that margarine be sold only in a package shaped like a cube; each state had its own separate design standards for water meters; two states forbade a type of heavy road vehicle that was allowed to operate everywhere else; and so on. All things considered, there was less impediment to trade and movement within the European Community than between the Australian states. The Australian economy, Hawke claimed, was 'balkanised'.

But Bob Hawke's speech was not intended as a litany of complaints about federalism, it was a call to arms to do something about it. He invited the states and local government to cooperate in a new spirit with the Commonwealth on a program of reform, a 'new partnership'. Hawke invited the premiers to attend a Special Premiers' Conference in Brisbane in October. Thus began Hawke's New Federalism. For the prime minister, the call for a new spirit of intergovernmental cooperation was a by-product of his government's most urgent priority: the need to improve national economic efficiency so as to make the Australian economy internationally more competitive. In pursuit of this overriding national priority, in 1990 public policy was in the midst of a series of major upheavals (Kelly 1992). Under challenge were the arbitration system in industrial relations, tariff protection, large-scale public enterprise, and much else that had been a familiar part of the Australian scene for nearly a century. A pro-competitive, neo-liberal policy agenda was taking hold, finding adherents across nearly the whole partisan spectrum and finally sweeping through all governments (Henderson 1995). Structural reform—commonly labelled in Australia 'microeconomic reform'—sought to improve economic efficiency by removing anti-competitive barriers, most of which took the form of various kinds of government intervention through economic as well as social policy (Butlin *et al.* 1982).

Much of this economic transformation required action by state governments. Commonwealth powers over economic policy, although considerable, were limited by the Constitution. Large sectors of essential industry and infrastructure provision, such as transport, energy and health services, were in the hands of the states. In 1990, only one state premier—Nick Greiner in New South Wales—was a genuine enthusiast for microeconomic reform, although other state governments were pursuing modernising programs of managerial reform in their public sectors. State premiers at that time were attracted to cooperate in Bob Hawke's 'new partnership' principally because they saw the opportunity to persuade the Commonwealth to embark on serious fiscal reforms and take other steps to improve their position as governments within the federation. Hawke acknowledged these concerns and included them on the agenda of issues to be tackled through cooperation. A linkage was made between economic reform and federal reform. In June 1990, the premier of New South Wales, Nick Greiner, had circulated a paper titled 'Micro-economic Reform of Commonwealth–State Relations'. Over the years that followed, in the Special Premiers' Conferences and at COAG, numerous intergovernmental agreements were signed, joint schemes of administration were set in train, uniform schemes of legislation were adopted, and intergovernmental bodies with national mandates were established. This book explores the impact of these experiments in collaborative federalism.

Federalism: The Problem or the Solution?

The claim is often made that divided government sets up 'artificial' barriers to solving problems that cross jurisdictional boundaries, while political decentralisation (in particular the power of states to defend their autonomy) impedes the development of common solutions. The practical examples are legion and provide many notorious cases of 'lack of coordination', as Bob Hawke's July 1990 speech reminded us: railway gauges, fire hose couplings, road vehicle regulations, and a host of other cross-border anomalies. The same problem in another guise is found in uncoordinated, overlapping service provision by more than one government, where the boundary problem is one for the citizen to solve in the search for appropriate service. Others argue that the 'problem' is created not by the boundaries themselves but by particular aspects of the division of powers, or the perversities of the system of financial allocations such that 'rational' cooperation is impeded (Forsyth 1995).

Coordination problems are endemic, and a different structure that divides interests or individuals from each other simply replaces one set of such problems—or boundaries—with another. The commonly advanced solution is centralisation to eliminate the fragmentation, but this embodies the fallacy that power, if centralised, is also both unified and made effective. Centralisation merely leads to new but equally troublesome (and equally artificial) horizontal divisions between departments and branches of the centre. So similar are such problems, whether or not there is a horizontal (departmental) or vertical (territorial) division of powers, that one seminal theorist of bureaucratic politics resorted to a territorial analogy to analyse the pathologies of self-serving interdepartmental conflict in centralised bureaucracies (Downs 1967, 211–22).

Another way of thinking about coordination problems is to see them as cases of the obstacles to cooperation where individuals (or governments) have different interests and face uncertainty about the actions of others. The heart of the problem in many such cases is that, even where it can be shown that benefits would accrue to each and all from cooperation to overcome anomalies or avoid perverse outcomes, the incentives to cooperate are typically not sufficiently strong or clear to outweigh the existing, perceived gains from uncoordinated action. Game theorists model such situations as a 'prisoners' dilemma' or a 'tragedy of the commons': the safest and most risk-averse course of action for each individual where behaviours are interdependent, in the absence of certainty about the future actions of others, turns out to be

6   COLLABORATIVE FEDERALISM

mutually self-destructive. What good does it do me to refrain from depleting the common resource to exhaustion—be it fish in the ocean or clean air—when I cannot be certain that everyone else will also refrain? No-one wants to be the sucker.

There are some special and particularly intractable problems of co-ordination in a federal system such as Australia's. What makes the federal condition especially problematic is that it is logically and practically impossible to divide functions or responsibilities of any kind so as to produce watertight boundaries and keep issues and problems from overlapping and out of the sphere of 'the commons' (R. Davis 1995; Leslie 1987, 48–63). The words used to make any distinctions will not actually constrain the activities by which interrelations are revealed. Technological change, for example, makes a mockery of any attempt to freeze definitions of the activities of governments in a form of words. The dramatic growth of interstate road transport is just one example where a jurisdictional minefield has been created by technological change, and has had to be resolved by intergovernmental cooperation. Moreover, governments being what they are, there is little likelihood that they will not seek at least to reach, and probably to extend, the limits of their jurisdictions. Invasion and overlap are the norm and voluntary vacancy is the exception. Hence increasing entanglement is, it seems, unavoidable. Indeed, this is part of Australia's federal history. While the initial response to new problems and issues is to call for a Commonwealth initiative, a common outcome is an intergovernmental arrangement of some kind, because the states often possess both the jurisdictional competence and the administrative capabilities. Thus over the years a complex array of intergovernmental programs and machinery has developed across very many policy sectors, leading in turn to new sites for expressing the dilemmas of overlap.

In a federal division of powers, the flip-side of *divided* power and jurisdiction is *shared* power and jurisdiction. Australian federal debates have been plagued by confusion about the nature of the division of powers, particularly the failure to observe a distinction between the division of functions and the division of the public power (or authority). The former is a blueprint for the fields of activity to be undertaken by the respective governments, but the latter sets up separate, democratic, quasi-sovereign entities. Rufus Davis (1995, 223) makes the same distinction: 'the division of power will connote (a) the creation of co-equal law-making authorities; and (b) the division of functions between these authorities'. The essential character of the division of functions in the Australian constitution is concurrence, that is, most functions are shared rather than being exclusive (Galligan 1995). But there are no constitutionalised mechanisms for pooling governments' law-making

NATIONAL PROBLEMS, FEDERAL SOLUTIONS

or executive authority to deal with these shared functions. Practical exigencies in fulfilling constitutionally sanctioned functions bring governments together, but at the same time the Constitution sets them apart as distinct political entities. This is one reason for the rich complexity of administrative and political machinery of intergovernmental relations. But this machinery can be a source of tension, because coming together arouses fears of loss of authority. Collaborative federalism is set against arm's-length federalism within the very fabric of the constitution. Some of those involved in the process emphasise the need to cooperate so as to make overlapping functions serve common ends; others emphasise the need to safeguard and foster the political basis of authority so as to preserve the separate systems of democratic accountability embodied in dual government.

In the 1990s, Australian federalism has become more collaborative. The executive branches have become more entangled, not only through the process of continual discussion and negotiation in and around COAG, but more significantly through the operations of new national schemes, where day-to-day executive action must be subject to uniform legislation and jointly agreed protocols, and where in some cases jointly mandated executive organs, advisory bodies or regulatory agencies exercise significant powers. Do these trends signal a sea change in the Australian federal system, the surrender of arm's-length, dual government to the needs of national, functional coordination? Is the constitutional paradox referred to earlier between functional concurrence and jurisdictional duality being resolved through submerging or blurring the latter?

The structure of the rest of the book is as follows. Chapter 2 reviews and extends Australian debates about federalism, focusing in particular on 'cooperative federalism'. This was the rallying call of Hawke's 'new partnership' and the underlying mission of SPC and COAG. The chapter traces the themes and arguments about federal reform and restructuring that were prevalent in the public debates and intergovernmental conflicts in the 1990s, relating them to underlying tensions or dilemmas in Australian federal institutions and traditions as well as to the contemporary debates and conflicts in SPC and COAG. For example, there is a tension between 'parliamentary federalism' and 'executive federalism', paralleling the tension already mentioned between dual government and functional overlap. Recently, state government leaders have articulated a model of 'competitive federalism' as a way of justifying their autonomy in a defence against possible Commonwealth domination of collaborative institutions.

Chapter 3 provides a detailed narrative of the trials and tribulations of SPC and COAG. The unfolding agenda of reform undertaken in these

8 COLLABORATIVE FEDERALISM

intergovernmental fora—including the items that were dropped from the agenda—is set in the context of unfolding political events, the personalities involved, and the changing economic and political climates. The Commonwealth's continued dominance of much of the proceedings of intergovernmental cooperation is noted, as well as the states' considerable powers of resistance. Interstate differences in positioning and perspective are also highlighted. Chapter 4 looks at the players in the SPC and COAG processes, the roles they occupied and the manner in which they performed those roles. The SPC process energised a new combination of existing actors and roles to operate in new frameworks of official action—committees, working parties, and the SPC and COAG meetings themselves. The analysis provides examples of the manner in which existing, settled networks of functional intergovernmental relations were interrupted and overlain by a new agenda and a fresh sense of urgency by the new players. 'Whole-of-government' actors—premiers and their close advisers—were injected into the process, with mixed results. New political priorities and new ideas were brought to play in both existing and new intergovernmental fora.

Having provided an analysis of the processes by which political leaders and officials forged new collaborative programs in recent years, we turn next to more general themes underlying the reshaping of federal institutions in a collaborative form. Chapter 5 is concerned with a detailed analysis of cooperative forms of joint administrative action on the ground, each of them arising in response to the dilemmas of functional concurrence. How has cooperation been pursued in practice? This chapter looks back at the historical development of such machinery and shows how the ground was prepared in earlier years for the initiatives undertaken through SPC and COAG. A vocabulary and framework for institutional analysis is developed and applied. The analysis provides a check-list of the sorts of institutional problems that arise when confronting issues of intergovernmental coordination, and the range of institutional solutions that have been applied to resolve them. In Chapter 6 this framework for analysis is extended and applied in a close look at some of the machinery of intergovernmental collaboration that has been created by SPC and COAG since 1990. A more formal and rigorous definition of 'collaborative federalism' is provided, enabling the contrast with arm's-length federal institutions to be specified more precisely. This analysis is undertaken through detailed examples and case studies, showing how new joint schemes and agreements have been structured, and how they have actually been operating. It is an open question whether or not the decision rules that have been agreed upon for many of these new spheres of joint action have actually been applied and followed, especially where they restrain the political freedom of manoeuvre of the participating governments. The outcomes from this point of view are mixed, but allow us to conclude that collaborative rather than arm's-length patterns of intergovernmental relations are in the ascendancy.

Chapter 7 focuses on an analysis of attempts to solve 'duplication and overlap' in policy, planning and service provision by state and Commonwealth governments. The same framework of institutional analysis is also applied in these case studies. Here, the neo-liberal agenda of public sector restructuring also enters the picture. The application of modern ideas and practices of public sector reform to intergovernmental management could have profound implications for the federal system of government more generally. In some cases, they reinforce collaborative, executive-centred forms of centralised joint action and undermine the achievement of a model of competitive federalism of the kind espoused by many neo-liberals themselves. The concluding chapter turns to an assessment of the trends evident from the foregoing analysis. We ask whether or not the kinds of collaborative arrangements that have mushroomed under COAG provide a blueprint for the future of Australian federalism, and whether or not we should welcome or resist these trends.

CHAPTER 2

The Theory and Practice of Cooperative Federalism

Bob Hawke's New Federalism was born of pragmatism rather than principle: his political agenda required the states' cooperation. Top of that agenda was success with economic reform, not federal reform. However, by taking a federal initiative, the Commonwealth both mobilised and became subject to a series of long-running federal debates. The language and imagery Hawke used to launch his initiative drew on contested presumptions, models and diagnoses of federalism, from which tensions and conflicts quickly became apparent. By offering the states a role on a new national stage, the prime minister opened the way for them to push their federal claims and arguments. At the same time, the states were vulnerable in this national forum in case they were swept up in a cooperative process not of their own making, in which their separate identities would be submerged in a drive for national uniformity and coordination.

The issues emphasised by the prime minister appeared disarmingly simple. First, the diagnosis—overlap, duplication and balkanisation; and second, the remedy—cooperative federalism. All that was being asked was a bit of housekeeping to remedy anomalies and make things neat and tidy. Quickly, however, it became plain that this language mobilised contradictory agendas. The states saw the problem of duplication in terms of repelling Commonwealth invasions of their jurisdiction, while the Commonwealth saw the problem in terms of a need for the states to submerge parochial concerns and agree to national standards and strategies. Sometimes, however, their interests coincided, and politicians and officials found themselves innovating and experimenting with new institutional, legal, financial and managerial techniques and instruments. But these cooperative solutions in turn raised new and

THEORY AND PRACTICE OF COOPERATIVE FEDERALISM 11

sometimes unexpected issues on which state and Commonwealth perspectives differed.

While the search was on for national solutions to a shared economic reform agenda, the fact that the processes were inescapably federal in nature gave prominence to the politics of intergovernmental relations. Federalism was put to the test. With both economic reform and federalism hitched to a 'closer partnership', the stakes were raised: not just the shape of future economic policy was in question, but also the rules of the game by which policy was made. Debates and arguments were set in train that had their own political dynamic. When the Commonwealth could not persuade the states to see the force of its argument, the point at issue became the right to disagree and the importance of diversity as ends in themselves, rather than an argument over the substance of economic reform.

The agenda of reform embarked on through Special Premiers' Conferences and the Council of Australian Governments (SPC and COAG) stimulated fresh political thinking about how to shape the future of federal relations and gave rise to new forms of federal politics, such as a much-heightened level of interstate cooperation. But the fields of battle were familiar ones: federal–state finances; the decision rules of intergovernmental fora at ministerial and official level; the division of powers; the appropriate executive instruments for joint, intergovernmental action and the accountability mechanisms that should accompany them; the methods of arriving at and maintaining uniform legislation; and so on. While the SPC process started in a climate of joint problem-solving, where a language of consensus briefly prevailed, with the passage of time the customary divisions between state and Commonwealth rose to the surface.

This chapter is concerned with drawing out the underlying federal arguments and models that were evoked and challenged in the process. As we shall see, the spirit of harmony was politically insecure and short-lived, possibly because it was so torn by internal tensions and contradictions. The respective positions drew on interpretations and images of Australia's federal traditions—the practical experience of federalism—but the arguments also rested in part on various strands of federal theory, and these will be briefly explored. The discussion begins with the critique of duplication and overlap. In comparing and contrasting state and Commonwealth diagnoses of this problem, we see that they were drawn to emphasise different dimensions. The states linked it with federal finance or vertical fiscal imbalance, under which the Commonwealth intruded on state jurisdictions, and the Commonwealth linked it with the need for national uniformity and harmonisation. Both

12   COLLABORATIVE FEDERALISM

sides for a time adopted the rhetoric of partnership. Not surprisingly, however, they held competing images of cooperative federalism: the Commonwealth had in mind a centrally managed, collaborative model, and the states mostly had in mind moving towards an arm's-length, balanced relationship of mutual respect, and were attracted to a model of competitive federalism.

Overlap and Duplication

An important stimulus to the agenda of the new federalism of the 1990s was a view, articulated by state and Commonwealth leaders alike, that overlap and duplication were responsible for excessive friction, conflict, confusion and waste. The broader climate of informed opinion almost universally accepted this way of framing the issue. Nick Greiner, in setting out an agenda for federal reform, sought a 'rationalisation' of functions to achieve a 'clean separation' (Greiner 1990). He went so far as to suggest a 'trade' of powers—for example, the Commonwealth should be given industrial relations in exchange for school education. A paper commissioned by the Economic Planning Advisory Council (Wiltshire 1990: 1) lamented the extent and growth of overlap and duplication, claiming that this outcome had 'distorted the original attempt at coordinate federalism and made any delineation of functions between levels of government extremely difficult'. But behind this claim and underlying Greiner's call for a 'clean separation' lie some common misconceptions as to the nature of the Australian federal design, the practicalities of policy and administration, and the principles and objects of federal theory.

As to Australia's constitutional design, Galligan (1995) convincingly argues that coordinate federalism in this sense is not a part of it. Such a model, in which the dual, sovereign governments enjoy distinct and separate spheres of jurisdiction, was enunciated by Bryce (1888), later elaborated on by Wheare as the classical federal model (1946), and more recently evoked by Mathews (1977) to characterise the pattern of intergovernmental relations in the first twenty years of Australian federation. Even if, in those early years, entanglement and overlap were relatively slight and unproblematic, reality never conformed with the coordinate ideal of cleanly delineated functions. Many of those framing the Constitution had read and admired Bryce and seemed to have had in mind a doctrine of separate spheres, but the actual division of powers turned out to be radically different (Warden 1992). The Constitution set out a system of concurrent or shared—not compartmentalised—jurisdiction (Galligan 1995, 192–203). Most of the Commonwealth's enumerated powers—those in Section 51—are not exclusive. The Commonwealth was given paramountcy in these areas of shared jurisdiction, in that its legislation would override that of the states, but this did not mean the states could not or would not continue to pursue their interests in these areas.

In any case, it is logically and practically impossible to enumerate powers, functions or responsibilities in such a way that the result is watertight boundaries. The delegates at the conventions 'failed to appreciate that simply naming powers was not tantamount to defining the ambit of those powers' (Warden 1992, 152). The words used to make distinctions cannot actually determine the activities by which the interrelation of governments and their activities is revealed over time (R. Davis 1995, 35). The world has changed and brought new roles and functions for governments: new technology has given rise to new problems and possibilities, new social movements have sprung up, and whole new fields of policy have been invented. The occupation by state and Commonwealth governments of this ever-changing policy landscape was shaped over time by their ambitions and resources. Both Commonwealth and state governments found their jurisdictions expanded. In some cases they interfered and clashed with each other, while in others they made adjustments and cooperated. This process, which inevitably produced overlap and often friction, was not a perversion of a classical Australian federal ideal.

The attempt to accommodate and work with overlap and duplication is a perennial one routinely experienced in federations. In the Canadian federation, with a very different starting point that enumerated provincial rather than federal powers, exactly the same pressures towards entanglement have been noted, and complex arrangements of cooperation and accommodation have evolved (Leslie 1987). Impatience with some of these arrangements in both Canada and Australia has led to a search for tidier arrangements, with a view to rationalising activities according to the 'layered dimensions to particular policy areas, which are appropriately dealt with by layered institutions of government' (Galligan 1995, 202). For example, Wiltshire suggests setting national standards for school curricula at the Commonwealth level, as against 'local design and delivery' of school systems by the states (1990, 17). However, debate at this point can quickly become entangled with arguments about the virtues of uniformity versus the advantages of diversity. As well, devising such layered arrangements creates difficulties of exactly the same kind as attempts to specify powers: the words used to attempt to distinguish national from local roles will not on their own constrain the activities.

The lack of an unequivocal conceptual or historical basis for agreement about the nature of the problem of overlap and duplication, or

14   COLLABORATIVE FEDERALISM

the kind of remedies it required, became clear as events unfolded after
the issue was placed on the agenda in 1990. The illusions of the classical
ideal of coordinate federalism persisted through some of the statements
in the initial Brisbane SPC communiqué (Galligan 1995, 197). This
'neat and tidy' vision of federal–state relations is also attractive to
modern advocates of smaller government (Kasper 1993). One way or
another, they argue, the Commonwealth and states must disentangle
themselves and sort out clear and distinct roles and responsibilities
(NCOA 1996). In practice, it is not so easy. State and Commonwealth
leaders often make suggestions about what areas of policy and
administration the other should vacate and hand over, but of course the
lists rarely coincide. Argument over roles and responsibilities continued
to dog COAG in 1997 after seven years of searching for agreements (see
Chapter 7), and despite widespread agreement that this, along with
fiscal problems, remained the most important issue for settlement
(Productivity Commission 1996, 172–4).

The states were highly critical of the levels of detailed oversight in
One aspect of the illusory language of consensus was the recourse to
the seemingly neutral terminology of efficiency—waste and delay—in
the critique of duplication. The Commonwealth government was keen
to improve efficiency in the delivery of government services, and this
led to an apparent consensus at some points that the complex and
burgeoning system of special-purpose grants and agreements needed
rationalising. Cost savings were potentially available, for example, if
consolidation of agreements along with new forms of monitoring of
outcomes replaced the plethora of funding agreements which, with
their detailed specifications, required costly oversight and compliance
reporting. A number of specific-purpose grant programs—road funding
for example—were already undergoing such changes (Painter and
Dempsey 1992). But Commonwealth departments and ministers were
not eager to stop trying to control aspects of (for example) school
education or community health. The aim was often a substitution of
new controls, not their removal or the surrender of jurisdiction.
Fletcher and Walsh (1992) accurately characterise the Commonwealth's
approach as a 'managerialist', top-down vision of federalism.

The states were highly critical of the levels of detailed oversight in
grant agreements and supervision, but their version of a more efficient
system was the removal of controls altogether. They also objected to the
use of special-purpose grants as indirect instruments for controlling
state expenditures, such as dollar-for-dollar or maintenance of effort
requirements which channelled state resources to Commonwealth
programs. At the Commonwealth level, departmental managers were
sympathetic to such criticisms because these methods of grant administration ran counter to latest management doctrine. For example,

THEORY AND PRACTICE OF COOPERATIVE FEDERALISM   15

controls that relied primarily on inputs—like funds—were ineffective and often counter-productive; duplication of effort in service provision produced confusion for the client and waste for the taxpayer; and objectives could best be met by controls 'at a distance' and devolved management, rather than detailed involvement in programs. But short-term political and policy concerns often overrode managerial rationales, with the Commonwealth continuing to be drawn to traditional instruments of control and direction in response to the concerns of clients and pressure groups. The deals struck with the states to reshape joint program funding and management in the early 1990s followed no particular logic or pattern at first, but were the outcome of case-by-case negotiations. In the case of disability services, for example, in 1991 the policy and program field was divided into separate compartments of state and Commonwealth program responsibility, with block funding for the states in their area of concern, but little joint strategic planning or management over the whole system (Yeatman 1996). In the case of vocational education and training, the new arrangements set up in 1992 involved a jointly mandated national authority, national standards, and pooled funds and close central monitoring of state outputs and performance across the whole sector (Taylor 1996; see also Chapter 7).

Hope for a consistent set of principles to bring order to the situation rose with the application of ideas and doctrine drawn from the new public economics and principal-agent theory, such as funder-purchaser-provider splits, and contracting out in a contestable market of providers (Edwards and Henderson 1995). These techniques, it was hoped, would provide a way of sorting out appropriate roles for levels of government in areas where it was recognised responsibility had to be shared. At the same time, modern techniques of data collection, storage and manipulation, plus agreement on desired program outputs and performance standards and indicators, would allow for joint planning and monitoring within national frameworks and goals. But these solutions often merely raised old problems in new ways: Who set the performance criteria and the standards, and how much diversity and experimentation was to be allowed in their application? Who determined the pace of marketisation of the provision of a service that was previously the responsibility of a state government public body? If funds were pooled and states and Commonwealth were joint funders, were the purchasers also to be national bodies, or state agencies? How were the standard-setting, monitoring and regulatory bodies to be constituted and controlled? And so on. The critical issues were still jurisdiction, autonomy, and political control of policy domains important to constituents.

16   COLLABORATIVE FEDERALISM

To sum up, when the states called for an end to duplication and overlap, it was code for removing the Commonwealth from areas of activity that state governments wished to control. In the state version of solving overlap, a link was drawn between three elements of duplication: first, removal of detailed program controls; second, the withdrawal of Commonwealth involvement in whole fields of operational policy; and third, the conversion of special-purpose payments to general-purpose revenue assistance. For the Commonwealth, the meaning was diametrically opposed: consigning the states to a subordinate role under the guidance of agreed (or imposed) uniform policies, guidelines and standards. The Commonwealth's agenda also had three elements, but they were different ones: to assert its role in achieving national, uniform outcomes in key areas of policy; to consign the states to the role of faithful agents in the performance of prescribed tasks; and to overcome resistance and obstruction by diminishing their power and discretion. These competing perspectives were both embodied in the concrete historical experience of, on the one hand, federal fiscal relations and, on the other, intergovernmental policy coordination, and we turn next to these aspects of federal debates.

Federal Fiscal Relations and Vertical Imbalance

The primary cause of the problem of duplication and overlap from the states' point of view was the Commonwealth's ever-expanding political ambition, which led it continually to invade new areas of state jurisdiction. From this point of view, one of the principal issues was the Commonwealth's acquisition over time of an effective monopoly of the two most important sources of revenue in the modern state: income tax (personal and company), and excise and sales taxes. This monopoly was achieved with the assistance of the High Court's interpretations of the Constitution. Although the states were left the residue of unenumerated powers, the court in construing Commonwealth powers has taken the view that 'the effect of any particular construction on the residue of state powers [was] irrelevant' (Zines 1989: 26). From about 1920 the High Court stopped applying two important principles that protected the states: one a doctrine of implied reserve powers, and the other a doctrine of implied immunities by which no government could use its powers to restrict the powers of another. In so far as the powers and prerogatives of the states were residual, implied and unstated, rejecting these doctrines left the states vulnerable.

Before World War II income tax was a joint area of revenue raising, but it was taken over by the Commonwealth as a wartime measure. The Commonwealth Labor government then sought to entrench its

THEORY AND PRACTICE OF COOPERATIVE FEDERALISM   17

occupation of the field and succeeded. It relied on Section 96 of the Constitution (allowing it to make grants and attach conditions to them) to legislate to the effect that any state which returned to raising revenue from a separate income tax would be penalised by a cut in grants of the same amount, while the uniform Commonwealth tax would still be levied. This stratagem was upheld by the High Court as the correct literal reading of the powers of the Commonwealth, even though the result was to deny a state the effective enjoyment of its own constitutional powers. As to excise and sales taxes, the High Court has persisted with a narrow interpretation of the meaning of the Commonwealth's exclusive 'excise' power, claiming that it extended to all taxes on the sale as well as production of goods, thereby excluding the states from levying such taxes (Galligan 1995, 174–7).

It must be pointed out, however, that this growth in Commonwealth jurisdiction and powers has not resulted in as dramatic a degree of centralisation as a literal reading might suggest. The political and administrative restraints on Commonwealth power consequent upon the existence of effective, active, democratically elected state governments remain significant. State political leaders are adept at exploiting Commonwealth intrusions with damaging 'anti-Canberra' political crusades; the relative impotence of the Commonwealth in areas of concurrent jurisdiction is often revealed by its lack of administrative resources and local knowledge compared with the states; and even in the case of federal finances, the system of grants results as much in a system of mutual interdependencies as in a structure of dominance (Sharman 1985, 113).

Nevertheless, the growth in the preponderance of the effective revenue powers of the Commonwealth has produced a very strong sense of impotence and frustration. The Commonwealth collects nearly 80 per cent of tax revenues but is responsible for just over half of outlays. About one-half of state revenues is in the form of Commonwealth grants. Many of these are tied or specific-purpose payments—they come from the Commonwealth with conditions attached, are directed at functions and programs that are of the Commonwealth's choosing, and bring with them a considerable degree of administrative involvement in program design and monitoring (Walsh and Thomson 1993, 1–15). In the 1980s and 1990s under the Hawke and Keating governments the proportion of tied grants gradually increased to over 50 per cent.

The consequences of such an extreme vertical fiscal imbalance include the lack of control of state governments over their own budgets and, in some cases, over their own agencies and programs due to Commonwealth funding and oversight. This, it has been argued, leads to fiscal irresponsibility and can produce difficulties in holding

18 COLLABORATIVE FEDERALISM

governments fully to account for their spending (Walsh 1992). For example, the preponderance of grants in state revenue sources has been criticised for its distorting effects on public expenditures: the states are more likely to be fiscally irresponsible because they are spending 'fifty-cent dollars' (i.e. they are accountable for raising only one-half of the revenue that supports their spending). In the process there is an observable 'fly-paper' effect (Walsh and Thomson 1993; Dollery and Worthington 1995), by which programs funded by grants attract disproportionately more state funds as well ('money sticks where it hits'), ratcheting up overall expenditures and at the same time skewing priorities.

Arguments such as these are consistent with the analysis of 'government failure', in which it is claimed that long-term trends in uncontrolled public-sector growth (both in spending and regulation) were due in part to these sorts of structural defects in public accountability and decision-making mechanisms. Prominent among the effects identified have been feather-bedding in state governments' public utilities and a heavy burden of anti-competitive state regulations covering occupations, professions, and the distribution and sale of goods and services. This critique brings together the issues of the division of powers, federal finances, and microeconomic reform: the states could blame the irrationalities of fiscal federalism for some of the inefficiencies of their inherited public sectors, or could link them with their difficulties in meeting the costs of putting their houses in order. Greiner (1990) made the point: 'Much of what has been perceived as irresponsible behaviour by the states has been the rational response to irrational incentive structures caused by a division of responsibility between Federal and state Governments.' This was not a linkage that the Commonwealth was ever keen to admit, although its economic policy advisers increasingly pointed it out (Carroll 1995; Industry Commission 1994).

Historically, while all Commonwealth governments have shown a reluctance to hand back financial independence to the states, Labor governments especially have sought to increase their financial and other capacities *vis-à-vis* the states, on the grounds that the Commonwealth has the primary role to play in delivering social and economic reform. A chasm was revealed between the Commonwealth Labor government's view of vertical fiscal imbalance and the states' perspective on it after Paul Keating became prime minister at the end of 1991. Keating, in a speech at the National Press Club earlier in 1991, had described it as the 'glue that holds the federation together', referring to the way in which the Commonwealth's possession of the dominant revenue-raising powers enabled it to pursue programs of national significance,

THEORY AND PRACTICE OF COOPERATIVE FEDERALISM   19

to engage effectively in national macroeconomic management through fiscal policy, and also to redistribute tax revenues in the form of equalisation grants. Keating may have been one of the more extreme centralist prime ministers, but Commonwealth governments of all political persuasions have not surprisingly been reluctant to surrender their fiscal control. The Howard government elected in 1996, despite paying lip-service to federal fiscal reform when in opposition, ruled this out at an early point. Indeed, its financial leverage over the states was employed ruthlessly to extract a 'contribution' from them in order to reduce the budget deficit in the government's first budget (see Chapter 3).

The historical record also shows that the states have been far from united or determined on a course of action to seek to alter the underlying situation of vertical fiscal imbalance. It can be fun spending fifty-cent dollars. The Commonwealth bears the odium of collecting the taxes, while state premiers look for the plaudits from bringing home a 'special deal' from the Commonwealth. While their rhetoric has described their mendicant status as an intolerable obstacle to their capacity to govern as quasi-sovereign constitutional units, their political practice has seen them often exploiting the situation rather than seeking to change it. However, the sense of grievance and unity of purpose among the states over the Commonwealth's fiscal powers were probably never greater than at the time Bob Hawke launched his initiative in the middle of 1990. The special deals had begun to dry up. For the first time since income tax collection had been centralised, the Commonwealth was embarked on a long, sustained process of cutbacks and budget reductions. The Commonwealth had for several years imposed a squeeze on general revenue grants to the states as a deliberate budget-cutting exercise, prompting the states to complain with some justification that the Commonwealth was deliberately shifting the burden of cutbacks to their budgets. They were also experiencing the adverse impact on state taxes and charges of a serious economic recession (for example, a downturn in the property market and building industries, and a consequent diminution in transaction fees and charges). The character and style of Treasurer Paul Keating fuelled their grievances. Keating relished more than most his ability to call the tune at annual Premiers' Conferences. Nick Greiner, for example, recalled his amazement after the first meeting he attended as premier of New South Wales at the manner in which the premiers were treated, and the arrogance and peremptoriness with which their attempts to make serious contributions were dismissed (personal communication).

When Hawke placed financial reform on the agenda in the spirit of partnership, it was seized on as the main issue by most state premiers.

20 COLLABORATIVE FEDERALISM

At stake here was an overlapping set of constitutional and policy issues, neatly brought together under the rubric of economic reform. The premiers could seek to argue that microeconomic reform entailed fiscal reform and a reduction in the proportion of tied grants. They saw the potential to win concessions from the Commonwealth on fiscal matters in return for cooperation on national standards and national markets. Cooperative federalism, the correction of vertical fiscal balance and microeconomic reform came together for the states as an inextricable package. But this was not the way the Commonwealth packaged the issues. It had an entirely different set of federal experiences and images of reform in mind. In line with the Commonwealth's views on the problem of overlap and duplication, its first priority was the creation of integrated markets operating under nationally uniform policies. From this perspective, remedying vertical fiscal imbalance could be depicted as a backward step, a stripping away of some of the 'glue' that held the system together. The next section turns to the issues of uniformity and coordination which so dominated the Commonwealth's agenda for the closer partnership.

Uniformity, Harmonisation and Problems of Coordination

Bob Hawke's rhetoric in his 1990 speech focused repeatedly on 'the national interest': 'we share a commitment to a single national identity ... Yet within this splendid unity, we have imposed on ourselves a burden of different rules and regulations and requirements which needlessly weighs against the tremendous advantages we can have as a nation-continent.' This rhetoric, backed by homespun examples such as railway gauges and margarine packaging, underscored Hawke's call for inter-governmental cooperation. The talk was of 'anomalies', 'fragmentation' and 'confusion'. It was powerful rhetoric, and it supported a fundamentally centralist view of the problems and the solutions. There was little serious reference in his speech to the advantages of diversity; rather, the presumption was that any difference, however minor, was an impediment to national efficiency. The assumption was that uniformity and national standards were desirable wherever there was any kind of interconnection, trade, or movement of people.

But nationalistic rhetoric aside, to show that there are boundary costs is not to demonstrate that there should be uniformity, at least until they have been weighed up against the boundary benefits. There may well be good reasons for differences due to local conditions. In a federal system people have the capacity to weigh the inconveniences against the benefits and to choose to pay the costs of anomalies. Another deception embedded in the rhetoric is the equation of harmonisation (or

THEORY AND PRACTICE OF COOPERATIVE FEDERALISM 21

coordination) with uniformity. 'Different' does not necessarily mean inconsistent or incompatible. Equally tendentious is the claim that national means uniform, and that the Commonwealth is the only government that can bring about desirable levels of harmonisation. Uniformity—or at least convergence towards uniformity—is indeed a common pattern in the evolution of state policy in many spheres, but it frequently occurs without either the direct intervention of the Commonwealth or the existence of national standards. Interstate co-operation and other processes, including emulation and imitation, often lead to harmonisation. Each government generates its own ideas and tries different things; one innovates, another resists, and the rest look on to see which succeeds. Mistakes made by one are avoided by others. The outcome is often a generally agreed course of action (a 'winning formula') which, because it works and because there is demand for it, could quite well become more or less uniform (Painter 1991a). In such a process, on the one hand local populations can express their differences and try new things that suit them; on the other, divided government and decentralised authority do not necessarily entail thwarting a society's capacity to act collectively in dealing with common problems.

While the Commonwealth's agenda on many of these issues of coordination and harmonisation was at heart centralist, not all state premiers had strong objections to many of Hawke's calls for greater uniformity. Inconsistencies, incompatibilities and boundary costs were in some cases significant burdens to them as well. Reaction to the Commonwealth's proposals for uniform schemes and the removal of cross-border anomalies varied from government to government and issue to issue. Greiner probably went furthest in calling for breaking down the significance of state borders, seeing 'no reason why we cannot have uniform commercial laws, uniform manufacturing standards, uniform consumer laws, food standards and public health regulations', not to mention a 'single, integrated [electricity] transmission grid for the eastern states' (Greiner 1990). Of course, the largest state would have the least to fear in calling for uniformity, as it would be in the strongest position to determine the standard.

In such a situation, interstate differences characteristically breed suspicion, fear and hostility. Resistance to change arises from a lack of certainty coupled with a lack of trust, often based on bitter experience of the manner in which power is wielded in federal politics. Even in areas of regulation and provision where most states—not just New South Wales—had begun to see the need for a reduction in anomalies and the benefits of harmonisation, the rhetoric of cooperation often hid an underlying fear of change. The problem in such cases—even where it can be shown that benefits would accrue to each and all from co-operation—is that the incentives to cooperate are often not sufficiently strong or clear to overcome the uncertainties bred by distrust, and a state 'sits pat' in a search for ever stronger assurances, resulting in inaction. Hawke's closer partnership and its vision of a new cooperative federalism was supposedly the answer to this problem: if political leaders all got around the table with goodwill, they would all be able to overcome their fears and distrust and agree on the kinds of solutions that were in the best interest of all. But was it that simple? The next section discusses the various origins and meanings of cooperative federalism, both in Australian federal experience and in federal theory, preparatory to looking at the contrasting state and Commonwealth views of how to overcome these coordination problems through cooperation.

Cooperative Federalism

Cooperative (like coordinate) federalism has become a much misused label. Some have used the term as a synonym for administrative federalism, that is, the networks and structures of routine information exchange and discussion, along with the specific delegations, joint programs and joint bodies set up to manage day-to-day relations: 'when the shouting was over it was the administrators who were left to sort out the ensuing mess' (Wiltshire 1977, 3). This purported inherent propensity to cooperate among administrators does not mesh with the experience of bureaucratic friction arising from intergovernmental jurisdictional battles—for example, in the case of fisheries (Haward 1991, 122–3), or companies and securities regulation (see Chapter 5). Indeed such is the propensity for friction, the adversarial nature of much federal politics and the Commonwealth's urge for domination and national uniformity (whatever the label attached to it), cooperative federalism might seem a contradiction in terms. Wiltshire prefers 'responsibility sharing' to highlight the jointness of the action, free of overtones about the form of the relationship, but he burdens this with an erroneous understanding of what it entails: 'it is a pity that the Australian Constitution divided the tasks of the public sector between governments. If only it had provided for joint responsibility in most areas and stipulated the means of cooperation, we would not have the kaleidoscope pattern of intergovernmental arrangements we have today' (Wiltshire 1977, 3).

As already argued, the Constitution does in fact embody concurrency. But Wiltshire is right to say that it does not institutionalise any formal, joint decision-making arrangements or 'means of cooperation'.

THEORY AND PRACTICE OF COOPERATIVE FEDERALISM   23

In constitutional terms, the governments are independent of each other. Constitutionalised cooperative or joint decision-making arrangements are exemplified by the German federal constitution: first in the composition and powers of the upper house, the Bundesrat, to which the provincial governments (or Lander) nominate representatives, and which has equal law-making powers with the lower house; and second in the 'functional' division of powers, with the principal law-making power over most matters lying with the federal parliament, and the provincial governments implementing federal laws and a plethora of ·'joint programs'. But the Australian Constitution (like the Canadian) sets up wholly distinct governing systems ('parallel rather than interlocking', Painter 1991a: 274), with separate sovereign parliaments and executive agencies. Any interaction or joint action has evolved out of practical exigencies, for political and administrative convenience. Despite the plethora of such arrangements, the original arm's-length relationship remains intact. Adversarial politics and joint administration coexist as a matter of course.

Cooperative federalism, then, is a slippery concept. It does however have its uses in the analysis of recent Australian federal experience. It is applied here to a particular style of intergovernmental relations that evolved out of a perception of a common agenda of problems (and, in some instances, solutions) at the level of 'high politics' (Galligan *et al.* 1991, 14–17). In dealing with this agenda, there was a deliberate attempt to institutionalise cooperative norms and procedures in and around SPC and COAG. But cooperation at this level in the Australian federal system is always conditional and voluntary. Sawer (1977, 6) makes the point: 'it is the assumption of "cooperation" that each of the parties to the arrangement have [*sic*] a reasonable degree of autonomy, can bargain about the terms of cooperation, and, at least if driven too hard, decline to cooperate'. Both political leaders and their officials, for all their apparent camaraderie, sense of common mission and search for agreement, still retain distinct (perhaps otherwise conflicting) purposes. If they agree for the moment on where they are seeking to go, they never forget where they come from; it remains true that 'where they sit determines where they stand'.

Intergovernmental cooperation is tactical, and it is normally temporary because it coexists with competition and conflict (even within the same room). While voluntary, it can be induced and maintained by sanctions, such as the moral sanctions that develop from a 'culture of cooperation'. By definition, however, if the capacity to impose sanctions is too unevenly distributed, we more than likely have coercion, as has been characteristic of the Financial Premiers' Conferences. Cooperation can be terminated as much by a recourse to coercion as by unilateral, voluntary withdrawal. Clearly, it is not possible to seal hermetically a forum designed for cooperation from the broader political context—it will reflect the character of other forms of intergovernmental relations going on at the same time, as linkages are made by the actors with other political arenas.

Richard Simeon (1972) coined the apt phrase 'federal–provincial diplomacy' to encapsulate the character of intergovernmental relations in Canada, and much of what he says rings true for Australia. He borrowed Lindblom's concept of 'partisan discussion', which captures the nature of much of the process (Lindblom 1965). The norms and tacit understandings of diplomacy and the dynamics and constraints of the artificial system itself—its sense of a closed world of arcane forms and mysterious practices—find their echoes in Common-wealth–state relations. There is the sense that, despite the differences and the claims to autonomy, the whole is still an important entity that stands above all else. The forms of cooperation that this produces are not just matters of style but also of substance—for example, the participants often focus on constituting rules and frameworks for making future policy in preference to the nitty-gritty of the substance of policy, because the latter brings out petty differences. There is a peculiar mix of mundane detail and high principle, so intergovernmental arenas are likely to exhibit forms of behaviour that swing unpredictably from unanimous and smooth agreement to rancour, threats and name-calling. The histrionics are not always signs of an end to cooperation, but may be simply part of the tactics of reaching agreement. Co-operation on the details of interdependency is not all sweetness and light, free of pressure or sanctions. The kinds of sanctions that maintain cooperation in the long run are those that the group can consensually wield against a recalcitrant member—ultimately perhaps expulsion, or at least non-participation in some collectively produced, shared and valued benefit.

In later chapters we look in more detail at the kinds of working rules and strategies that actually characterise federal institutions that arise from a cooperative process, contrasting them with other intergovern-mental arenas and drawing on historical examples and precursors. If cooperative federalism has some of the character just described, however, it is important also to note that it has its limits in the real world of federal politics. There was not, as discussed earlier, agreement over the basic nature of many of the problems and solutions, even if there was a recognition of interdependency and of the need for joint action of some kind to deal with the issues, as variously defined. Neither was there always a 'cooperative spirit'.

Collaboration versus Competition

One of the difficulties presented for the development of a clear working notion of cooperative federalism is that it has been used as a slogan, and the meanings are politically contested. The ways to achieve cooperation, that is the manner in which it was to be undertaken, have been matters of dispute. The Commonwealth's vision of cooperative federalism was closely allied with its managerialist perspective, with its drive for collectively agreed uniform strategies and smooth implementation of outcomes. This was a collaborative image of intergovernmental joint action. This image homed in on the nuts and bolts of commitment to joint action, such as binding intergovernmental agreements for uniform legislation, to lock state governments into joint ventures with agreed, national objectives.

This approach is not a new one, but the SPC and COAG processes brought it to such prominence that the potential exists to set Australian federalism on a new course, largely by stealth. It is essentially a model of interlocking rather than arm's-length federalism. Unlike the German model, however, where collaboration is institutionalised in legislative structures and law-making processes, it is a system of interlocking *executive* federalism. The institutions of collaboration—ministerial councils, officials' committees and joint administrative bodies—are executive bodies, and the lines of authority and accountability are based on consultation, clearance and agreement by ministers. To achieve this, highly formalised structures and procedures may be set out in the intergovernmental agreements. One vital step towards making these structures effective instruments of pooled executive power is the surrender of the veto in favour of majority voting rules for many decisions. In this way ministerial councils, for example, take on an executive life of their own, rather than being purely constituent bodies. With state and Commonwealth powers transferred to such bodies of joint decision-making, and to similarly mandated intergovernmental administrative and advisory agencies, the question clearly arises as to whether 'intergovernmental cooperation smothers its federal features' (Crommelin 1986, 46).

Not surprisingly, despite all their apparent enthusiasm for co-operation, some state premiers became suspicious of this emerging collaborative model. In fact, in so far as state premiers did collaborate in such developments, they revealed a fundamental contradiction or tension in their political strategies. As discussed earlier, for the states the central issues on the agenda of cooperative federalism were Commonwealth jurisdictional invasion or intrusion and vertical fiscal imbalance. Joint action to solve problems of coordination over implementing microeconomic reform was sometimes secondary. In addressing overlap and fiscal reform, the states were seeking to assert and assure their autonomy as self-governing units in the federation. They wished to retain the capacity to act independently and to set their own political course and policy priorities, and for this they had to escape the domination of the Commonwealth. They sought a restoration of balance or equality in an arm's-length federation of separate executives and of quasi-sovereign, distinct parliaments. Their experience was of a system where the Commonwealth had come to possess the power to act unilaterally in ways that all too often put the states on the losing end, and of the Commonwealth's hierarchical models of administrative cooperation in which the states were suborned or coerced to do its bidding. This was a perversion of an arm's-length federal model, in which Commonwealth unilateralism and coercion had between them brought about a process of creeping centralisation.

The danger was that, unless these perceived deficiencies were corrected, the participation by the states in cooperative arrangements would provide yet another way in which the Commonwealth would entrench its dominance. Cooperation to achieve agreed outcomes would, without a sure basis for each participant to have recourse to independent action, depart so far from a situation of mutuality among equals as to become a process of coercive closure (like the Financial Premiers' Conferences). Any cooperative arrangements arrived at in this setting would be so loaded with Commonwealth interests and priorities as to be centralism in a new guise.

As has been the case throughout the history of the federation, the smaller (less populous) and more peripheral states had more to fear from a collaborative process than the large eastern states, and more to lose by departing from an arm's-length, more adversarial federal politics. Significantly, however, the longer the SPC and COAG processes went on, the more united became the states' alternative position and the more coherent their contrasting image of the future of federalism. There was a conscious effort to reach a common view. As described in later chapters, the states set up their own distinct forum for reaching common positions and advancing their views. At a meeting in November 1991 they agreed to four principles that would guide their approach to federal affairs (see Chapter 3). A sphere of distinct Commonwealth activity in national affairs was acknowledged, but a claim was also made for a say in defining the national interest. And there was an attempt to reconcile the fact of cooperation and collective action to solve joint problems with the existence of vigorous, independent state governments, through a firm statement of the subsidiarity principle on the one hand (stressing the benefits of decentralisation and diversity) and the

THEORY AND PRACTICE OF COOPERATIVE FEDERALISM   27

need to remedy vertical fiscal imbalance on the other. Accountability was also highlighted, significantly through reaffirming a model of dual government:

> Integrated policy depends on the capacity of each government to coordinate and integrate the range of issues affecting its jurisdiction. The interests of citizens, the efficiency of government and accountability to electorates are all enhanced by developing the capacity for integrated decision making at each level in the federation.
>
> ... Accountability to Parliaments should be a major focus, and this would be enhanced considerably by reform of the vertical fiscal imbalance, of the nature and conditions of tied grants, of the allocation of responsibilities and of the processes of intergovernmental relations. [Premiers and Chief Ministers, communiqué, November 1991, attachment]

While not reconciling the accountability dilemmas of joint collective action among executives (in particular the problems of parliamentary scrutiny of such action), these statements begin to acknowledge the fundamental importance to state governments of escaping the embraces of a one-sided, collaborative system engineered via a cooperative process. In the states' image of a balanced, arm's-length federation, co-operation would be on the basis of 'legitimately shared objectives, a relationship of mutual trust and economic incentives to cooperate rather than confront' (Premiers and Chief Ministers, communiqué, November 1991, attachment).

This last point hinted again at the question of finances. It echoed Greiner's argument in his July 1990 speech about the 'irrational structures' of federal–state relations, particularly financial relations. That type of argument has been taken further. First, fiscal autonomy, including taxing powers, is a *sine qua non* of any properly constituted, independent government. Second, in a federal system where powers are shared, the distribution of fiscal capacity must coincide with the allocation of functions. There must be 'fiscal equivalence'—that is, each government financing its expenditure from funds it raises in its own name: 'Inefficient compromises, free-riding and much political conflict are then avoided ... Fiscal equivalence would create many incentives for state and local governments to cultivate their own tax base by pursuing good, far-sighted development policies and by competing to attract mobile capital and talent' (Kasper 1993, 174). Cooperation in a context where the economic incentives are perverse (e.g. in the case of vertical fiscal imbalance) is likely only to compound the distortions and inefficiencies, encouraging collusion, and further blurring transparency and accountability (Sproule-Jones 1975). Such a view has been put by Australian critics of COAG (Nahan 1995). They argue that 'cooperation' is either a process in which politicians and bureaucrats get

28 COLLABORATIVE FEDERALISM

together to enlarge the scope of public power for their individual benefit, or a sham behind which the Commonwealth concentrates its power *vis-à-vis* other governments (or perhaps it is both). From this perspective, fiscal equivalence and a clean division of functions are essential elements in a properly constituted federal system. There is another presumption as well: that the constituent units—the states—should be the prime movers, and the central government should be severely limited in scope and powers. Kasper (1993, 175) espouses a classical, coordinate model of the division of powers in which the Commonwealth looks after 'foreign affairs, defence, monetary probity, rules for nation-wide transport and communications, laws and regulations concerning civil and business interaction, and not much else'.

This view calls on a model of competitive federalism in which competing governments strive to offer the most efficient and responsive packages of goods and services (Breton 1985; 1996). The theory of competitive federalism has its origins in an economic analysis of systems of decentralised government, in which multiple jurisdictions offer distinctive bundles of services and policies, each attracting different firms and residents and, in the process, competing with each other: innovating, experimenting, specialising and (in aggregate) maximising both political responsiveness and economic efficiency. Dealing with spillovers and achieving any economies of scale would be tackled via inter-jurisdictional cooperation as much as through a federal government. This, too would occur best as a direct result of the unimpeded responsiveness of governments to the demands of their citizens.

As already pointed out, elements of this model are far removed from the reality of Australia's federal Constitution, which entrenches concurrence. Critics also point out the negative potential of interstate competition, encapsulated in the phrase 'the race to the bottom', and best illustrated by the counter-productive bidding wars of incentives and concessions state governments engage in to attract investors (Industry Commission 1996). Nevertheless, the image of competitive federalism (albeit much blurred and muddled) is not confined to a few economic liberals, but has entered the public realm as part of a rhetoric in defence of the states against the Commonwealth. Wayne Goss in a speech in July 1995 enunciated the principle as follows:

> In a federation, states compete 'horizontally' for jobs and investment through different regulatory, taxation, investment and expenditure policies. This also enables the states and Territories to offer different fiscal and social policy mixes. This has the capacity to advance national efficiency while encouraging states and Territories to act as 'laboratories of democracy' in experimentation with particular expenditure programs. [Goss 1995, 7]

THEORY AND PRACTICE OF COOPERATIVE FEDERALISM   29

Two different models of 'competition' are being muddled: first, a cut-throat war to win market share, each jurisdiction picking its own winning formula based on distinctive attributes, talents, or policies; and second, a somewhat more benign version, where one state innovates and others emulate if it succeeds. The first leads to diversity (indeed it logically depends on it); but the second can lead to uniformity, assuming everyone follows the winning formula (Painter 1991a).

Logical consistency aside, some of the themes are appealing. Goss put a 'national efficiency' spin on his appeal so as to tackle the Commonwealth on its own ground—the importance of microeconomic reform to improving international competitiveness. This is a point on which the states agree: it is one of the four principles (the 'structural efficiency principle') of the November 1991 leaders' communiqué. But the way to achieve it from the perspective of a model of competitive federalism would not be via collaboration, but via arm's-length competition coupled with cooperation only where absolutely necessary. In this view, most areas of microeconomic reform would proceed more effectively if the states and the Commonwealth left each other alone to get on with it, with the states seeking to make the best of their own 'natural advantages' by picking distinctive strategies and picking up clues from each other's successes and failures, striving to outdo each other, and accelerating the pace of reform in the search for competitive advantage and growth. In contrast, collaboration (understood in this context as cooperation on the Commonwealth's terms in SPC and COAG) blunts and undermines the competitive dynamic and produces an unnecessary level of conformity that stifles initiative and experimentation.

The image of competitive federalism mobilised by state leaders in the public debates is somewhat distant from the economists' theoretical formulations. Its main point is to package the states' major claims in an attractive wrapping: remedy fiscal imbalance; remove unnecessary financial controls and replace special-purpose grants with block grants; get the Commonwealth out of whole domains of traditional state policy; and devolve functions. In the climate of the 1990s this might seem to be a winning formula. It echoes neo-liberal sentiments about small government, and it strikes at a number of commonly perceived sources of government inefficiency. Indeed, the Howard government's National Commission of Audit in 1996, although not a strong supporter of competitive federalism *per se*, supported all of these propositions (although in some cases, in seeking a clean separation of powers and functions it allocated one or two to the Commonwealth that the states wanted for themselves). The National Commission of Audit also took the claims about cost savings arising from removing duplication at face value: where a function was devolved to the states along with a block

30 COLLABORATIVE FEDERALISM

grant, the grant should amount to only 90 per cent of the previous level of funding (NCOA 1996, 32). All of this was a bit academic in any case. The Commonwealth's response in 1996 was to accept only half of the package: devolve some of the functions, but not the funds, much less the fiscal power.

The linking of competitive federalism with microeconomic reform as part of a political strategy to advance the interests of the states against the Commonwealth could be a double-edged sword for other reasons. Competition can get nasty. It is divisive. Larger, richer states begin to see even less reason for fiscal equalisation, for example: doesn't equalisation, by smoothing out diversities, contradict the whole basis of competitive advantage? But the smaller states, seeking to create for themselves new niches in the international scramble for investment, vigorously assert both their right to a 'fair go' through fiscal equalisation, and also their right to develop policy and reform packages embodying special concessions and attractions to business, with a view to stealing investment from the metropolitan magnets of Sydney and Melbourne. When Wayne Goss halved the transaction tax on stock exchange dealings in May 1995, and announced the location of a new exchange in Brisbane, the premiers of New South Wales and Victoria cried 'foul'. The New South Wales treasurer called for an interstate agreement on harmonising tax rates, fearing a race to the bottom and the further steady erosion of state tax bases under this form of competition. Indeed, the potential for competition to deplete and distort the tax base and to result in less than optimal collective provision of public goods is a real one, and as much a potential source of perverse incentives and collective ruin as is vertical fiscal imbalance (Industry Commission 1996).

On all matters of policy and politics, the states as a group cannot be viewed as a permanent, solid bloc. Their unity over federal fiscal reform in recent years has been unusual and it has not extended to all aspects of financial relations, particularly fiscal equalisation. In so far as they share common ground as part of a defence of state jurisdiction against the Commonwealth, they also share certain underlying positions about the nature of the federation. As discussed in this chapter, the states have mobilised some distinctive models and images of federalism to challenge the centralist elements in the Hawke agenda of cooperation. This battle of rhetoric and imaging has been one part of the attempt to shape the course of events and defend their positions on SPC and COAG during the process of change. But the states are inevitably caught in a double bind in so doing, for the very fact of cooperating and framing common positions mutes their distinctiveness and suppresses their individuality. In so far as this is part of an adversarial, arm's-length,

THEORY AND PRACTICE OF COOPERATIVE FEDERALISM

political process, it might strengthen the states; but as following chapters show, the search for unity and common ground in a collaborative setting such as COAG is a different matter, and fraught with dangers for the sustenance of their federal traditions and visions.

Conclusion

In this chapter, a vocabulary of competing conceptualisations of Australian federalism has been elaborated, drawing on a review of different images and models of federalism. Hawke's New Federalism and the challenges of coping with the agenda of microeconomic reform brought to the surface fundamental issues of federal design. The participants in the process themselves picked up on many of the issues and mobilised a variety of federal ideas. The rhetoric of cooperation that developed around such issues as overlap, duplication and problems of harmonisation disguised a division of views between state and Commonwealth perspectives, and some divisions between the states themselves.

But images, models and rhetoric aside, what actually has been happening? Is it the case that SPC and COAG have contributed significantly to the resolution of coordination problems? If so, what exactly have been the institutional forms that have been applied to the task, why were they chosen, and how have they operated? From a closer look at the record, should we label it a cooperative episode in Australian federal history? Or was it a Commonwealth-inspired episode of yet more centralism? Has the result been a set of collaborative institutions modelled in such a way as to suppress diversity, and has this thwarted the potential for a more dynamic, competitive federalism? These questions are answered in the following chapters. We will then be in a position to ask: Is Australia's federal future as a system of interlocking, executive collaboration, guided by a dominant Commonwealth, or is there the possibility of a resurgence of arm's-length federalism?

CHAPTER 3

SPC, COAG and the Politics of Reform

The main aim of this chapter is to provide a narrative account of the work done by the Special Premiers' Conferences and the Council of Australian Governments (SPC and COAG) between 1990 and 1997. A couple of themes will emerge: first, that a considerable number of cooperative schemes and collaborative institutions were created during this period; but second, that the politics of reform was typically adversarial, and that the outcomes in some cases remained strongly contested by some of the protagonists. One recurring issue was the threat of Commonwealth domination, and in response the challenge of state resistance. For the sake of economic reform, the Commonwealth needed state cooperation. The Commonwealth had taken the lead during the 1980s, with deregulation of the financial markets in 1983–84, the ending of the two-airline policy and commercialisation of business enterprises, tariff reductions in 1988 and beyond and, by the end of the decade, halting steps in a privatisation program. It was now over to the states, as many saw it: electricity, gas, water, the transport industries, education and training, health and so on were all state-managed industries, while the states also were responsible for the existence of interstate barriers to free movement of goods and services, and a plethora of state regulatory regimes and instruments. The states were depicted as laggards. As Bob Hawke put it in his July 1990 speech: 'microeconomic reform ... is absolutely essential if we are to have a more competitive economy. My Government has acted to reform ... areas of virtually exclusive Commonwealth control. We still have unfinished business ... In advancing to the next stage, the co-operation of the states is essential ...'.

In fact, state governments by 1990 were already embarking on their own programs of economic reform. The inefficiencies of their public

SPC, COAG AND THE POLITICS OF REFORM 33

enterprises were an increasingly difficult burden to bear—particularly in a context of growing fiscal scarcity brought on by Commonwealth budgetary tightening—and they began to turn to commercialisation, pro-competitive reform and, in some cases, privatisation, for remedies. There had been important harbingers in some states of elements of such an agenda, such as the programs of deregulation and financial reform of the short-lived South Australian Liberal government elected in 1979 (Painter 1987). In the 1980s Labor governments in Victoria, South Australia and New South Wales implemented managerial reforms to some state enterprises and public service departments (Halligan and Power 1992; Laffin and Painter 1995).

But none of these governments saw public sector restructuring primarily in terms of policies of economic liberalisation. The Greiner government that came to office in New South Wales in early 1988 was the first in Australia elected with a program of structural reform that drew on a philosophical commitment to economic liberalism (Laffin and Painter 1995). It embarked on a program of commercialisation, including widespread application of contracting out and the corporatisation or privatisation of government business enterprises. State enterprises shed labour, contracted out much of their work, sold off unwanted assets, cut back on uneconomic services to the public, and restructured their charges so as to remove cross subsidies (mostly to the benefit of business customers). They began to make substantial profits and return handsome dividends to the state budget—indeed, state governments rather than customers were the principal beneficiaries of reform (Painter 1995; BIE 1995, 91). Where New South Wales had started to go, others followed. A growing economic and fiscal crisis in Victoria in the late 1980s and early 1990s, involving the collapse or winding down of key state economic development agencies (the Victorian Economic Development and Victorian Investment Corporations and subsequently the State Bank) triggered the resignation of Premier Cain, a reappraisal by Labor, the sale of the bank and—ultimately—the election of the Kennett government in October 1992, with a radical neo-liberal reform program. Labor governments also lost office under similar circumstances during 1993 in South Australia, where Dean Brown was elected premier, and in Western Australia, where Richard Court defeated Carmen Lawrence. Kennett and Brown embarked on major austerity and labour-shedding programs, and cuts to services, along with contracting out and privatisation programs. Meanwhile, the Goss Labor government in Queensland also pursued significant programs of public enterprise and regulatory reform, but stopped short of privatisation. The Greiner and Fahey governments, having run into political difficulties in New South Wales, were succeeded by the Carr

34 COLLABORATIVE FEDERALISM

Labor government in 1995. Far from turning the clock back or seeking an alternative way, this government seemed intent on outdoing its predecessors in the microeconomic reform stakes.

A fillip to a growing national focus on state government economic reform performance was provided by the Industry Commission. From 1989 (with its anti-protection agenda seemingly all but fulfilled), the commission was asked to turn its attention to microeconomic reform. In its inquiries and reports it focused increasingly on public enterprise and regulatory reform at state government level (Carroll 1995). It noted progress in New South Wales and in some other places, but constantly urged faster and more widespread change. It tended to highlight the national, rather than state, dimensions of these issues —that is, the extent to which problems had significance for national economic performance and required cross-jurisdictional remedies.

Thus the growing pace of reform in the 1990s was due to a combination of circumstances, including partisan factors. The states themselves increasingly determined and shaped the agenda. They felt the most immediate pressures to press on with reform, and by the mid-1990s had become the front-runners. This spread of the reform agenda in the 1990s through the different jurisdictions might in itself be said to be a feature of a federal system, where experimentation and emulation can assist in the diffusion and implementation of reform (Nahan 1995). There was a considerable degree of cross-fertilisation and learning—for example Queensland's Green Paper on corporatisation was published after 'having studied the experience of the Commonwealth, New Zealand and New South Wales' (Halligan and Power 1992, 199). The states faced similar pressures and adopted similar responses, albeit with significant variations. For example, the Goss Labor government inherited a very sound fiscal position and was able to proceed relatively cautiously with commercialisation and corporatisation, without any pressure to institute severe economy measures or 'sell off the silver'. There was also intense competition between the states to attract investment by offering low taxes, along with efficient, cheap infrastructure and services and a positive business climate. Ratings in the financial markets became particularly important following the relaxation of central controls over state borrowing under the Loan Council, culminating in 1994 in virtual deregulation. The rating agencies reflected prevailing doctrines and expected the states to press ahead with market-liberalising policies and structural efficiency measures in the public sector. In sum, the pressures to outdo each other in microeconomic reform intensified in the national and international political and economic climate of the 1990s.

Commonwealth–State Interdependencies and Economic Reform

Ironically, reform in the states was impeded by Commonwealth policies. Commonwealth tax policies and the prevailing Loan Council rules provided severe disincentives to corporatisation and privatisation (Sturgess 1990; Painter 1995). For example, a privatised government trading enterprise, instead of paying dividends to the state government and enjoying the status of corporate tax exemption as a statutory body, would pay a proportion of its profits as company tax to the Commonwealth. This was a serious issue for state governments facing fiscal strains. The Greiner government was able to balance its budget only by taking large dividends out of its public monopolies (Painter 1995). Greiner was not willing to transform this into a windfall for the Commonwealth government, particularly as he perceived that its strategy was to diminish state government power and autonomy by tightening the financial screws. This was one of the reasons that Greiner saw the issue of federal financial relations as a key item on the federal reform agenda in 1990.

Commonwealth leadership was seen to be required for another reason: to provide a means of breaking the log-jam of cross-boundary coordination problems. Many of the items in this area that appeared subsequently on the SPC reform agenda had a long history of inaction or slow progress, despite a growing recognition of the need for harmonisation. In some—such as road transport regulation and rail—the Commonwealth had become increasingly involved, even though the primary responsibility remained with the states. This nationalisation of policy issues and reform effort has been a long and seemingly inexorable process (Nelson 1992), but the urgency of economic reform gave it a new emphasis.

There were some in Canberra who argued for vigorous, unilateral Commonwealth action—for example, more aggressive use of the corporations power—but the government opted for a less confrontationist strategy. Several state leaders had begun to express a willingness to cooperate, and the signs looked good for such a strategy. Nor can we discount the significance for this choice of strategy of Bob Hawke's personal predilection for a consensual style of politics. But the main, underlying reason for seeking cooperation was that there were strong doubts about the limits of the Commonwealth's constitutional powers, and hence a valid fear of uncertain and damaging political outcomes. Three general reasons have always provided strong arguments for the Commonwealth to tread cautiously in such instances. First, the unpredictable outcome of any challenge to the High Court from an invasion of state jurisdiction can sometimes create more problems for the Commonwealth than it resolves—a negotiated political settlement offers

36   COLLABORATIVE FEDERALISM

at least the certainty of influencing the outcome. Second, the invasion
creates political friction that state governments and opposition parties
can often exploit to their advantage, particularly when a government is
politically vulnerable for other reasons, such as the state of the economy.
Third, the occupancy of new jurisdiction in a climate of hostility brings
with it material costs and burdens that the Commonwealth may be ill
equipped to bear, particularly because of its deficiencies in administrative capacity and knowledge. The possession of these capacities by the
states often tips the balance towards cooperation.

The Launch

In the months leading up to the June 1990 Financial Premiers' Conference, Hawke had suggested on more than one occasion that it was
time for a new initiative in intergovernmental relations. Responses were
mostly positive. Just before the conference John Bannon, then the
senior premier, launched an 'eleven-point plan' to reform federal–
state financial relations. Four years earlier, he had sought to launch a
similar initiative, without success (Bannon 1987). Nick Greiner responded by circulating a paper titled *Microeconomic Reform of Commonwealth–State Relations*, drafted by Garry Sturgess in his Cabinet Office,
containing proposals to rationalise finances, functions and program
relations. Encouraged by these signs, Hawke placed microeconomic
reform on the agenda of the June financial conference, and also
signalled the possibility of a further 'special Premiers' Conference'
(*AFR*, 13 June 1990). His opening speech at the June conference
promised a new start, to 'manage our relationship across a wider range
of federal issues more effectively and cooperatively ... not merely to
correct this or that particular defect but to begin a process leading to a
genuine partnership' (*AFR*, 29 June 1990).

But as it turned out, Hawke had chosen an inauspicious moment to
launch a cooperative initiative. The deepening recession called for a
firm strategy on the budget surplus and cuts to expenditure. As a
consequence, the June conference was a bitter, acrimonious event from
which the premiers departed angry. The Commonwealth's 1990
financial offer significantly tightened the screws on the states' own
budgets by offsetting increases in special-purpose grants with decreases
in general-revenue grants, capital assistance and borrowing approvals.
Bannon's eleven-point plan for reform targeted precisely these aspects
of the Commonwealth's approach to fiscal relations. The premiers
reacted to the offer on the afternoon of the first day of the conference
by unanimously rejecting it. Bannon acted as spokesperson at a press
conference, earning himself the lasting ire of the treasurer. Paul Keating

SPC, COAG AND THE POLITICS OF REFORM 37

was obdurate and dismissive, telling the states they could take it or leave it. Of course, they had no choice. The premiers' grievances over finances were deep-seated. Not only had they experienced the tightest fiscal squeeze since World War II, but the Commonwealth had at the same time rapidly increased the proportion of total grants disbursed as special-purpose payments (Edwards and Henderson 1995). The premiers felt betrayed. Who was running the show, Hawke or Keating?

The prime minister was facing up to the same question. Never far from the surface at this time were questions about the leadership succession and a possible challenge by Keating. Hawke's speech at the National Press Club on 19 July, with its rhetoric of closer partnership, was an attempt by him to save face, reassert his leadership and recapture the initiative. Microeconomic reform was the priority, but he also mentioned the environment, duplication of services, constitutional reform, industrial relations, federal finances and social justice. In addition, he 'would welcome further suggestions from the Premiers as to what they want discussed'. A further conciliatory gesture was his announcement of a hand-over to the states of the bank accounts debits tax. He announced the setting up of a Commonwealth–state officials' committee chaired by the secretary of his department to prepare the agenda, and the establishment of a new unit in his department to provide continuing support.

Nick Greiner's instinctive response to journalists who informed him of Hawke's speech was to applaud it. One week later he also gave a speech at the National Press Club, in which he promised his firm commitment to an agenda of federal reform. He raised many of the same issues as Hawke and offered his own gesture of goodwill—to hand industrial relations over to the Commonwealth (Greiner 1990). It could well have suited Greiner as the lone non-Labor premier to take a more sceptical, negative view over the months ahead. Some of his ministerial colleagues could see the pitfalls of getting too close to what had been, up to this point, a centralist Labor government. But Greiner showed his hand. He could not resist the prospect of extending his economic reform ambitions to the federal stage and of being part of a national, coordinated effort (Laffin and Painter 1995). As to the other states, it was partly a matter of falling into line. All were Labor premiers, and the combined forces of Bannon and Hawke were enough to bring them on board. Above all they were attracted by the prospect of financial reform.

The Brisbane Conference, October 1990

The rancour of June and the gulf between the states and the Commonwealth on federal financial relations were not forgotten, but over

38   COLLABORATIVE FEDERALISM

the months leading up to the Brisbane conference, premiers and the prime minister bit their tongues and echoed the rhetoric of goodwill and cooperation. The open invitation to put matters onto the table for discussion was an important stimulus to cooperation. It was not without risks, but the process of formulating the agenda for October was carefully managed so as to try to avoid them. The head of the Prime Minister's Department met with his state counterparts to set up a process, including a series of working parties, to ensure a smooth passage to and beyond Brisbane. As well as the headline issues in the Hawke and Greiner speeches, such as duplication, federal finance, the national economic market and environmental policy, other items presented themselves from an already existing agenda of intergovernmental joint action: proposals for a national rail freight corporation and for co-operation on harmonisation of road transport regulation and charging were already well advanced, for example; national food standards and uniform building regulations were also under discussion. Hurdles to agreement on these matters remained, but much of the groundwork had been done. New South Wales put corporatisation and privatisation of government trading enterprises on the agenda. The peak officials' meetings divided up the work required to bring matters to a point fit for presentation in October. In some cases, machinery was already in place and simply needed a new stimulus; in others, work had to be newly assigned. The object was a series of position papers with recommen-dations for agreement by heads of government on key topics. For example, the New South Wales Premier's Department was given the job of drafting proposals on government trading enterprises. Some items were left to the states to agree on and to present 'state papers'. A joint Commonwealth–state group of officials prepared a paper on duplica-tion of services.

Hawke needed progress on economic reform, but the states, while not hostile to this agenda, remained primarily concerned with their financial grievances. The price they tried to extract for cooperation was a serious commitment by the Commonwealth to look at these issues. In striking this deal, political tensions quickly became apparent. Neither the political rhetoric nor the smooth work of officials entirely submerged these tensions. In the weeks leading up to Brisbane, the public sparring began in earnest. The states were seeking either new revenue powers or a more satisfactory revenue-sharing deal, and a restructuring of financial grants so as to reduce the proportion of special-purpose payments. Treasurer Keating did not see vertical fiscal imbalance as a problem but as a virtue, because it allowed the Commonwealth to control national fiscal outcomes as part of its role in macroeconomic management and gave the Commonwealth the necessary levers to direct expenditures through special-purpose grants. Keating, with the support of many Commonwealth spending ministers, put these views forcefully in cabinet and caucus, and obtained from Hawke a public commitment that the Commonwealth would not surrender any control over national economic policy.

The Brisbane conference, however, went relatively smoothly. Press releases, media interviews and public reporting presented an image of goodwill and partnership. So, too, did the carefully worded communiqué. The first item announced a major review of financial relations which acknowledged both the 'need to address ... vertical fiscal imbalance' and the 'national responsibility for effective macroeconomic management'. The gulf at this stage was only papered over. More firm was a commitment to reduce tied grants and to undertake reviews of duplication of services. Agreement was reached on the need for a single, commercial national rail freight corporation; general principles for a national scheme of road transport regulation and charging; a scheme of uniform regulations for non-bank financial institutions; a series of committees working to specific timetables on regulatory reform to create a 'national market'; the desirability of an intergovernmental agreement on the environment; and an investigation into setting up of a national electricity grid. Additional SPC meetings, with their agendas already guaranteed to be crowded from these and other initiatives, were scheduled for May and November 1991.

To Sydney in July 1991

Due to a snap election for May 1991 called by Nick Greiner, the May SPC meeting was postponed to July. The May Financial Premiers' Conference dealt with two items of business from the October 1990 meeting: a national scheme of regulation for non-bank financial institutions and a deal on freeing government trading enterprises operating on a commercial basis from the global borrowing controls of the Loan Council (along with agreement by the Commonwealth to provide temporary financial assistance to state governments undertaking restructuring of their trading enterprises, e.g. for redundancy payment schemes). In fact the arrangements for exempting these enterprises from Loan Council controls set such tight guidelines on commercialisation that no enterprise qualified (EPAC 1995, 140).

The July SPC meeting merely noted progress and acknowledged interim reports from working parties on the financial issues, with the matter set down for further consideration at the October SPC. The major achievements were in microeconomic reform: signing of agreements on setting up a National Road Transport Commission to bring in

COLLABORATIVE FEDERALISM

uniform heavy-vehicle regulations and charging; the setting up of a National Rail Corporation; the establishment of a National Grid Management Council to oversee integration of electricity supply and distribution into an interstate market; and agreement in principle on implementation of a mutual recognition scheme for state regulations covering goods and occupations. The agreement on road vehicle regulation was accompanied by the untying of $350 million in Commonwealth road grants and agreement by the Commonwealth to delineate more precisely its field of responsibility for roads to restrict it solely to a system of national highways. A joint working party also was set up to consider a national approach to competition policy.

So far, so good. As we discuss in Chapter 4, the negotiations and discussions surrounding some of these issues and agreements involved a great deal of brinkmanship, strong-arm tactics and complex, ingenious deals and compromises. The road and rail agreements, for example, nearly came unstuck at the last minute. But the pressures to agree and to show concrete achievements were strong. They arose partly from the high public expectations set in motion back in October, and partly because political reputations were on the line as a result of the strong commitment to the process shown by the political leaders, a commitment that had grown with the frequency and intensity of personal interaction. Regular meetings of key state and Commonwealth advisers and officials also built up a momentum of their own, with each of the teams of advisers working closely with their respective political leaders.

November 1991 in Adelaide

All nearly came disastrously undone in October and November. The root of the problem was Hawke's insecurity as leader of the Labor Party. Paul Keating resigned as treasurer in June 1991 and unsuccessfully challenged Hawke for the prime ministership. Keating retired to the backbench, but no-one doubted that a further challenge was coming. Hawke's New Federalism was one of Keating's targets in his campaign during the second half of 1991. In a speech in October 1991 (also, like those of Hawke and Greiner in July 1990, delivered to the National Press Club) he mounted a strong critique of the whole process, condemning it for taking place out of the public eye and, above all, for threatening to surrender to the states vital powers that, he claimed, a national government must retain. His principal target was the new deal being mooted on federal finances, and his views echoed rumblings and protests from several ministers and within caucus. Hawke was vulnerable and under attack. Doubt and confusion grew in early November, with the leaking of drafts of the officials' reports to COAG and their use by the opposition in the federal parliament to sow division in the government's ranks. The reports revealed the divisions that existed between state and Commonwealth views, and expressed doubts and reservations about each of the options. They were handy weapons for those seeking to undermine the process. Caucus demanded reassurance from Hawke that the outcome would not be the kind of 'surrender' that Keating had depicted.

Three options had been identified to remedy vertical fiscal imbalance: a separately identified state income tax within a national collection scheme; a guaranteed share of Commonwealth income tax collections; and a hand-over to the states of some excise taxes. Talk of a state income tax raised public fears. State premiers were loath to use the phrase and some of them rejected it outright. Opponents of federal fiscal reform in the federal Labor caucus and cabinet succeeded in making the spectre of a state income tax the symbolic battleground of the whole issue. Versions of the first option for reform created a state income tax in all but name by allowing some discretion for an individual state to vary the rate levied on its portion of the collections. Under increasing pressure, at a caucus meeting on 4 November Hawke and Treasurer Kerin ruled out a state income tax, threw cold water on the transfer of excises, and spoke against any scheme for a fixed or guaranteed share of revenue. State premiers were angry, claiming that every possible option had seemingly been rejected. Premiers Lawrence and Bannon both threatened to call off the November meeting if none of the options was on the table.

The states, stung into action, reached an agreed public position on a shared national income tax system. A single assessment and collection system would remain, but a base rate (proposed at 6 cents) would be collected for the states. Over time, this rate could be varied by an individual state. An Australian Council of the Federation would meet annually to harmonise tax rates in the light of national fiscal and macroeconomic considerations. Greiner and Bannon talked with Hawke about the proposal. Concessions were discussed to meet anticipated objections: the capacity of a state to vary the rate could be phased in after a period (three years); and the Commonwealth might be given a power of veto (although the states could not agree on this proposal). Cabinet on 11 November 1991 rejected the premiers' plan, and in response the premiers carried out their threat and withdrew from the November SPC. These events were a severe blow to Hawke's political stature. He had invested greatly in the 'closer partnership', and it had come unstuck. He had been unable to carry either party or cabinet with him to fulfil his commitment to reform federal–state relations. For their part, the states had refused to back down or

42 COLLABORATIVE FEDERALISM

compromise merely for the sake of Hawke's personal political future. The prime minister sought to revive the process, but to no avail. Not long after, Keating mounted a successful party room challenge and became prime minister.

The state and territory leaders, having cancelled the conference planned for Perth, went ahead with their own meeting at the appointed time in Adelaide. It continued progress on important business that had been part of the SPC agenda, including agreement on a scheme of mutual recognition, to begin in January 1993, under which the states would refer the power to the Commonwealth to apply uniform legislation; formal agreement in principle on the non-bank financial institutions scheme; agreement on further extension of the role and scope of the national road vehicle regulation and charging scheme; and approval in principle of the need for a national competition policy (with the reservation that extension of the Trade Practices Act to cover exempt areas under state jurisdiction would 'remain the prerogative of each government on a case by case basis').

The meeting also reaffirmed the states' agenda for financial reform and their determination to pursue it. Two other initiatives demonstrated a growing sense of common purpose among the states. First, they firmed up their earlier proposal for a Council of the Federation to provide for a 'permanent, deliberative forum'. High on the list of items for it to consider would be fiscal reform and the division of powers and functions, but mention was also made of 'promotion of the economic union' and 'supporting continuing reform and efforts to improve the structural efficiency of both the Australian Federation and the economy'. The prime minister was invited to become the council's first chair. Second, the states and territories agreed on four principles for the allocation of roles and responsibilities among levels of government:

1. The 'Australian Nation principle' affirmed the need for national policies in the national interest but, staking a claim for state and territory involvement, calling for 'cooperation, involving collective action on the part of all levels of government' and asserting that 'in the articulation of the national interest the Commonwealth has a primary but not exclusive role'.
2. The 'subsidiarity principle' called for devolution to the maximum extent possible consistent with the national interest.
3. The 'structural efficiency principle' affirmed the need for continuing microeconomic reform with a special focus on 'the allocative and productive efficiency of governmental arrangements' (including federalism itself).

4. The 'accountability principle' called for 'democratic accountability and transparency' in intergovernmental arrangements (first and foremost, reform of vertical fiscal imbalance).

Agreement on joint, public affirmation of the four principles demonstrated the heightened sense of cohesion among the premiers that had come out of their participation in the SPC process. The Adelaide meeting reaffirmed the strength of commitment to their own vision of federal reform, while offering the Commonwealth an opportunity to keep the process of joint decision-making alive.

Newly anointed Prime Minister Paul Keating had every reason to distance himself from Hawke's New Federalism. Nevertheless, despite scorn for much of his predecessor's legacy, it soon became apparent that something would have to be put in its place. Keating seized the position of prime minister in the midst of a severe recession. He needed quickly to assert his leadership and produce some initiatives to cope with the economic crisis. His first major response was a package of expenditure and other economic measures announced at the end of February. The government dubbed the economic statement *One Nation*. The symbolism was not without irony, as many of the announced schemes required state-government involvement. The thrust of the package was to prime the pump through public investment, but in a way that achieved microeconomic reform objectives. Just as Hawke had found in 1990, many of the big-ticket structural reform issues facing the Keating government lay in state jurisdictions. Keating had reinvented much of the SPC agenda. Among the more ambitious plans were large-scale expenditure on railways (through the new National Rail Corporation) and investment in the proposed national electricity market. A new deal was proposed on technical and further education (TAFE)—to this point almost exclusively a state function, but subject to a Commonwealth takeover proposal in November 1991, which had been discussed and rejected by the premiers in Adelaide.

As had been the case in 1990, the majority of premiers were Labor, and this assisted in getting the states and the Commonwealth around the table again in 1992. The premiers in the one breath could congratulate Keating on the *One Nation* package while urging him to consider seriously their proposal for a Council of the Federation. Careful efforts were even made to take some of the heat out of the takeover plan for TAFE (*AFR*, 2 March 1992). Keating signalled he had an open mind on the states' proposals to revive the cooperative process (*AFR*, 10 March 1992), but it was clear that he could not be seen to have surrendered the initiative to them or to have lost face. When his approach to the states came in March, it laid down conditions. Most

44 COLLABORATIVE FEDERALISM

notably he insisted that the states' financial reform proposals would not be part of the agenda of a new round of meetings, although he agreed to consider other ways to provide them with more fiscal certainty and flexibility. He rejected the proposal for a Council of the Federation in the precise form proposed by the states, but showed a willingness to institute some new arrangement. This shadow-boxing opened a further exchange of conciliatory statements in which, once again, potential points of friction and grievances were submerged.

The Commonwealth and state heads of government met on 11 May 1992. They agreed to set up a Council of Australian Governments (COAG), chaired by the Commonwealth, to meet at least once a year, in addition to the annual Financial Premiers' Conference. Apart from a general injunction to facilitate 'increasing cooperation', the statement on its role referred to achieving 'an integrated, efficient national economy and a single national market ... [and] continuing structural reform of government' and consultation on issues including international treaties and major items emerging from ministerial council deliberations. Reference was made to rationalising and regularising these separate, functional ministerial councils. On finances, the Commonwealth shifted the agenda, focusing attention on the upcoming June Premiers' Conference with a proposal for greater medium-term national fiscal coordination and planning. The Commonwealth acknowledged also a more limited agenda of reform to meet state grievances, referring to 'predictability, flexibility and growth of state funding'. The meeting also picked up outstanding SPC items, including confirming the Commonwealth's role in the agreed mutual recognition scheme, and reaffirming commitment to the work of the National Grid Management Council, National Road Transport Commission and National Rail. The matter of vocational and technical education was put off until the June Financial Conference.

Keating and the States, 1992–93

Keating let his centralist predilections show in public more frequently than had Hawke, and his style was more abrasive and aggressive. But during 1992 the states won some important concessions. For example, the Commonwealth's need to see the economy pick up before a 1993 federal election assured them a relatively generous financial deal (although not generous enough either to satisfy the premiers or to prevent some from using the outcome as an excuse to raise state taxes), and Keating agreed to a formula that provided a guaranteed growth factor to general-revenue grants. In July, the conflict over TAFE funding was resolved with a compromise under which the Commonwealth

SPC, COAG AND THE POLITICS OF REFORM

retreated significantly from its initial position, agreeing instead to an arrangement under which a new National Training Authority would disburse funds in accord with agreed reform objectives. It would be supervised by a ministerial council. On other issues the states were outflanked. For example, they refused to participate in a proposed national review of competition policy which, however, went ahead in any case in October when the Commonwealth appointed Professor Fred Hilmer to conduct an independent review.

Federal–state politics entered a more adversarial phase during 1992, and omens were not good for the first COAG meeting set down for December. With the passage of time, new figures had appeared on the scene and a more abrasive partisan climate had developed. In February 1992, Liberal Ray Groom replaced Michael Field in Tasmania. In the middle of the year, Nick Greiner was replaced by John Fahey as Liberal Premier of New South Wales; in September John Bannon was swept from office by the State Bank collapse and replaced by Labor colleague Lyn Arnold; and in October, the Liberals under Jeff Kennett won the Victorian state election. Most of the initiators of the new federal partnership in 1990 had left the scene. Table 3.1 shows the level of turnover that had occurred by 1993, including the marked shift in partisan balance. Kennett's advent was perhaps the most significant development. His stunning victory in 1992 posed a serious challenge to Labor's grip on the economic reform agenda, and the extent of the Labor rout in Victoria directly threatened the party's national electoral fortunes. Keating had to take him on, and he chose to make a major issue out of Kennett's proposal for industrial relations reform. The Commonwealth government invoked the external relations power to pass legislation that provided Victorian unionists with a 'haven' of Commonwealth arbitration provisions so that they could escape the coverage of new anti-union state laws.

Conflict and division on this issue was bitter and rancorous, and centred on states' rights. The industrial relations issue threatened to overshadow the December 1992 COAG agenda. Indeed, it led to heated debate at the meeting, as a result of which the prime minister moved not one inch on his plans to override the Victorian law. There was some irony in this debate, in that one of the flourishes in the initial spirit of give-and-take in July 1990 had been a proposal by Greiner to cede industrial relations powers to the Commonwealth (even more ironic was that four years later, in November 1996, Kennett unilaterally ceded industrial relations powers to the Commonwealth). The proposal had been rejected in 1990 by the Labor premiers for fear of what might happen under a future Canberra Liberal government, given the federal opposition's industrial relations reform policies. Now that Kennett was

COLLABORATIVE FEDERALISM

Table 3.1: Parties and premiers, 1990–97

Year (July)	Federal	NSW	Vic.	Qld	SA	WA	Tas.	NT
1990	ALP Hawke	Lib./NP Greiner	ALP Kirner	ALP Goss	ALP Bannon	ALP Lawrence	ALP Field	CLP Perron
1991	ALP Hawke	Lib./NP Greiner	ALP Kirner	ALP Goss	ALP Bannon	ALP Lawrence	ALP Field	CLP Perron
1992	ALP Keating	Lib./NP Fahey	ALP Kirner	ALP Goss	ALP Bannon	ALP Lawrence	Lib. Groom	CLP Perron
1993	ALP Keating	Lib./NP Fahey	Lib. Kennett	ALP Goss	ALP Arnold	Lib. Court	Lib. Groom	CLP Perron
1994	ALP Keating	Lib./NP Fahey	Lib. Kennett	ALP Goss	Lib. Brown	Lib. Court	Lib. Groom	CLP Perron
1995	ALP Keating	ALP Carr	Lib. Kennett	ALP Goss	Lib. Brown	Lib. Court	Lib. Groom	CLP Perron
1996	Lib./NP Howard	ALP Carr	Lib. Kennett	Nat./Lib. Borbidge	Lib. Brown	Lib. Court	Lib. Rundle	CLP Perron
1997	Lib./NP Howard	ALP Carr	Lib. Kennett	Nat./Lib. Borbidge	Lib. Olsen	Lib. Court	Lib. Rundle	CLP Stone

ALP: Australian Labor Party
CLP: Country Liberal Party
Lib.: Liberal Party
Nat./Lib.: National–Liberal coalition
NP: National Party

implementing very similar measures in one state, he could win unqualified support only from his Liberal counterparts Groom and Fahey. But there was broad support from the states for another proposal, seeking to restrain the Commonwealth from indiscriminately, and without consultation with the states, using its external affairs power. A ministerial committee was set up to look into the issue.

The COAG meeting of December 1992 was short on major initiatives. A rationalisation of ministerial councils was agreed to in principle, along with new protocols to improve their decision-making procedures. A National Forest Policy was signed by all states other than Tasmania, and among other agreements was one on a national Asian Language Development Program. The go-ahead was given to do more work on setting up the national electricity market and to undertake a review of the removal of barriers to interstate trade in gas. Besides the apparent decline in cooperative spirit due to the changing personnel and the heightened political tensions arising from new partisan divisions in Commonwealth–state relations, another factor was also taking the gloss off the achievements of the SPCs and COAG. Difficulties were by now being experienced in implementing some of the agreements. The national electricity market was getting bogged down, with the issue reappearing regularly on the COAG agenda as deadlines marking steps towards the final goal were postponed. Reform of interstate barriers to a national gas market was also meeting resistance. The National Rail Corporation was embroiled in protracted negotiations with the unions on a new set of employment conditions for railway workers, pending which the expenditure of Commonwealth *One Nation* funds on infrastructure to complete a national standard-gauge network was frozen. Meanwhile, state doubts and suspicions were growing over national competition policy. Only one premier—John Fahey in New South Wales—showed any public enthusiasm for the proposal.

However, competition policy, which was seized on by the Commonwealth as the next major step in microeconomic reform, became a reason for Keating once again to seek to revive cooperation with the states. In May 1993 the Hilmer Committee was given an extension on its reporting date and asked to consult more closely with the states. Keating and his advisers publicly stated they could achieve most of their competition policy objectives unilaterally, but privately they were admitting that the risks might be too high, due to constitutional uncertainties and the capacity for uncooperative, recalcitrant states to take evasive action to protect their monopolies from pro-competitive reform. When the report was released in August, it recommended a cooperative approach.

At the June 1993 COAG meeting in Melbourne, microeconomic reform was given fresh impetus with the establishment of an intergovernmental working group to identify an agenda of new policy initiatives. The June meeting also revived the issue of Commonwealth–state roles and responsibilities with a working group to report to the next meeting. In principle, all governments publicly supported economic reform, and key state as well as Commonwealth policy advisers—such as Ken Baxter, Kennett's chief public servant in Victoria —were prominent in urging more action. But this did not prevent friction over detailed aspects of the agenda of reform already agreed on. The South Australian government, for example, resisted pressure to conform with the Commonwealth's vision of a national electricity grid, refusing to separate complete ownership and control of its transmission network from its generating facilities. South Australia also rejected plans for free trade in gas on an interstate pipeline network (*AFR*, 10, 17 June 1993). Here as in other disagreements there was a divide between small and large states, with a tendency for Victoria and New South Wales to align more closely with the Commonwealth on measures to create national markets. There is a long history of attempts by the small

48 COLLABORATIVE FEDERALISM

states to protect themselves from commercial domination by Melbourne and Sydney, as well as political domination by Canberra, and many of the interstate barriers to free movement of goods, services and labour were the legacy.

The June COAG meeting was overshadowed by yet another outbreak of rancour resulting in deadlock, this time over the High Court *Mabo* judgement on Aboriginal land rights. Keating sought to use the meeting to set in motion a comprehensive, joint approach to resolving the issues of land titles and claims that arose from the judgement, but he did little to prepare the ground. State differences and resistance were so great that discussion proved fruitless. The recently elected Richard Court from Western Australia was among the most determined in resistance to Keating's proposals for a national response. There were now three aggressive, determined, confident and recently elected leaders, (Keating having just won the May 1993 federal election), each with publicly stated views that presaged confrontation rather than cooperation in intergovernmental relations.

To make matters more difficult for a smooth COAG outcome, John Dawkins as treasurer was in no mood in 1993 to be generous to the states over financial matters. In the lead-up to the Financial Premiers' Conference in July, he told the states that they were neither taxing to their full capacity nor doing all they could to restrain expenditures, so their calls for more money were futile (*AFR*, 28 June 1993). Tax competition between the states, he argued, had eroded their tax base. Before the Commonwealth could consider adding to their revenue-raising capacities, they should restore those they had voluntarily surrendered.

Following this round of exchanges, the Commonwealth's termination of previous policy on compensation for state government privatisation of major enterprises came as no surprise. Such compensation was defended on the basis of the loss of tax equivalent and dividend revenue from the state to the Commonwealth, but its origin was two special deals struck by Keating as treasurer with Labor governments in Victoria and South Australia, each desperate for financial help following the collapse of state-owned banks. Dawkins argued that compensation—which might amount to more than $10 billion in the foreseeable future—was unjustified, as any loss of tax equivalents would be offset by reduced interest payments following the sale of the asset. Each state was now restricted to one such compensation payout (including those already made) for a major state bank or insurance company. When this reversal was announced at the 1993 Financial Premiers' Conference, the result was a further fierce and bitter argument between the premiers on the one hand and the treasurer and prime minister on the other.

SPC, COAG AND THE POLITICS OF REFORM 49

At the same meeting steps were taken to deregulate state borrowings by rewriting the Loan Council rules, and to implement a coordinated state and Commonwealth process of aggregate budget forecasting and reporting under the name of the *National Fiscal Outlook*, including such things as nationally agreed debt targets. This had been foreshadowed by Treasurer Dawkins, and had been the subject of extensive consultation between state and Commonwealth Treasury officers. It was potentially a significant new tool of national fiscal management. Premiers Fahey and Kennett, in their remarks to the conference, complained once again about the atmosphere of take-it-or-leave-it, proposing instead a more thorough, extended conference of cooperative decision-making to take a 'more coordinated approach to economic and industry policy' (*Australian*, 6 July 1993). But the states also squabbled among themselves over fiscal equalisation, with a strong bid by Victoria and New South Wales to move to a per capita funding basis.

1994: Hobart and Darwin

The COAG meeting scheduled for the end of 1993 was postponed due to an election in South Australia, won by the Liberals under Dean Brown. Only Wayne Goss of Queensland and Marshall Perron of the Northern Territory were now left of the original SPC group of leaders, and Goss was also the only remaining Labor leader (see Table 3.1). In February 1994, on the eve of the postponed meeting set down for Hobart, Western Australia's Richard Court launched a strident attack on the Commonwealth's past and current invasions and abuses of states' rights in his 'Audit' of the powers 'usurped' by Canberra since federation. In the lead-up to that meeting, strong representations were made by the Business Council of Australia to both Commonwealth and state governments to bury their differences and make significant progress on competition policy, energy, and other items of microeconomic reform. Competition policy was now the key item on the Commonwealth's national reform program. But no state was keen to agree to the Commonwealth's version of a national scheme without vital guarantees and safeguards. Kennett, Court and Brown, in particular, would not wish to miss the opportunity to win plaudits from their home supporters for resisting Keating's 'power grabs', or at least for showing suspicion. In that context, the Keating government's industrial relations legislation, overriding that introduced by Kennett, was a key point of division.

Several premiers saw an opportunity to revive their claims for financial reforms. While Keating again dismissed any such proposal, reaffirming his centralist position on fiscal federalism in a speech at the Australian National University, he offered the smallest possible olive

50   COLLABORATIVE FEDERALISM

branch by at least admitting that the states had a right to exist and that
a cooperative approach was needed to implement economic reform
(*Australian*, 24 April 1994). But competition policy and state finances
were inextricably bound together, because a sticking-point for the states
in accepting the scheme was the loss to their revenues that would follow
from breaking up state monopolies and making their pricing policies
subject to outside, independent scrutiny. However, only Western
Australia had voiced objection to the underlying principles or objectives
of a national competition policy. The premiers and chief ministers met
briefly before the COAG meeting to discuss tactics, and Court's strident
opposition was toned down. Victoria and New South Wales were lined
up behind the objectives of the policy as a result of pressures from their
business communities, while Goss was under strong pressure from
Canberra not to break ranks with his Canberra party colleagues. He
took a conciliatory position in public statements amidst the posturing
and sparring, and played a vital role in brokering a peace. Despite some
strong reservations of other state and territory leaders, they agreed to
accept the broad principles of competition policy. But they decided to
insist on Commonwealth assistance for their loss of revenue, and to link
agreement with their demand for serious progress on a reduction in tied
grants. The leaders also agreed to meet at a longer session before the
next COAG.

The Hobart COAG meeting in February 1994 was relatively amicable,
with the states' common position forming the final basis for an agreement. It involved an acceptance of the Commonwealth's proposed
principles for competition policy, including some form of uniform
legislation, along with an agreement by the Commonwealth to look into
a limited form of compensation. Legislation and a series of agreements
were to be drafted for subsequent approval at COAG. Minor Commonwealth concessions were made on a timetable of implementation. The
communiqué also contained significant Commonwealth conciliatory
gestures on duplication and special-purpose grants, including a statement that proposed reviews would 'include consideration of tied grants
with a view to reducing their incidence'. State premiers hailed this as a
'breakthrough' (*AFR*, 28 February 1994). Closer attention to the communiqué, however, suggested otherwise: the issues were referred to
functional ministerial councils, out of the grasp of central agency
reform enthusiasts. The Working Group on Commonwealth–State Roles
and Responsibilities, which had been set up in June 1993, would have a
'monitoring' role. The fine print aside, the crux of the issue of competition policy from the states' perspective remained the Commonwealth's
continued refusal to see intergovernmental cooperation as a set of
linked issues, at the centre of which was fiscal relations. Once again, the

SPC, COAG AND THE POLITICS OF REFORM 51

Commonwealth was asking the states to embark on a process that promised the hope of long-term benefits but guaranteed the certainty of short-term pain.

The March 1994 Financial Premiers' Conference included an agreement to implement a full and consistent tax-equivalent payments regime for all state and Commonwealth business enterprises. Government-owned state enterprises would be 'taxed' by their own state treasuries at a rate equivalent to their direct and indirect tax liabilities as if they were private corporations. The aim was to achieve competitive neutrality, but one other consequence was to highlight starkly the revenue benefits to state governments of their continued ownership of business corporations.

The states held out hopes of some progress on duplication and tied grants, but this was not immediately forthcoming. Attempts to link these issues with the Commonwealth's push on competition policy were not productive. Although the Commonwealth proved conciliatory in regard to discussions on the details of implementing the Hilmer recommendations, there was only hostility to the attempts to strike a financial deal as a price of agreement. As the Darwin COAG in August 1994 approached, the states began to take firmer positions on the need for financial compensation and to demand special arrangements for regulation of their own utilities. At the end of July, the state and territory leaders met in Sydney and once again asserted that financial reform was their main priority. The Leaders' Forum was formally instituted as a twice-a-year event, its principal aim being to make progress towards a 'new federation' involving a 'removal of duplication' and a 'guaranteed revenue base for the states'.

Support for the principles of competition policy was reaffirmed, but the need for the states to offset revenue losses through access to the revenue gains flowing to the Commonwealth was asserted in the leaders' communiqué of 29 July. The states also opposed the National Competition Council as currently proposed and demanded greater powers to grant exemptions from the new national regulatory regime. The Commonwealth, in response to the demand for a financial deal as part of a Hilmer package, went on the offensive, threatening to go it alone if a cooperative approach was not forthcoming and denying vehemently that there was any 'entitlement' to compensation (*Australian*, August 1994). However, some form of special grant was not ruled out as a transitional arrangement.

The Darwin COAG meeting in August 1994 fell into disarray in a rancorous dispute about these financial issues (see Chapter 4). The conservative premiers, led by Kennett, were determined to place finance at the top of the agenda. At the meeting itself, they chose to go on the

52   COLLABORATIVE FEDERALISM

attack. The demand for a revenue-sharing agreement arising from competition policy reform put on the table the general issue of federal financial relations, which Keating had firmly stated was not the business of COAG. State premiers used the opportunity to raise a number of continuing doubts and objections to aspects of a national approach to competition policy. The result was an impasse. At the end of the day, a face-saving formula was found in which the Commonwealth agreed that 'all Governments should share the benefit' and that the Industry Commission should undertake a study to help COAG at its next meeting to determine 'the appropriate percentage share' of any increase in Commonwealth revenues that might be transferred to the states (COAG communiqué, 19 August 1994). However, the major object of the meeting—to conclude formal agreements on legislation and the regulatory regime—was not achieved. The only other item agreed to at the meeting concerned a program for further progress on electricity reform. Discussion of a substantial report on duplication and tied grants, and a number of other agenda items, were deferred.

The political and media reaction was largely critical of the states' 'provincialism' and 'obstructionism', with talk of the 'death of COAG' and the collapse of the reform process. In the following weeks and months the Business Council of Australia and other groups exerted growing pressure on the states to drop their objections. The Industry Commission report, when it was circulated in draft form to the states in December, argued against substantial compensation of any kind. There followed a long and ultimately fruitful process of technical discussions about some of the methodology and assumptions of the report, with state treasuries winning considerable ground in pointing out errors. At the Leaders' Forum at the end of February 1995, with the report almost finalised, the states arrived at an agreed strategy which ultimately provided the basis for a settlement with the Commonwealth. The Industry Commission report, released in March, made dramatic and ambitious claims about the overall economic benefits of full implementation of competition policy and indicated that there would be revenue increases for both the states and the Commonwealth in the long run. It argued that the state contributions to economic gains through reforms in their jurisdiction far outweighed those of the Commonwealth, and also pointed out that the gains to Commonwealth revenue came primarily from state reforms. In quantifying these effects the Industry Commission report at the same time set feasible and realistic limits to the grounds on which a compromise, in the form of an equitable share in the competition policy 'dividend', might be possible (Industry Commission 1995).

SPC, COAG AND THE POLITICS OF REFORM   53

The COAG meeting of April 1995 was combined with a Financial Premiers' Conference—the latter in the morning, followed by COAG in the afternoon. The financial meeting was relatively free of rancour and well managed. At COAG, with the Hilmer recommendations the only major item, the states agreed to a series of competition policy payments beginning in 1997–98, conditional on their making progress on implementation of the Hilmer agenda (see Chapter 4 for a fuller account of the events). The deal also included a guarantee of permanency for an arrangement decided on at the financial meeting, where an agreement had been struck to maintain for three years the real per capita value of annual general-revenue grants (with the 1994 levels as the base). Projecting this guarantee forward as a permanent arrangement added an estimated $3 billion to the outcome by 2005–06 (*AFR*, 12 April 1995). Importantly, the states felt they had won a level of certainty in general revenue grants that they had never enjoyed over the life of the Labor government. Some premiers believed they had finally clawed some substantial financial gains out of the SPC–COAG process. The gains were illusory, however, as a little over twelve months later a new government intent on deficit-cutting clawed some of this back.

This meeting of COAG also saw some signs of progress on the long-standing issue of roles and responsibilities, particularly overlap and duplication in housing, health and welfare services. Some broad principles and a program of implementation were agreed to, with further reports called for on progress in 1996. A further matter on the agenda was the vexed issue of the Commonwealth's treaty-making powers and the demands by the states to be consulted where these treaties could form the basis of the use of the external affairs power of the Constitution to allow the Commonwealth to step into traditional areas of exclusive state jurisdiction.

Howard and Costello

A federal election was due before the middle of 1996, and no COAG meeting was held in the meantime. The November 1995 meeting was cancelled by Paul Keating. In opposition, the Liberals were increasingly cautious about making big promises, but Shadow Treasurer Peter Costello reacted sympathetically to the states' demands to redress vertical fiscal imbalance and restructure roles and responsibilities. Keating sought to make an election issue out of the states' demands for tax reform, seizing on a report commissioned by the Western Australian government which recommended a state income tax set at 15.6 per cent. He proposed a constitutional referendum to confirm the

54 COLLABORATIVE FEDERALISM

Commonwealth's monopoly of income tax powers. The Liberal Party toned down its support for tax reform, and the premiers and first ministers (most of them with an eye to the fate of their Liberal Party federal colleague) at their November 1995 Leaders' Forum in Brisbane rejected the state income tax option and reiterated the call for a guaranteed tax-sharing arrangement.

The Leaders' Forum was by now a regular, twice-yearly event. As a result the states and territories were able increasingly to speak with a united voice on major issues affecting relations with the Commonwealth. Its level of cohesion was assisted by the fact that only one of the leaders—Bob Carr in New South Wales—was Labor (see Table 3.1). In the lead-up to the election, the forum was a means of keeping state issues in the public eye. Following the election of the Howard Liberal government in March 1996, the April forum provided the opportunity for the states to position themselves in the light of their perceptions of the new government's likely agenda. This meeting reasserted a series of principles that had been enunciated at the first forum in 1994, which had elaborated on those agreed to in November 1991. The more comprehensive statement of principles read as follows:

- that the Federation enable government to be close to the people and responsive to local and regional needs;
- that the Federation enhance the cohesiveness of the Australian nation by being responsive to the needs of regional diversity, rather than dismissive of that diversity;
- a Federation in which the states are dedicated to the delivery of quality services to the Australian people;
- a Federation which delivers cost effective services for our taxpayers and which removes duplication between the various levels of government;
- a Federation that fosters a competitive national economy based on the fundamental principles of 'competitive federalism';
- a Federation in which there is a guaranteed revenue base for the states and Territories to match their expenditure responsibilities;
- a Federation which continues to be accountable to the people through their Parliaments.

The states had some cause to be optimistic about the possibilities for reform under the new Howard government. They prepared a detailed joint submission to the National Commission of Audit (NCOA), set up to undertake a review of finances and service provision, in which they attacked vertical fiscal imbalance and argued the need for the Commonwealth to vacate large areas of policy and to reduce the incidence of special-purpose payments. Submissions were also made on some recent

SPC, COAG AND THE POLITICS OF REFORM 55

innovations arising from COAG with which they were dissatisfied, most notably the Australian National Training Authority. The NCOA gave them a sympathetic hearing and, in a long section in its report on intergovernmental relations, it accepted most of their case about the costs of duplication and the desirability of sorting out roles and responsibilities, mostly with a view to limiting the role of the Commonwealth to a more arm's-length one of setting national frameworks. Most notably, the NCOA's June 1996 report included support for remedying vertical fiscal imbalance (albeit, as it acknowledged, a matter outside its terms of reference), either through the Commonwealth relinquishing income tax powers or collecting earmarked revenue for the states (NCOA 1996, 52).

However, even before the NCOA report was released, the states had received a rude awakening. The sixth meeting of COAG in June 1996 was tacked on to the Financial Premiers' Conference. It agreed to the setting up of a Treaties Council and adopted a revised set of consultative procedures; it made some progress on reforms to roles and responsibilities in health and housing; and it included New Zealand in the mutual recognition scheme. But these achievements were overshadowed by drama and brawling over finances. The treasurer had already signalled a tough budget to attack an inherited deficit, and had indicated that the states would be expected to make a contribution. Treasury wheeled out an old favourite to help with this strategy: the removal of state and local governments' exemption from wholesale sales tax. Treasurer Costello announced this proposal not long before the Premiers' Conference, pointing out the 'rorts' it encouraged, such as tax-free cars for top public servants. It was calculated that the annual cost to the states of removal of the exemption was about $1.2 billion. A number of anomalies emerged during the course of the following public exchanges, making the proposal look half-baked. It was pointed out, for example, that public schools and hospitals would now pay sales tax, but their private counterparts would remain exempt.

State premiers presented a united front, and directed a considerable amount of personal anger at the treasurer. Howard—who, ironically had been the one in cabinet to seize most enthusiastically on the idea—was forced to rescue him. The proposal was withdrawn at the Premiers' Conference as part of a deal in which the premiers agreed on the need to 'make a contribution" to overall deficit reduction, and to forgo about $700 million in each of the next two years in foreshadowed growth funds from the Commonwealth. These funds had been locked in by Keating in 1994 and 1995 as part of the arrangements surrounding the adoption of the National Competition Policy. The agreement to forgo the money was, the states, insisted, only a temporary measure, and the funds should

56   COLLABORATIVE FEDERALISM

flow again after two years. What appeared publicly as an embarrassing defeat for Costello in fact netted him a satisfactory financial outcome. Ironically, despite their complaints about vertical fiscal imbalance, the states were in a relatively healthy financial position because of several years of debt reduction, belt-tightening and financial reforms, and with an economic upturn making revenue projections look strong.

One other item appeared on the June COAG communiqué—confirmation of the deal struck on tougher gun laws by federal and state ministers in the police and justice ministerial council. This deal was a spectacular success for the prime minister. A horrific mass murder in April 1996 by a man armed with automatic weapons at Port Arthur in Tasmania led to a public outcry for tougher gun control. Several states (including Tasmania) had relatively relaxed gun control laws, while others had much tougher regimes. The least strict state regulations governing the sale and purchase of weapons set the effective level of national regulation. Howard put his personal authority on the line and pushed ahead with a radical proposal for uniform gun laws, prohibiting the sale of automatic weapons and requiring the surrender of those already owned by private individuals. Rural Australians were most severely affected, and the National Party had to be pulled into line. Resistance from several state premiers was also strong, but the prime minister skilfully and ruthlessly rode the wave of public sentiment in favour of tougher laws, driving the issue to a conclusion that brooked little if any compromise. The states agreed—in some cases very reluctantly—to adopt uniform legislation, and the Commonwealth agreed to foot most of the bill for compensation for surrendered weapons, including the imposition of a special levy on all taxpayers. This example of cooperative federalism was *sui generis*, owing all to the drama and horror of the original event and to the high level of public support for the prime minister's strong stand. It occurred almost entirely outside the realm of COAG.

The housing and health reforms signalled at the June 1996 COAG ran into further difficulties in following months. In the case of housing, agreement to divide responsibilities so that the Commonwealth looked after the income-support and rental-subsidy aspects of housing, and the states looked after housing provision and regulation, was agreed to in principle (indeed, this proposal had already been well advanced under the previous government). Funds previously going to the states direct for public housing provision would now be diverted to rental assistance, leaving the renter to seek private or public rental housing wherever it was available, with the states having to fund their public housing stock (if they chose to retain it) from charging closer to market rents. The sticking-points, not surprisingly, were the amount of funds being proposed for the rental assistance scheme and the termination of direct capital grants for public housing construction. The sums simply did not add up, as one of the Commonwealth's objectives was to break down the discrimination that existed in levels of rental subsidy between public and private tenants. With no additional funds, the implication was that existing public tenants would receive less in subsidy. The states would be expected to make up the difference, charge higher rents to maintain the revenue stream for public housing provision, or let their housing stock run down. The states refused to agree to the proposal until some method of providing them with a 'revenue-neutral' outcome was found.

In the case of both health and housing, the states were emboldened by the NCOA's recommendations, and by their own unity on the subject, to link the issues of funding and provision with the broader issue of tax reform. Jeff Kennett in particular pressed hard for wholesale tax reform, and put the issue of a goods and services tax back on the agenda. Costello and Howard, however, had stated on several occasions that federal finances, and tax reform more broadly, were not issues they were prepared to consider in their first term of office. Kennett's campaign was a political irritant, as it reminded observers of the gap between the identified microeconomic reform agenda and the caution of the prime minister not to leap ahead of public opinion. The housing issue was turning into a political negative, with no solution in sight. Health, housing and financial reform were the issues highlighted for the November Leaders' Forum. On none of them was the Commonwealth ready or willing to deal along the lines being proposed by the states. When, on the very eve of the COAG meeting scheduled for November 1996, Richard Court called an election in Western Australia, the prime minister took the chance to postpone the next day's Brisbane meeting. The new government's commitment to COAG as an institution was clearly not whole-hearted. It presented a series of awkward problems but no immediate solutions. Howard had won his personal battle with the premiers over gun laws outside COAG, and the government had struck its deal over the budget at the Financial Premiers' Conference. COAG was a Labor idea, in any case. In the same week that the November COAG was cancelled, the prime minister announced a restructuring of his department in which the Commonwealth–State Relations Division —COAG's guardian—was disbanded, and its work split up among functional policy divisions. All that remained was a small secretariat.

The Commonwealth remained deaf to the demands for further progress on reform to federal fiscal relations until the middle of 1997, when a High Court ruling outlawed the states' business franchise fees on tobacco, alcohol and petroleum products, on the grounds they were

58   COLLABORATIVE FEDERALISM

de facto excise taxes and hence exclusive to the Commonwealth. The High Court case had been instigated at the initiative of the states in the hope of establishing a more certain revenue base. The adverse judgement was a blow, but it also highlighted the need for a lasting resolution to the problem of vertical fiscal imbalance.

The immediate effect was to remove approximately $5 billion in state tax income from state budgets, or about 16 per cent of state-owned revenue. A rescue package was put in place by agreement with the states, under which the Commonwealth provided a safety-net of measures. The Commonwealth increased its own taxes on the affected products and returned the revenue in the form of grants. These measures were fraught with difficulties. Commonwealth taxes on some of these products were based on different principles, making a simple transition impossible. Levels of fees and methods of collection had differed significantly from state to state, and in Queensland there was no fuel franchise fee at all. The Constitution does not allow the Commonwealth to discriminate between the states in levying taxes, and it was left to the states to implement a system of reimbursements so that businesses would not pay more tax than under the old system. Disputes were bound to arise about the amounts and methods of reimbursement. An additional measure was a Commonwealth windfall gains tax of 100 per cent to recoup any amount obtained for refund in the case of a successful legal challenge to the new regime. The constitutional legality of this measure was a moot point, and litigation was expected to follow. In sum, the rescue package was only a stop-gap, and a long-term solution was seen to be necessary.

The immediate political effect was to exert intense pressure on the Commonwealth government to address tax reform more broadly. Eight days after the judgement, and seven days after the announcement of the rescue package, the Commonwealth announced a Taxation Task Force of Commonwealth officials to focus on the need for a new broad-based indirect tax and concomitant major reductions in income tax. The task force was also instructed to address the reform of federal fiscal relations (Prime Minister's press release, *Taxation Reform*, 13 August 1997). Later in the year, at a meeting of the Leaders' Forum on 31 October, the states agreed to a set of principles to guide this process and urged them on the Commonwealth:

- no increase in overall tax burden
- reductions in personal income tax
- reductions in business taxes
- state and territory access to broad-based growth taxes to replace some existing, narrowly based state taxes

SPC, COAG AND THE POLITICS OF REFORM

- reduction in vertical fiscal imbalance
- abolition of Commonwealth grants, other than for Medicare, fiscal equalisation, and assistance to the smaller states and territories
- direct access to taxation revenue sufficient for the states and territories to carry out their roles and responsibilities
- long-term certainty and consistency in the tax system.

One week later there was a meeting of COAG, after which the premiers and prime minister had a discussion of tax reform. All that could be agreed for public announcement was that there would be no increase in the overall taxation burden. COAG itself did not address any of the issues, but tied up some loose ends on gas reform and the allocation of roles and responsibilities in environmental policy.

It remained to be seen (as of December 1997) what the outcone would be for federal fiscal relations. Progress on issues associated with fiscal relations had stalled under the Howard government. Work had ground to a halt on the broad issue of allocation of roles and responsibilities, and little reform was being achieved in specific sectors such as health and housing. The tax reform agenda was dominated by the goods and services tax, and federal reform, including fiscal relations, was not high on the list of political priorities.

Conclusion

The launch of Hawke's New Federalism brought together a bundle of related but separate issues, some to do with federal reform, others to do with economic policy, and others rooted firmly in the short-term political ambitions of the participants. Looking back on the achievements of the SPCs and COAG up to 1997, it is clear that the Commonwealth's priorities and policy objectives were the dominant element. The states went along in the first place in part because one or two premiers shared some of these objectives, but primarily because they hoped to win achievements on their own agenda of fiscal reform. This agenda brought a flurry of early activity at the official level and some brave political commitments, but nothing came of these, and the issue was deliberately excluded from consideration by COAG. But the states signed up to a large number of agreements for harmonisation and national administration through joint action. The principal feature of most of these agreements was that they achieved significant elements of the Commonwealth's aims without an overt, potentially confrontational, unilateral occupation of the field. At the same time, many of the joint schemes and policies were perceived by most of the states to bring them benefits as well, in some instances assisting them in what they had

60 COLLABORATIVE FEDERALISM

already intended to do. Where there was friction or a reluctance to sign up to a cooperative national scheme, important concessions were sometimes made to state interests. Some of the joint schemes were primarily designed and negotiated among the states, and the Commonwealth was an onlooker or facilitator.

Yet alongside this cooperation and the private negotiations that brought it about, the normal, adversarial forms of federal politics went on unabated in the public arena. Indeed, some of the fiercest conflicts arose at COAG itself. However, it was not so much that there was a gap between rhetoric and reality as that rhetoric and reality expressed parallel but different political agendas. Australia's federal system is clearly one where both collaborative and adversarial strategies are part of normal politics, side by side. This is to be expected from the manner in which the federal design embodies a tension between cooperative and arm's-length modes of action. In practical terms, SPC and COAG were the latest in a line of institutional solutions to resolving this tension, where new energy and incentives were organised around a cooperative effort while the other side of federal politics, adversarial and arm's-length, was still very much in evidence. While bearing this in mind, in the next chapter, we turn to look more closely at what was particularly noteworthy about SPC and COAG as institutions of cooperative federalism.

CHAPTER 4

Achieving Cooperation: Players and Processes

The aim of cooperation was clearly set out in the charter of the Council of Australian Governments (COAG), stated in a communiqué of May 1992:

- increasing cooperation among governments in the national interest;
- cooperation among governments on reforms to achieve an integrated, efficient national economy and single national market;
- continuing structural reform of government and review of the relationships among governments consistent with the national interest;
- consultation on other major issues by agreement ...

Cooperation—the search for common ground as a basis for joint action—is one among several ways of resolving problems of coordination. It is voluntary and 'signifies a relationship between entities capable of non cooperation—of divorce (or secession), competition or conflict' (Kincaid 1991). Thus, it is the outcome of a process of strategic choices by partners, in this case governments in a federation, who retain the capacity to resist or opt out. In this situation, even when cooperating they can still retain distinct (perhaps otherwise conflicting) purposes. Indeed, it may be more useful to think of intergovernmental relations in its 'natural state' as an arena of separate and mostly conflicting interests, and cooperation as an artefact that arises from conscious effort. What factors in Australia's federal system lead to cooperative strategies rather than to perpetual conflict? What sort of effort is required, and what circumstances are conducive to it?

Conflict, if unmitigated, can in practice interfere with cooperation, but the two are not mutually exclusive. In a stable federal system a measure of mutuality can be expected to evolve naturally, even in the presence of underlying conflict. Regular interaction, including repeated

61

62 COLLABORATIVE FEDERALISM

conflict, can engender habits and norms of trust and mutuality which are conducive to cooperation. Conflict is limited by being grounded in a set of routinely reinforced understandings and norms. The participants in Australian executive federal politics share some crucial characteristics. First, they are part of the same federal political system and culture. They share a Constitution and a common set of political traditions and institutions. Second, they nearly all belong to a handful of national political parties with state branches, and share with some of the other participants common ideological and programmatic ambitions. Even with respect to partisan opponents, the language and forms of partisan conflict are well understood, as are the presumptions and limits of opposing positions. Third, as members of a single federal polity they participate in a set of parallel but interlocking federal institutional arrangements. As political executives, each understands the other's parliamentary dilemmas and legal or financial constraints, for example. Moreover, the mere existence of the Commonwealth as a national government confronts each of the others with a common, overlapping partner. On the one hand, they share a common enemy, but on the other hand they share a common partner, even if they mostly quarrel. But ultimately, 'the national interest' is a powerful unifying symbol, and the Commonwealth has a unique legitimacy in invoking it.

In an arm's-length federation, different political dramas go on in parallel, and occasionally overlap. Political leaders face separate constituencies, colleagues and cabinets; they have separate programs and different political opponents in their home jurisdictions. When governments 'play away', and come together to consider a common agenda, they may actually be focusing on entirely different things. For example, the political reactions in Western Australia to a proposal to increase taxes on long-distance heavy vehicles are very different to those facing the Victorian government. The games are both segmented state by state, and layered depending on the level of attention they attract. Premiers play one set of games, their ministers another, both within their own jurisdiction and in relations beyond it; meanwhile central agency officials are playing another set of games and functional agency officials yet another. Friends and enemies change from one game to another, even within the same problem field or issue area. Cross-border alliances occur both within and between jurisdictions. No one set of players can continually regulate or control this 'ecology of games' with any confidence of success.

The existence of overlapping but separate games can add complexity to a process of joint decision-making, but can also greatly simplify matters when cooperation over a particular issue is sought. Many things that need to be agreed matter crucially only to a small number of players, while the rest of the players are relatively indifferent because they are playing different games. Finding a pathway through the 'zones of indifference' is sometimes the key to an outcome. Log-rolling— trading off support across issues between parties to whom different issues of principle and interest are critical—is a common tactic in such situations. Issues may be repackaged so as to sideline a series of identified crucial concerns, perhaps putting these matters off to a later date, while doing no serious damage to other core objectives. Co-operative action in such a system might be primarily a product of tolerant indifference between parties with different agendas, rather than requiring sacrifice for the common good.

Thus the key to success might be simply to overcome the initial inertia and energise a process. The cooperative process needs direction and coordination. It may be shaped in outline by a set of institutional arrangements, such as regular meetings and the 'proper channels' of consultation and clearance, that is a set of habits and norms, but it is also a process of organising by the people concerned to achieve particular outcomes. The process of moving from a disjoint to a conjoint policy-making process in any issue area requires some such process of building commitment by the people concerned. In the next section, we identify those characteristics of the Special Premiers' Conferences (SPC) and COAG that help us understand the extent and level of commitment to cooperation: what was new and different that enabled the system to move as far along the path to cooperative, joint decision-making as it did? We look first at some general characteristics of the system, and then at some illustrative cases and examples.

The ingredients of cooperation

People

Observers of the initial phases of the SPC process all remark on the important part played by a shared sense of commitment among a particular group of political leaders. First, there was in mid-1990 a conjunction of Labor premiers and prime minister, with the exception of Nick Greiner (see Table 3.1). Second, these leaders were cast in a similar mould in other respects, notably the common experience of and commitment to public sector reform and economic restructuring in each of their jurisdictions. They shared a common mindset that valued good management and economic rationalism, and Hawke's July 1990 speech was in the language that many of them used in their own pronouncements about economic reform and intergovernmental relations.

64 COLLABORATIVE FEDERALISM

There was genuine intellectual commitment and enthusiasm on the part of several premiers, at least at the level of principle and generalities: at various times, Hawke, Greiner, Goss and Bannon, for example, articulated in public similar views about federal reform. Third, this group of leaders developed a sense of teamwork in the initial months of preparations and at the first meeting of SPC. Hawke and Greiner struck up a close personal relationship and found much common ground, while the state Labor leaders were all well known to each other from other contexts and occasions. Finally, this particular group, following the public relations successes of the launch and of the Brisbane SPC meeting, had invested something of their personal reputations in the venture, and were committed to seeing it succeed.

In bringing to the fore these factors of personality and political style, it is not intended to subscribe to what Aynsley Kellow (1995, 211) calls the 'astrological' interpretation of intergovernmental relations, in which the right 'alignment of planets' is necessary. The partisan factor, for example, can be over-emphasised, and sometimes works in reverse. Labor premier Carmen Lawrence was one of the most strident in the lead-up to the ill-fated Adelaide SPC in 1991, with her threats to withdraw altogether unless a satisfactory financial settlement was reached, precisely because the state opposition was accusing her of being indistinguishable from her Canberra 'Labor mates'. In response, the premier had to make special efforts to distance herself from Canberra. The conjunction of personalities, their partisan relations and so on, were not unimportant, but more significant was the way the process itself worked to establish a distinctive setting for cooperative styles of action. A process of team-building was set in train by the initial flurry of enthusiasm, and a virtuous circle of escalating commitment followed as each step of the process was taken. The personalities and friendships were often important, for example in facilitating last-ditch efforts at settlement through personal intervention, but again the crucial factor was probably not so much the friendships as the investment of personal political reputations in the success of the project.

Equally important were the intellectual enthusiasm and personal energy behind the project shown by senior officials and ministerial advisers. In some cases, this was a reflection of the role of these officials as personal appointees of the leader. In such cases, the *personae* of political leaders and their closest advisers were sometimes hard to separate. Greiner and his enthusiasm for federal reform cannot be separated from Garry Sturgess, the head of his Cabinet Office and a driving force in the reform program of his government (Laffin and Painter 1995). Sturgess was a strong advocate of federal reform and invested much time and effort in it (Sturgess 1993). Standing at Wayne

ACHIEVING COOPERATION: PLAYERS AND PROCESSES   65

Goss's shoulder and echoing his commitment to the venture was his chief adviser, Kevin Rudd; and ever present in the process in its early days was Mike Codd, the head of the Prime Minister's Department, whose conciliatory and measured style matched nicely Hawke's language of consensus. Just as their leaders found common intellectual ground and struck up close personal and professional relations, so too did these officials. This was not new, but built on existing links and networks. Sturgess, for example, sat on Kevin Rudd's selection committee in 1991 when he won the job of chief executive of the Office of the Cabinet (G. Davis 1995, 76). Indeed, as Glynn Davis tells it, Goss got his idea of setting up such an office from personal contact with Sturgess: the networks and personal contacts that oiled the machinery of cooperation sometimes crossed the divide of official and politician, as well as party and place.

Offices

The people we have just mentioned were all at the centre of government. SPC and COAG were meetings of heads of government, and the leaders' political reputations were bound up in their success or failure. With the announcement of the SPC initiative came a focusing of official effort on a successful, joint outcome. Hawke quickly committed his department head to coordinate the process, and also announced the establishment of a special division that would guide and monitor the hard, detailed work of preparing the agenda and putting flesh on the bones of any subsequent agreements. Later we describe the administrative machinery that was set up to make SPC and COAG work as meeting places and the executive instruments that were created to implement some of its decisions.

SPC and COAG would not have got off the ground without the existence in each jurisdiction of a whole-of-government capacity to organise preparatory work and commit to subsequent action. In some measure, this has always been present in the embodiment of the political leader, but the range and complexity of issues on the SPC agenda required far more in the way of coordinating capacity than could be found in one person or office. During the 1970s and 1980s, state governments and the Commonwealth built up elaborate and sophisticated policy and coordination machinery at the centre of government, reformed cabinet processes to make them more efficient and effective, and put in place policy and planning instruments that facilitated prioritising and policy review (Painter 1987). Glynn Davis (1995), in comparing Forgan Smith in the 1930s with Goss in the 1990s (both strong, centralising premiers), highlights the sea change that had

66   COLLABORATIVE FEDERALISM

occurred such that 'central coordination' required far more than a strong leader with a few simple levers of control over some key departments and sectors. It now required large amounts of information, sensitivity to diverse interests and concerns, openness to many channels, ability to intervene in numerous arenas where decisions might be irrevocably made, and a diversity of instruments of influence and control to affect outcomes. John Warhurst (1983) was among the first to emphasise the significance of the growing complexity of inter-governmental relations for the development of this more sophisticated coordinating capacity. It allowed governments to respond in a consistent way across the whole of government to threats and opportunities in intergovernmental arenas and to prevent various arms of government doing deals on their own, without the knowledge of central agencies or cabinet. The monitoring and coordination of intergovernmental relations was a significant function of the policy arms of the 'new' Premier's Departments of the 1970s and 1980s, as well as in state Treasury Departments. By the early 1990s, this function was indistinguishable from overall policy and political strategy, and was often to be found embedded in the cabinet or policy divisions of the first minister's office.

As will be seen from some of the case studies presented in this and later chapters, it was of crucial importance for the conduct of relations on SPC and COAG that these internal coordinating mechanisms were in place and in good order. Central agency officials were key actors in energising some of the joint decision processes in particular areas of policy. In several cases their intervention, backed up by the commitment and urgency generated by their political leaders' investments in the process, transformed the pace and scope of joint action. With the whole of government mobilised to deal with a broad agenda of sectoral coordination problems, negotiations between departmental officials and portfolio ministers on ministerial councils, and on their supporting officials' committees, were transposed to new levels, where central agency officials took a lead role. The 'central agency club' (Weller 1995) took over. Within governments, what were formerly minor inter-agency squabbles or niggling obstructions became subject to the keen eye and impatient attention of the premiers' fixers. Cabinets themselves had to get involved directly in sorting out some of the details, because the issues of territory and policy were intensely felt. For cabinet to review negotiating positions and bring together disparate agency views on SPC and COAG agenda items, the machinery for cabinet clearance and coordination had to be in good working order. This machinery had been transformed in most states in the preceding ten or fifteen years, allowing for the more effective processing of business, the greater exercise of strategic oversight, and the more expeditious management of conflict so as to prevent obstruction and delay (Painter 1987; G. Davis 1995; Halligan and Power 1992). Weller (1995) argues that the SPCs and COAG led to a strengthening of these procedures and put more muscle behind the efforts of those in the central agencies who maintained them, making it easier for premiers to 'corral ministers'.

A special role in the central agencies club fell to the Commonwealth Department of Prime Minister and Cabinet, which was at the hub of things by the very nature of the Commonwealth's position in the federation. It provided many of the chairs of committees and working groups, undertook much of the drafting of reports and communiqués, and kept track of business for the forthcoming agenda. The roles of the officials of the department were often ambiguous, including serving the prime minister as a protagonist in federal politics; mediating and representing Commonwealth interdepartmental politics and positions; maintaining the health and integrity of the SPC and COAG process; and acting as honest broker in seeking agreements among governments. During this period the Commonwealth–State Relations Secretariat in particular developed a reputation for fair dealing, even if on occasion the tensions between roles produced frustration and mistrust.

In sum, the prior existence of appropriate institutional capacities within each of the participating governments was an essential precondition for the extent and level of cooperation required to fulfil some of the expectations of SPC and COAG. But these capacities were not, of course, sufficient conditions for success. Institutions and protocols had to be developed to manage the intergovernmental arenas themselves.

Committees

SPC and COAG spawned a plethora of working groups and standing committees to prepare agendas, undertake detailed policy work, and hammer out the finer points of agreements. The prime minister's July 1990 speech announced 'a Commonwealth–State Steering Committee chaired by the Secretary of my Department with equivalent State Government representation. Its main role will be to arrange for the preparation of papers for this first Conference and then in broad terms to coordinate and advance future work.' The October 1990 SPC communiqué recorded that this Steering Committee would be 'ongoing' so as to undertake work for future SPCs, of which there was to be at least one each year. Heads of Cabinet Offices or of first ministers' departments continued to meet regularly throughout the life of SPC and COAG, in particular during the period leading up to each meeting; they prepared the agenda, saw that recommendations and agreements were in place, prodded other committees or working groups into action, intervened to overcome log-jams, and so on. The final job before each meeting was to prepare the communiqué, a task that was undertaken by the Department of Prime Minister and Cabinet for the first meeting, but which became a more collaborative effort in later years.

The proposals and papers submitted to the first SPC drew on the work of a number of existing working groups, or were drawn up by Commonwealth officials and, in some cases, officials from particular states. The program of work and the submissions were agreed to by the Steering Committee. One of the outcomes of the first SPC meeting was to mandate a series of specific-purpose committees and working groups to prepare reports on matters earmarked for joint action. The matters on which such groups were to report ranged from a scheme to regulate non-bank financial institutions to the formulation and implementation of new standards and charges for heavy road vehicles. In each case, the setting up of a group was accompanied by a timetable, with a reporting date for a specified future SPC meeting (either May or November 1991). In some cases, the Steering Committee was charged with overseeing and pulling together a series of reports on a common subject, for example regulatory reform. Other channels of inquiry and reporting were also utilised—for instance in the case of duplication of services, an 'ongoing process for review of all functional areas [will] be established, reporting back through Ministerial Councils to heads of Government'.

Over time, the working parties and task forces proliferated. Some disappeared once an agreement was reached; others were transmuted into implementation bodies until more permanent arrangements came into being. In 1995, the committees comprised the Steering Committee; three standing committees on treaties, microeconomic reform and regulatory reform; and specific-purpose committees on health and community services, child care, electricity reform, free and fair trade in gas, legal profession reform, the centenary of the federation, statehood for the Northern Territory, ecologically sustainable development, and water reform. Finally, a Steering Committee had been set up, headed by the chair of the Industry Commission, under the COAG umbrella to collect and publish performance indicators on service provision by the states. Most of these bodies were chaired by the Commonwealth, but New South Wales chaired two specific-purpose working groups and Victoria one.

The key ingredient in this layered system of committees was the manner in which central agency and heads of government perspectives and timetables were introduced. In the case of the standing committees, central agency officials provided most of the members. In some of the working parties, they sat as members alongside representatives from line

ACHIEVING COOPERATION: PLAYERS AND PROCESSES   69

agencies. SPC and COAG looked to the chief officials of the central agencies to oversee the work of these committees, and they all reported to the heads of government meetings through the Steering Committee. What provided this machinery with its driving force was the close association of the coordinating role of the Steering Committee with the might of the heads of government themselves. In some cases, this rested on the personal authority that these officials carried as trusted advisers of their premier or prime minister—they spoke with the latter's authority as well as their own. When Mike Codd took a negotiating position or made a commitment, others knew that nine times out of ten the prime minister would stick by it as well. His successor, Mike Keating, worked with a very different prime minister. Paul Keating kept the business of making deals more to himself, and the power of the centre was more likely to be exercised through political directives following crisis meetings by the heads of government. Either way, this new federal coordinating machinery transmitted the political authority of whatever common ground existed at the centre.

Protocols

The existence of SPC and COAG focused attention on improvements to processing the business of cooperation. Protocols and operating procedures were developed, and extra attention was devoted to developing the most effective manner of guiding issues to successful fruition. Much of this work was undertaken by the Commonwealth–State Relations Secretariat in the Prime Minister's Department, but continuous consultation and mutual learning among the central agency club also took place. These officials already had a wealth of experience from their coordinating roles in their own governments. Their expertise lay in channelling and processing of business to ensure effective whole-of-government decision-making and accountability. This expertise was put to use in crafting the workings of SPC and COAG.

The officials of the central agencies learnt how to channel business and to manage issues in these more complex intergovernmental arenas. Edwards and Henderson (1995), drawing on experience from their positions in the Commonwealth–State Relations Secretariat, have provided a distillation of this practical knowledge. For example, they record how careful attention came to be given to selecting items for discussion at each SPC or COAG, with others for noting of progress in out-of-session discussions. They emphasise the importance of such things as advance circulation of papers, and clarification of the options in unresolved issues passed up to higher levels. They describe the judicious use of outside chairs of committees or working groups so as to overcome any question of insider partiality. Weller remarks that these independent chairs 'could negotiate more readily with all parties and try to bring them together', and they were particularly useful for working on an issue where a whole-of-government view was broadly agreed on, and what remained was 'to manage the opinion of line agencies within those limits and bring them to a negotiated conclusion' (Weller 1995, 18). Another important point of procedure was the value of having an external, independent source of expert advice: either to trigger an issue and set the parameters of a search for solutions, or to ease a faltering process through a difficult roadblock. The Industry Commission was particularly important in this regard. Its report on public housing (Industry Commission 1993) was vital in setting the agenda for COAG deliberations on housing reform (albeit ultimately not successful, but for other reasons); and the use of the Industry Commission to report on the growth and revenue implications of the Hilmer reforms provided a vital circuit-breaker in a situation of potential deadlock (see below).

This heightened attention to both process and protocol led in 1992 to an agreement for new operating rules to apply to all ministerial councils. In June 1993, following a review and a report to COAG, it was agreed that ministerial councils be restructured and reduced in number from forty-five to twenty-one. The protocols covered such things as representation, reporting, timing of public announcements, drawing up and circulating agenda items, and mechanisms for joint consultation between ministerial councils. For example: 'It is the responsibility of Ministers to ensure they are in a position to appropriately represent their Governments at council meetings ... Council arrangements should include processes for ensuring that all parties have input to the development of agendas and that agendas are agreed at the earliest possible date prior to meetings' (DPMC 1994, 1–5). Attention at this level of detail to such basic matters of procedure illustrates the heightened awareness of the nuts and bolts of intergovernmental relations that accompanied the emergence of SPC and COAG as working institutions.

Consultation

Beyond the relatively closed worlds of SPC and COAG working parties and committees was a plethora of attentive publics and pressure groups interested in the subjects on the reform agenda. In structuring the processes by which SPC and COAG made progress on joint schemes and national policies, the importance of managing the involvement of these publics and groups was recognised. It would be going too far to say that COAG's minders conceived of the possibility of incorporating this involvement in one all-encompassing collaborative process. Nevertheless, they did pay deliberate attention to managing processes of public consultation. Intergovernmental relations are notoriously opaque and hard to access for the public, with conventions of secrecy and bureaucratic habits of confidentiality dominant most of the time. However, the processes of inquiry and deliberation that led up to many SPC and COAG decisions often included deliberate efforts to involve relevant publics. These efforts were aside from those that individual ministers, departments or governments undertook on their own account, and were part of the coordinated effort of collaborative decision-making.

The opposition of key producer groups (in some cases, including the public utilities) to economic reform was recognised as a potential obstacle by the central agency club. For example, the process leading up to the adoption of the mutual recognition scheme in 1991 included the public release of a discussion paper and a series of formal public consultations, with a view to defusing hostility and suspicion among key groups. The process of framing of mutual recognition policy was managed primarily by the New South Wales Cabinet Office, particularly Garry Sturgess. The discussion paper was made public following approval by the July 1991 SPC, and submissions were called for, to be delivered by September. Agreement of governments was gained on the appointment of former Labor premier of New South Wales, Neville Wran, as a 'champion' of the mutual recognition scheme to facilitate a series of public seminars in the state capitals (Sturgess 1993). 'Consultation' may be a misnomer here, as these seminars were designed to educate, to assuage fears and to 'spread the message'. This, of course, serves to emphasise the central point: that a key ingredient for making progress was the effective management and diffusion of public opposition, through deliberate strategies managed by the central agency coordinators.

Elizabeth Harman (1996) has described aspects of the complex process of pressure group, partisan and intergovernmental politics that accompanied the adoption of a national competition policy. The intergovernmental negotiations managed through COAG, which are described later in this chapter, were only a small part of a wider process of political management. Several Commonwealth ministers and their political offices were involved in various phases of this process, dealing with submissions from and negotiations with the unions and with public interest groups. Like the Labor Party as a whole, ministers were by no means united on the benefits of the policy, with some seeing it as a threat to traditional Labor conceptions of the role of the public sector, others reflecting the views of particular client groups (such as the consumers' movement or the Business Council), which in turn had very different perspectives. State ministers, meanwhile, were themselves subject to pressures from a variety of sources. The size of the stakes

72 COLLABORATIVE FEDERALISM

involved and the degree of contentiousness of the issues meant that moderating the processes of interest representation and consultation in this case was far beyond the capacity and scope of intergovernmental managers.

The COAG central agency club and others involved sought directly to incorporate consultative mechanisms in the COAG deliberative processes on certain issues. The chosen issues tended to have a less clear partisan dimension and to be rather narrowly industry-specific, allowing for a relatively precise targeting of the relevant client and constituency groups, and containment of the ramifications. In cases such as creating a national electricity market and gas reform, the principal participants were relatively few in number, albeit with an intense commercial interest—the stakes were very high. Notwithstanding the efforts to include such stakeholders on deliberative committees, or to invite detailed submissions at regular intervals, there was intense conflict on some of the finer details of implementation. Some of this conflict arose from the resistance mounted by the states' monopoly electricity authorities to their loss of control of the industry as a result of marketisation, and in such cases the central agency club was keen to strengthen the reform process by ensuring that other industry interests in favour of greater competition were given a hearing.

A very different industry context was evident in the case of proposed reforms to the manner in which health and welfare services were delivered—the issue of the respective 'roles and responsibilities' of different governments and agencies. Here, the COAG task force issued a public discussion paper in January 1995 in order to obtain feedback from welfare groups, especially the peak bodies such as the Australian Council of Social Service. The issues were of a general nature, at the level of basic principles and general structures of service delivery and its organisation, and, in hindsight, somewhat academic. More fiercely contested, and less amenable to smooth management, were deliberative processes surrounding specific proposals for both organisational and financial reforms, where winners and losers could be identified, as in the case of housing policy reform. Here, despite the existence of channels and opportunities to make submissions, welfare lobby groups were more likely to feel excluded and to view the intergovernmental arena as a closed, exclusive one in which the only interests and players that really mattered were governments and their agencies.

Actors and processes: two cases

Wayne Goss, premier of Queensland, introduced to the agenda of the first SPC the issue of regulation and prudential supervision of non-bank

ACHIEVING COOPERATION: PLAYERS AND PROCESSES   73

financial institutions. Fresh in the minds of all were several collapses or crises of building societies and credit unions, notably a major default by the Pyramid Building Society in Victoria. Independently, the Queensland government had been undertaking a major review of the area, and the report provided a framework for further consideration of the issues. The industry and the financial sector at large were in favour of uniform regulation and a single regulatory body to replace the states' separate schemes. The Commonwealth was not seeking to occupy the field, but was prepared to let the states take the running if they could agree to the need for a national scheme. The October 1990 SPC asked a working group to report by 31 March. The May 1991 Financial Premiers' Conference agreed in principle to a national scheme and to its general principles. The working group continued to meet, and set up a task force to draft legislation. The meeting of premiers and first ministers in Adelaide in November 1991 agreed to the details of a uniform scheme, including uniform legislation and a national (but not Commonwealth) regulatory body.

In coming to this agreement, the major players were the states. A regular forum of states' registrars of building societies and credit unions had met and discussed common interests for many years. Under the immediate stimulus of industry events and pressure, SPC provided the convenient setting for a major review and reform. The working group set up in October 1990 comprised representatives of state Treasuries and Departments of Attorneys-General, plus representatives from the Commonwealth Treasury and Reserve Bank. Its secretariat was provided by the Queensland Treasury. The group met regularly and communicated with frequent conference calls. There were sticking-points in the process, most notably the more cautious attitude of the Victorian government, which was suspicious of light-handed forms of supervision and self-regulation because of the backlash against the collapse of Pyramid. As the work got more into the detail, some state registrars and their ministers began to object to the surrender of jurisdiction. One participant described how these objections were overcome:

> Some of the states were indifferent and stood back to let Queensland, Victoria and New South Wales take the running. They all had to share ownership, though. In the end, Victoria had to go along with the majority view. The industry pressured them, and being at the heart of the financial system they could not stand outside it ... In New South Wales, Greiner was terrific. The minister was not supporting it, but his officials followed the government's line rather than the minister's. Some officials suffered for it ... There were good dynamics in the group, it searched for a rational, defensible position to achieve the objectives we had been given. For the most part, you wouldn't have known which state they were from. [personal communication]

74   COLLABORATIVE FEDERALISM

This was perhaps an unusual case, in particular because the Commonwealth was only involved on the fringes, and because there were no serious political difficulties for any of the states or territories in arriving at the agreement. The obstacle was in large part inertia, arising from the complexities of devising a common scheme from a starting-point of varying local legal traditions, such as the different ways in which friendly societies, cooperatives, building societies, credit unions and so on were constituted and operated in each state.

A very different case was the establishment of the Australian National Training Authority. As was the case in many areas of reform under SPC and COAG, the issue had been brought to the surface before 1990 by important independent inquiries, and had been considered in the existing fora of a ministerial council and officials' committee. Opinion converged on the view that the area of technical and further education (TAFE) was suffering from neglect. Bob Hawke floated the idea of a Commonwealth takeover in 1990, but the states for the most part would not countenance it. In late 1991 the Commonwealth revived the take-over offer, along with a major injection of new funds. Keating put a proposal on the table for the May 1992 meeting of heads of government, under which a national training authority would be set up. The states would share in its 'ownership' by forgoing financial assistance grants, and would have a 'seat on the board'. The Commonwealth's fall-back position was to enter the training market as a direct purchaser.

The surrender of responsibility for the TAFE system was seen by some premiers and their advisers as a possible plus. Industry was complaining about the adequacy of services; the TAFE unions were militant; and there was high unmet demand. Many senior TAFE managers and central agency officials in New South Wales and Victoria supported a takeover, but other stakeholders in the system in those states feared the consequences. In New South Wales, Greiner could not convince his cabinet that a hand-over was a good idea. In the smaller states, the TAFE system was seen by state politicians as a significant instrument of local development policy and one of the last bastions of exclusive provincial jurisdiction. The lowest-common-denominator position for the states was to push for more money for the existing system. What emerged was agreement over a version of the Commonwealth's national training authority, under the supervision of a ministerial council. If the Commonwealth were to enter the market as a direct purchaser, it would rival state governments as an independent policy force in the sector, with significant leverage over the states' systems of provision. States saw this as a threat. The Commonwealth agreed to offer growth money to the states, in return for a concession from the smaller states that they would accept a maintenance-of-effort clause.

ACHIEVING COOPERATION: PLAYERS AND PROCESSES 75

The negotiations that led up to an agreement at the June 1992 Financial Premiers' Conference were conducted under the umbrella of COAG, but not primarily through the well-oiled machinery of its committees. The issues were highly politicised. The education policy-makers in the states' TAFE systems had conflicting views, and were as much concerned to escape from the supervision of state Treasuries and, (in some cases) their ministers, hoping thereby to win freedom to implement reform in their systems. State central agency officials, some of them suspicious of an unholy alliance between TAFE managers and Commonwealth funders, took the lead, acting as personal emissaries of their heads of government in a process akin to shuttle diplomacy. The chief players at various stages included the prime minister's chief adviser, Don Russell, Garry Sturgess from New South Wales, and Kevin Rudd from Queensland. Some of the hard bargaining was done bilaterally between the political leaders themselves. Wayne Goss was hostile to the Commonwealth's takeover bid and fought hard on the side of the smaller states. One of the keys to a final settlement was a deal between Paul Keating and Wayne Goss to set up the new national training authority in Brisbane. Not surprisingly, one of the professional educational managers involved in the process described the final stages, when he was squeezed out, as 'chaotic', and the outcome as a 'dog's dinner' (personal communication).

This was a political deal struck in a climate of suspicion and hostility over the Commonwealth's motives. Some might argue that it does not belong in a discussion of cooperative federalism, but this would miss the point. The key was some old-fashioned wheeling and dealing in money and a down-to-earth parochial inducement for Brisbane, but the habits and contacts of the central agency club were also important. Equally important was the inclusion in the settlement of a set of institutional arrangements that promised to provide federalist safeguards against a complete takeover, and to preserve the interests and independence of the smaller states. These arrangements, to be described more fully in a later chapter, were by 1992 typical of SPC and COAG outcomes, and echoed the kind of collaboration that underlay the spirit of cooperative federalism. The experience of cooperation in SPC and COAG provided a set of ready-made solutions that guided even the most divisive issue towards a settlement.

Road transport reform: cooperation out of conflict

The case of road transport reform also shows the importance of the linkage between jointly agreed outcomes and the crafting of purpose-built institutional rules. In this case, under the pressure for agreement,

76   COLLABORATIVE FEDERALISM

non-negotiable positions that threatened irreconcilable conflict were dealt with by cordoning them off under rules for future decision-making. For a group committed to a cooperative process and wanting to avoid deadlock, sometimes the only kind of agreement that is possible is one that puts off the confrontation by laying down new decision rules: that is, a non-decision rather than a tough one.

Efforts by state roads authorities and others to cope with the co-ordination problems created by the gradual growth of interstate road transport began long before the issue was placed on the agenda of SPC in 1990. But the emergence of a scheme for regulating and charging heavy vehicles that resolved these problems required a shift from a slow, measured process of voluntary cooperation to a system of tightly regulated joint decision-making to achieve agreed, uniform outcomes. Here was a clear case of the institutionalisation of collaborative federalism. How did it come about? The constitutional power to regulate road freight transport and to impose associated vehicle charges lies, in the first instance, with the states. Regulatory regimes originated in the 1930s, at a time when interstate road traffic was insignificant and, until the 1970s, they evolved piecemeal and largely independently. Although, under Section 51(i) of the Constitution, the Commonwealth has the power to legislate on trade 'among the states', the story until the late 1980s was largely one of purely interstate cooperation, with the Commonwealth looking on. The Commonwealth was potentially also a major player in the field of charges and road cost recovery through fuel taxes, and via its road grants to the states (Painter and Dempsey 1992).

Heavy vehicle regulations include such things as vehicle dimension limits; speed limits and other traffic codes; systems of vehicle inspection; noise and exhaust emission regulations; and vehicle mass limits to inhibit road damage (ISC 1988, vol. 1, 10–16). State licence fees and charges accompanied these regulations. Both charges and regulations varied extensively between the states, and many cross-border anomalies developed. Vehicle operators fled to the states with the lowest charges and the least constraining regulations. States with more congested roads imposed tougher regulations and higher charges (Painter 1992, 64–5). Meanwhile, other jurisdictions pocketed the licence fees and charges, enforcement costs were high, and evasion was rife. Vehicle operators, who were largely owner-driver contractors working for freight for-warders, were not only fiercely independent and highly opportunistic, they were also capable of well-organised, militant action. In 1979 and again in 1988, they voiced protests over taxes, charges and regulatory anomalies through highly successful road blockades. Both actions accelerated the involvement of the Commonwealth in regulation and charging (Painter 1992, 71).

The pressures for harmonisation of regulations were strong from within the industry. Until 1990, the focus for efforts to harmonise regulations was the Australian Transport Advisory Council (ATAC), a ministerial council set up in 1947. Under the umbrella of ATAC, a number of national bodies, assisted by industry representatives, facilitated harmonisation (ISC 1988, vol. 1, 36–7). The Vehicle Standards Advisory Committee, chaired by an officer of the Federal Office of Road Safety, drafted Australian Design Rules, the first of which were implemented in 1970. The Australian Motor Vehicle Certification Board was a Commonwealth-funded body overseeing vehicle testing by manufacturers. In 1989, the Commonwealth enacted the Motor Vehicle Standards Bill, using powers under Section 51 of the Constitution. It was largely uncontroversial, and retained the existing advisory committee structure and approval mechanism involving the states (Cwlth *PD*, HoR, 23 May 1989, 2689). Other regulations, for example vehicle inspection and maintenance, depended for their implementation on state and territory legislative instruments and enforcement regimes. Periodic codification and consolidation through interstate agreement under the ATAC umbrella gradually brought greater harmonisation.

An important role in harmonising vehicle mass and dimension regulations was played by the National Association of Australian State Roads Authorities (NAASRA), an interstate body dating back to 1934. The outcome of a study in 1976 was the adoption by ATAC of a recommended schedule of limits, which differentiated between the eastern states and the remainder because of different road conditions and road costs. The schedule was subsequently enacted by most of the states, resulting in 'a high degree of uniformity' (NAASRA 1985, 1). A full-scale review of these regulations was conducted by the national association in 1984–85. Industry demands were by now strong for uniformly higher limits in order to increase the productivity of the road freight industry and to take advantage of technological improvements. However, agreement in ATAC could again only be reached on the basis of differential limits (ISC 1988, vol. 2, 23–4). In 1987 Victoria and New South Wales introduced special permits and charges to allow for vehicles over 38 tonnes. Amended dimension limits adopted by ATAC were implemented uniformly in all states other than South Australia by the end of 1988.

After the election in 1983 of the Hawke government, with a more expansive view of national transport policy than its predecessor, the Inter-State Commission was revived (Coper 1989) and a National Road Freight Industry Inquiry was set up. In 1984 the inquiry recommended a new national registration system for interstate vehicles, a proposition that received the support of ATAC. The result was the Commonwealth

78 COLLABORATIVE FEDERALISM

legislated Federal Interstate Registration Scheme, which offered owners of vehicles that were exclusively for interstate use the option of federal registration. Revenue from registration charges went straight back to the states. Agreements with all the states and territories gave effect to new charges in January 1987. Following a recommendation of the Inter-State Commission, the Commonwealth in 1988 legislated to override separate state permits and charges for interstate vehicles (ISC 1990, 41–2). But states and territories continued to impose separate and varying charges for vehicles registered in their own jurisdictions. Proposals by the Inter-State Commission for a national uniform set of charges produced fierce opposition from the industry and from the low-charging jurisdictions. The fundamental obstacle remained differential charging. In January 1991, a 42.5-tonne articulated truck paid a federal registration charge of $3385; the charge for a similar vehicle in the Northern Territory was $510, in South Australia, $2684, and in New South Wales, $6749 (OAG 1991, Attachment C).

The evolution of these measures created a complex tangle of anomalies. Every solution seemed to create new problems. Governments had gone some way down the path towards harmonising regulations, stimulated by pressure from the transport industry, the potential gains for regional economies, and a growing consensus among the technical experts in the transport policy community, but much remained to be done. The 1990 report of the Inter-State Commission sought to document the efficiency gains of further harmonisation and of cost recovery, and to demonstrate that these were only achievable under a 'national scheme'. Here was an ideal agenda item for the Special Premiers' Conference. The timing was perfect. The Commonwealth's agenda paper on the subject for the Brisbane conference led to agreement in principle on a 'national heavy vehicle registration scheme together with uniform technical and operating regulations and nationally consistent charges'. The agreement left open the implementation options of a referral of powers to the Commonwealth or complementary legislation, and flagged 'variations in standards to take account of different regional conditions'.

The significance of the shift in decision arenas from ATAC to SPC was profound. It provided a new impetus: a whole-of-government commitment to microeconomic reform supported by a first ministers' declaration of principle and intent, as distinct from a sectoral concern for an industry's local and technical requirements. New personnel appeared around the bargaining table. A working group—subsequently referred to as the 'Overarching Group on Transport' of Commonwealth and state officials—was set up to report to the next SPC, under the oversight of the Steering Committee of central agency chiefs. Twenty-

ACHIEVING COOPERATION: PLAYERS AND PROCESSES   79

four state and Commonwealth officials (many of them from the central agencies) attended its first meeting on 30 November 1990, and in turn set up three technical working groups on heavy-vehicle charging, registration and regulation, and road-funding responsibilities. The Overarching Group itself focused on the legislative mechanisms for a national scheme, the possible role for a national body, and revenue matters associated with new charges. After setting out terms and reference and a work program for these bodies, the group agreed to meet a few weeks later to hear representations from—among others— the Road Transport Industry Forum, the Transport Workers' Union, the Business Council of Australia and the National Farmers' Federation.

The process of drafting an agreed report and then reaching a formal agreement for the next SPC was long and tortuous. The issues in dispute were many and complex. Industry pressures and signals were mixed, ranging from in-principle support from major peak bodies to outright hostility from some operators in low-cost jurisdictions and from rural producers in remote areas such as northern Queensland. State cabinets in the less-urbanised states were particularly sensitive to their local transport industries and users, and some were also divided internally. In Queensland, for example, where there was a relatively low level of cost recovery from charges, the Transport Department generally supported microeconomic reform in the industry, and cost-recovery measures that removed effective rural subsidies from the transport budget. But it faced the wrath of the Department of Primary Industry, along with the vocal and well-organised opposition of the rural sector. This conflict was also played out in the Queensland cabinet, and dogged the premier's ability to take a clear position on the issue up to the last minute. Officials of the Premier's Department were directly involved in the negotiations, and sought an agreement that reflected the reservations and concerns of the Queensland government. But cabinet (and the premier) had to tread a fine line between the pressure to reach an agreement and the constituency politics of rural Queensland.

Sharp divisions and hostilities emerged between states and territories, as well as with the Commonwealth. Northern Territory ministers and officials, for example, were highly suspicious of the high-charge regimes being mooted to meet the goals of road cost recovery of New South Wales and Victoria, seeing them as the continuation of measures to protect the revenue of their inefficient, state-owned railway systems (although, in fact, central agency officials in the eastern states supported higher road charges as leverage for imposing full cost recovery on their railways as well). The 'western states' demanded special concessions and regional variations to perpetuate the existing low-charge regimes for road trains and other vehicles in outback Australia.

80 COLLABORATIVE FEDERALISM

Well-orchestrated leaks of official discussions, and mooted new charges, fuelled outback fears and opposition (e.g. *QTN—The Management Magazine for Transport Operators*, 28 June 1991).

In this climate it proved impossible to produce a unanimous report from the Overarching Group that resolved the issues. Many of the recommendations were qualified by reservations; the scale of charges included in the report was clearly identified as 'indicative' and 'for illustrative purposes only', and it was 'noted but not endorsed' by the July 1991 SPC; and many unresolved matters were referred to the proposed national commission for future determination. The Steering Committee and the chair of the Overarching Group (a deputy secretary of the Department of Prime Minister and Cabinet) now faced the problem of finding a formula to which the premiers could sign their names at the forthcoming meeting. The delay in the date of the second SPC from May to July 1991 was helpful, but even then the final agreement was stitched together at the last minute. In early July, on the initiative of New South Wales, separate meetings were held to consider an agreement restricted to the eastern states and the Commonwealth. Queensland managed to extract further concessions on the length of time to be taken to phase in new charges. The Commonwealth did not relish the prospect of an agreement that excluded three states, and by now was reluctantly willing to countenance a proposal, originating with Western Australia, that the agreement make reference to high- and low-charging zones. The Commonwealth's last-minute proposal detailed a separate set of decision rules on the ministerial council for eastern and western states, to enable them to set their own 'zonal' charges.

In a last-minute flurry, the Queensland cabinet switched zones and moved in with the west. The Queensland cabinet's preferred position was to seek a delay, but pressure from the prime minister to reach agreement was strong. The perceived danger was that an alignment with the eastern zone would fuel the fears of the rural community that concern for regional impacts would be swamped by the southern majority. If agreement was to be forced on Queensland, the safest path was to placate the local constituency. The zonal decision rules were incorporated in the agreement signed by the premiers on 31 July 1991. The Northern Territory remained dissatisfied and did not sign.

The agreement was thin on substance, but focused instead on institutions, because this was the basis on which cooperation was achievable. The procedures themselves were a mix of those that were designed to smooth the way to effective joint decision-making and others that were patched in so as to placate individual states. We look more closely at these aspects of the agreement in Chapter 6, when we look at how the newly crafted institutions actually operated as instruments of

ACHIEVING COOPERATION: PLAYERS AND PROCESSES   81

cooperative federalism. An important element in the agreement was a national commission, which was given the responsibility of making recommendations on specific matters to do with both regulation and charging. These recommendations would be adopted unless the ministerial council disallowed them. A timetable to adopt uniform legislation was agreed on. A ministerial council would approve this legislation and exercise oversight of the national commission. Different aggregation formulae applied to different ministerial council decisions, most of them requiring majority rather than unanimous approval (see Chapter 6). A majority of states in each zone made decisions about the level of charges for their zone. On South Australia's insistence, one-third of the ministerial council could block any proposed scheme of charging principles. The level of detail in the enunciation of the voting rules was a principal ingredient in reaching agreement. So too was the referral of a number of thorny issues of substance to the national commission for later consideration.

Competition Policy: Cooperation Tested

The agreement on road transport reform was a product of the early months of the SPC process, when the spirit of cooperation was at its strongest. Nevertheless, conflict was intense, a number of sticking-points were encountered, and agreement had to be cobbled together. The process leading up to the agreement on a National Competition Policy (NCP) was even more fraught. The policy was a product of COAG, and of a set of leaders most of whom had not been involved in the launch of the SPC process. However, elements of the policy had their origins in earlier initiatives. The July 1991 SPC agreed that a 'national approach to competition policy' was desirable to achieve the greatest benefit from the sectoral microeconomic reforms already implemented. A working group was set up to review the appropriateness of current competition policy, with special reference to government trading enterprises, marketing authorities, unincorporated bodies, and government procurement policies. The group was to recommend on the need for reforms to the Trade Practices Act, such as extending it to cover state-owned bodies, and removing the power of governments to exempt restrictive practices sanctioned by specific legislation. Problems were identified, but the deliberations provided no clear basis for a way forward.

The prime minister contacted the states with a proposal for an independent review, and the November 1991 meeting of premiers and first ministers called for it to be conducted by an 'agreed independent consultant' under the oversight of a small steering committee. In the event, Prime Minister Paul Keating in October 1992

82   COLLABORATIVE FEDERALISM

unilaterally appointed Professor Fred Hilmer. The states, in a joint letter
of response to Keating's proposal for the inquiry, questioned whether 'a
single national policy or law can be formulated to deal sensibly with all
cases of competition'. In May 1993, Hilmer was given an extension of
time and asked to consult with state governments. This was a concession
to the states, and Keating now agreed explicitly that the report would be
considered by a joint working group of state and Commonwealth
officials, before a proposal went to COAG. Hilmer's report, published
in August 1993, recommended a cooperative approach, with a jointly
appointed National Competition Council overseeing policy, and a
Commonwealth authority, the Australian Competition Commission
(replacing the Trade Practices Commission) to implement it. Hilmer
considered that unilateral Commonwealth action to change the law and
implement policy was feasible, but favoured a 'cooperative approach to
extending the coverage of general conduct rules in the interests of
comity, simplicity ... and certainty'. However, this preference was 'tem-
pered by the need to provide streamlined decision-making', and Hilmer
warned that 'unilateral Commonwealth legislation would be prefer-
able to ... any unreasonable delay in progressing cooperative reform'
(Hilmer 1993, xxxv–xxxviii). The constitutional uncertainties concerning Commonwealth jurisdiction in the event weighed heavily in the
strategy not to proceed unilaterally, but to seek an agreement with the
states before implementing a national policy. But the states remained
wary, as Keating had only reluctantly accepted that the reform process
was a partnership with the states.

The agenda for the National Competition Policy covered many areas
that were already subject to jointly agreed reform processes, such as gas,
electricity, rail and water, while state governments themselves were
acting on their own programs of microeconomic reform. The policy was
seen by some as an attempted Commonwealth takeover of these
reforms, with only token gestures to COAG and cooperation. COAG at
its June 1993 meeting set up a Microeconomic Reform Working Group
of senior officials to review the progress of joint reform. The stimulus
for this came from some of the states—in particular Victoria. Jeff
Kennett was keen to show he was outrunning Paul Keating in the
economic reform stakes, and wanted to reassert COAG's role in anticipation of future developments. State premiers—most of them by now
Liberal were not opposed in principle to the aims of competition policy.
However, they had strong political reasons to want to control its pace
and direction. The reform of gas and electricity had run into snags
as particular states sought to adapt it to suit their own industry
conditions. Much of the impact of competition policy reform would
be on state-owned monopolies and other forms of state regulation of

ACHIEVING COOPERATION: PLAYERS AND PROCESSES   83

trades, occupations and commerce. Initial state responses to the Hilmer Report were not uniformly enthusiastic, in large part because it was seen to be unsympathetic to the specific and often different concerns of particular states. For example, South Australia was worried over the pace of reform of its utilities and the threat of being swamped by competitors from interstate, with $140 million in electricity authority dividends at risk (*AFR*, 28 February 1994); Victoria wanted to retain its own system of regulation of its privatised monopolies; and New South Wales, like South Australia, relied on large dividends from its electricity generation authority to help balance the budget. Over the next few months, state concerns focused on the link between competition policy reform and state revenues, in particular the loss of freedom to set prices and to extract dividends from state-owned monopolies. The states began to talk of 'compensation', and the 'one-way street' of the Commonwealth's view of reform, which imposed all the pain on the states.

In the lead-up to the February 1994 COAG, there was a public war of words over the states' demand for their interests and views to be taken seriously. The Commonwealth talked tough in public, but made concessions on the day. COAG agreed to some general 'principles' of competition policy, along with a series of understandings and commitments that expressed some of the states' reservations and anxieties. The process of drafting legislation was to be a joint, cooperative one; a report for the next meeting would establish the 'practicalities' of applying the principles; Commonwealth compensation to the states for 'loss of monopoly rents' would be considered; officials would explore how to accommodate the states' requirements to 'exempt, temporarily, particular conduct, practices or arrangements'; and so on. But the states were clearly not in control: as the *Sydney Morning Herald* headlined the announcement, 'states back PM's reform plan' (26 February 1994).

The COAG Microeconomic Reform Working Group, under the close watch of the Steering Committee of chief officials, was given the job of putting together the details of a package to reform national competition policy. Most of the officials were from the central agency club. One of their first tasks was to identify the precise impact on state businesses and regulations. To achieve this, an audit sub-group was set up, under an independent chair. This group coordinated an examination in all states and territories of the impact of the new measures. Some of the findings were reassuring to the states: the effects of extending the Trades Practices Act were less dramatic than had first been thought. The impact of associated reforms that Hilmer had recommended to promote competition (such as competitive neutrality with respect to government-owned businesses, independent prices oversight to prevent governments extracting monopoly profits from

84   COLLABORATIVE FEDERALISM

their enterprises, and third-party access rights to network infrastructure) would be much greater, but most state governments were already proceeding down these paths and the issues were of timing and scope rather than principle. A second sub-group worked on the impact on state legislation. Legal opinions differed, but some state governments were of the view that the impact on the 'sovereign powers' of state governments had been seriously underestimated by Hilmer and by the Commonwealth's legal advisers (Charles 1995, 113).

The states insisted on a number of safeguards and measures to facilitate the implementation of a national policy in the context of their different local circumstances. For example, they would set their own timetable and undertake their own separate reviews of regulation to remove those that were against the spirit and letter of the National Competition Policy; and states would implement their own regimes of access to essential facilities, and prices surveillance mechanisms for utilities, in accord with a set of agreed principles, but not necessarily following the same uniform approach or methods. A demand that the states could continue to grant exemptions from the Trade Practices Act was only agreed to 'subject to a Commonwealth override' (COAG communiqué, 19 August 1994).

The states met together at a Leaders' Forum two weeks before the August 1994 COAG meeting and set out their principal remaining objections. The depth of opposition differed, with Western Australia in particular still opposed in principle to a national scheme. The communiqué did not accept that a new National Competition Council was necessary. The capacity to continue to make exemptions was one demand; another was 'to share financially in the benefits of sustained reform', in particular through being able to 'access Commonwealth revenue'. The states called for further consultation and to put off a decision until February 1995. Treasurer Willis responded by threatening that the Commonwealth would 'go it alone', and Paul Keating referred to the states' response as a 'dance of the brolgas' (*AFR*, 10 August 1994).

The COAG meeting of 19 August had before it a draft agreement and legislation, drawn up by Commonwealth officials following the working group's deliberations, and a draft communiqué. Aspects of these documents were sufficient to trigger a heated response from the premiers. Anger was directed at their own officials for 'agreeing' to some of the matters in them, and the meeting proceeded with officials absent. Paul Keating was forced to concede that some aspects of the package did not conform with earlier commitments agreed at Hobart. At the same time, it was apparent that some state premiers had not apprised themselves of the full significance of some of these agreements, but were better informed about some of the grievances of

ACHIEVING COOPERATION: PLAYERS AND PROCESSES 85

affected interest groups (Churchman 1996). Jeff Kennett led the charge, with an ambit claim for 50 per cent of the Commonwealth's revenue gains from the National Competition Policy and insistence that his state be in control of reforming its own legal profession, and not be subject to national control and oversight. A number of amendments were agreed to in the legislative package, and the Commonwealth also agreed to an Industry Commission inquiry into the states' claims for 'compensation'. Importantly, the communiqué pronounced agreement that 'all governments should share the benefits to economic growth and revenue from Hilmer and related reforms to which they have contributed'. Further consideration of the legislation, the intergovernmental agreements and the plans for financial arrangements were delayed until the next meeting of COAG.

The events of this meeting were interpreted by some as the final breakdown of whatever was left of a cooperative process of reform. Comment and reactions from peak industry groups and the financial press were negative and pessimistic. Premiers themselves were increasingly critical of COAG, likening it more and more to old-fashioned Financial Premiers' Conferences. At the next Leaders' Forum a few months later, they went on the attack again, calling for fundamental reform to restore the place of the states in the federation. Kennett used COAG as an example of creeping centralisation: 'I think we get rolled every time we go into COAG, whether we agree on something or not. It's the nature of the beast. While there is said to be discussion, invariably the Federal Government does what it wishes' (*Australian*, 25 November 1994). The gloom deepened when Paul Keating postponed the February 1995 COAG meeting to April.

Officials shared some of the disillusionment. One participant reflected on the events leading up to the August meeting:

> An approach based on consensus is particularly open to lack of clarity about agreements and the outcomes of discussions at meetings. Several times objections had to be raised to minutes that recorded unanimous agreement on issues that had majority support, but on which several states or territories in fact maintained a vigorous opposition. At times, this caused difficulties, with officials having to explain to their leaders that the state position had been put, despite appearances to the contrary from the written reports.
>
> ... Change may be needed, but it must be in a way that strengthens the federal system. The challenge ... is to build trust and a willingness to cooperate, based on mutual respect. There were times when the COAG process on national competition policy was not characterised by this approach.
>
> ... The Darwin COAG was probably the climax of the mistrust I have described. [Charles 1995, 114]

86   COLLABORATIVE FEDERALISM

Some of the change in tenor and climate was due to the accession of Paul Keating, who saw COAG as at best a necessary evil. His first preference was for the Commonwealth to act unilaterally, and his personal style was adversarial and abrasive. Not for him the smooth workings of a club of officials, presided over by a benign guiding hand, but the dramatic personal intervention of the leader at the chosen moment of drama, face to face with his antagonists around the table. As one who was close to the action recalls:

> Keating would not allow his Department Head to go out and make major deals in his name. Hawke was different, he trusted Codd and would back him up on whatever agreement he went back with from the senior officials' meetings. Paul Keating had to be directly approached by Goss and Kennett with a deal before the competition policy was stitched up, that was his style. [personal communication]

Another contributing factor was the change in state leaders, and the fact that several—notably Richard Court and Jeff Kennett—revelled in responding in kind to Keating's barbs and insults, hoping thereby to enhance their own popularity ratings. Clearly, there were major differences in the manner of doing business in COAG compared to the early days of Hawke's SPC. The Darwin experience was not unique. Following the landmark High Court *Mabo* judgement, Keating had put the issue of Aboriginal land rights to the June 1993 COAG meeting. The result was angry words and deadlock. The issues raised by *Mabo* were settled in other places, using other mechanisms, and the positions of several state governments were overridden by the assertion of Commonwealth powers. Things seemed to be going the same way with competition policy.

The Industry Commission's draft report was circulated in December 1994. It contradicted most of the claims of the states that they deserved 'compensation' for revenue losses by pointing to the economy-wide gains of reform. The states questioned some of the assumptions and data in the analysis, and provided the Industry Commission with detailed criticisms and suggestions. For example, it turned out that most of the imputed gains to state government finances were based on an assumption that implementation of the National Competition Policy would mean an end to railway subsidies. The New South Wales Treasury convinced the Industry Commission that this was a separate policy issue and could not be assumed to flow from competition policy implementation. The final, published report put a different spin on the distribution of benefits and costs (Industry Commission 1995). In the first place, it reassured the smaller states that the process was not

ACHIEVING COOPERATION: PLAYERS AND PROCESSES   87

inevitably going to lead to domination within a national market by economic power from the east. The more states joined the process, and the more sectors were reformed, the bigger would be the total benefits and the more widely would they be distributed. Second, the report depicted the distribution of revenue gains in such a way that both sides of the argument could claim that they were right. The states would not lose revenue so much as see their share decline, because the tax system fed more of the revenue gains (particularly in company tax) to the Commonwealth. The reforms undertaken within state jurisdictions would contribute \$19 billion per annum to gross domestic product, compared with \$4 billion per annum arising from Commonwealth reforms. Commonwealth revenues would rise \$5.9 billion in real terms, compared with \$3.0 billion for the states. The argument was no longer so much about 'compensation', with its negative-sum connotations, as about 'sharing in the revenue gains' (a positive-sum process) according to revenue contributions.

By now, the pressure from business interests on both Commonwealth and state leaders was intense. The Business Council of Australia orchestrated a public campaign to try to ensure that the policy would be approved, and in each state business leaders were mobilised to lobby premiers and other ministers. The heat was turned up on the five state Liberal premiers in particular. The result was that most went to the Leaders' Forum in Adelaide on 24 February 1995 convinced of the need for a common position that might be acceptable to the Commonwealth, in order to see the policy adopted at the forthcoming COAG. Those holding out for various reasons were put under pressure (Hendy 1996, 114). State officials had for some time been cooperating closely on formulating detailed positions on remaining points of concern (Churchman 1996, 99). Despite strong reservations from some, the states agreed to accept a process to ensure uniform legislation similar to that used for the national companies legislation (see Chapter 5), under which a template law would be passed in one jurisdiction and automatically applied (along with subsequent amendments) by state 'application laws'. Western Australia remained sceptical, but finally came on board when the remaining states agreed to insist that the Commonwealth accept equal voting rights on proposed legislative changes following any agreement. The leaders also announced that they did not seek 'compensation' but expected a 'fair share of the "competition dividend"'.

This united front put the pressure back onto the Commonwealth. A deal was now in the offing, and further detailed work was done in the officials' working group. The consensus among the leaders

88 COLLABORATIVE FEDERALISM

> produced a change of mood at officials' meetings. The next meeting of the Microeconomic Reform Working Group was productive and positive. The Commonwealth was prepared to listen to the states' problems and treat them as genuine. The states expressed their willingness to believe that the Commonwealth would do its best to solve these problems. [Charles 1995, 116]

Jeff Kennett and Wayne Goss put the bones of the agreement to the prime minister, and a deal was struck. The voting rules for the approval of changes to the competition code gave the Commonwealth two votes and a casting vote, but at least embodied the principle that a vote was needed, not just a consultative process with the states. The financial arrangements were the core of the deal. As we have seen, the meeting of COAG on 11 April 1995 was preceded by a Financial Premiers' Conference in the morning. The financial meeting was relatively free of rancour, and well managed. At COAG, with the Hilmer Report the only major item, the states agreed to a series of Commonwealth 'competition policy payments' beginning in 1997–98, conditional on their making progress on implementation of the Hilmer agenda (including 'related reforms' such as restructuring the gas and electricity industries). The Commonwealth at the last minute got the states to agree to a sign a formal agreement tying the grants to these milestones of achievement. The total amount to be distributed was $4.8 billion over ten years, building up to about $600 million a year by 2001, or about 40 per cent of the tax gains. The Commonwealth also gave a guarantee of permanency for an arrangement decided on at the Financial Premiers' Conference, where an agreement had been struck to maintain for three years the real per capita value of annual general-revenue grants (with the 1994 levels as the base). Projecting this guarantee forward as a permanent arrangement added an estimated $3 billion to the outcome by 2005–06 (*AFR*, 12 April 1995). Importantly, the states felt they had won a level of certainty in general revenue grants that they had never enjoyed over the life of the Labor government. Some premiers believed they had finally clawed some substantial financial gains out of the SPC and COAG process.

The final competition policy agreement was the product of a long, complex and conflict-ridden process. The outcome was a clear compromise, with the Commonwealth accepting a number of measures of substance that retreated from Hilmer's original blueprint, in particular by leaving much of the initiative in implementing competition policy to the states within a binding national framework that applies only at a general level of principle. The states were left to create their own separate access regimes, although they would need to be confirmed by the new national body. The ability of a state to seek to make exemptions to the application of the Trade Practices Act was another concession.

ACHIEVING COOPERATION: PLAYERS AND PROCESSES 89

What comprised 'compliance' with the agreed milestones also left scope for variation from a uniform, national policy (Harman and Harman 1996). The range and scope of the concessions on both sides, in a highly complex package of related matters, reflected a long and ultimately successful process of negotiation within a cooperative framework. Nevertheless, the states bound themselves firmly to a national scheme and subordinated their legislative 'sovereignty' to a collaborative process, an outcome that was not easy for all to swallow.

Conclusion

This chapter has analysed the nature of the processes operating in and around SPC and COAG from the viewpoint of its cooperative aims and objectives. It is clear that the institution provided a framework that facilitated reaching agreement on joint action on a range of issues. This was because it provided new opportunities and resources for actors following an agenda of joint action to persuade others to get on board. The politics of SPC and COAG were a reflection of the wider political forces in the federation, in particular the Commonwealth's dominant fiscal position and its advantage in occupying the high ground of 'the national interest'. The driving force behind putting an issue on the agenda for joint action was more often than not the Commonwealth, through its insistence on the existence of a national dimension. Conversely, the Commonwealth could ignore the states' claims for the urgency of fiscal reform and insist that this item should be left off the agenda. There was something of the traditional take-it-or-leave-it approach here.

But the institution was more than a mere reflection of existing, wider federal forces. It made a difference in those areas where inertia, timidity or lack of organisational and political capacity would otherwise have thwarted concerted action. Merely by being there, it caused officials and leaders to keep working at reaching agreement. It provided deadlines, and it focused public attention. The internal working rules and relationships generated by the SPC and COAG framework were also important in driving concerted action to achieve reform. They gave new and vital positional and other resources to key actors, most notably the central agency club and heads of government themselves. Advocates of reform in the wider community placed high expectations on SPC and COAG, and thwarting them became a thing to be avoided in itself. In this respect, as Weller (1995, 17) notes, the importance for SPC of some early runs on the board in 1991 was crucial. The more SPC and COAG achieved, the higher the stakes and the greater the investment of reputation and commitment.

COLLABORATIVE FEDERALISM

SPC and COAG had some unintended consequences as well. The case of the National Competition Policy, for example, showed the extent to which the states increasingly came to coordinate their actions through COAG and the Leaders' Forum. These bodies became a focus of state resistance to Commonwealth intrusion, as well as of initiatives for the states' own agenda of reform. The growth in political muscle that this exhibited was also in part a reflection of the wider political climate of the times, with the Keating Commonwealth government increasingly isolated and embattled due to the aftermath of a serious recession and growing public disenchantment. Nevertheless, after 1995 it is evident that the Commonwealth was increasingly reluctant to convene COAG for fear of giving the states a forum to flex this collective muscle.

Set against these short-term shifts in the alignment of federal political forces is the longer-term significance of the new institutional arrangements. One feature to emerge from the case studies, aside from the importance of COAG, its committees and protocols, was the extent to which the SPC and COAG agreements created new, associated institutions that facilitated future, routine forms of joint decision-making in particular sectors. The intensity and regularity of intergovernmental contacts on topics of joint and continuing interest focused attention on the scope and nature of intergovernmental machinery for joint policy-making and implementation. Not only in COAG itself where, as we have seen, protocols and other mechanisms were institutionalised, but also in other arenas where joint schemes were being implemented, the limits and possibilities of different institutional forms were under scrutiny. Institution-building was often a matter of great substance in the SPC and COAG negotiations themselves. The obstacles to joint agreement that were confronted were often overcome by putting off the substantive issues to later so that agreement could be signed and sealed: for example, by setting out detailed decision rules in order that signatories could feel some confidence that these issues would be settled with their interests properly represented. Intergovernmental bodies and protocols were gaining heightened importance as part of the fabric of political settlement and the shaping of policy. The stakes were often high, even if the subjects of negotiation were narrow, technical matters such as who was on what joint committee or agency, and what voting rules would apply. These arrangements redefined the contours and boundaries of jurisdictional ground. They were an acknowledgement of interdependence, and a recognition that future benefits would probably flow, even if individual 'sovereignty' was being watered down. The potential existed for a longer-term realignment and reshaping of the institutional map of Australian federalism. In the next chapter, we turn to a more detailed look at some of this machinery. We begin with a survey of the repertoire of institutional forms that is part of Australia's rich federal tradition, surveying the historical development of inter-governmental machinery and seeking out patterns and trends. We discover that the seeds of collaborative federalism had already been sown. In later chapters, we show how they began to sprout and in some cases flower in the hot-house climate of SPC and COAG.

CHAPTER 5

The Machinery of Intergovernmental Relations: An Institutional Analysis

Australia inherited the Westminster parliamentary system, with its strong executive tradition; the result is that intergovernmental relations are dominated by the executive arms of government. As well as the long-standing annual Premiers' Conferences, specific-purpose ministerial councils—for example a meeting of ministers of agriculture—and supporting officials' committees and working parties provide regular fora for consultation. A large number of ad hoc or standing administrative groups and other arrangements add to the complexity (ACIR 1984). These bodies are the media for information exchange and may deliberate on and oversee specific financial and program relations. Some of these relations are conducted under the auspices of formal intergovernmental agreements to enable joint action, in a number of cases being accompanied by schemes of uniform legislation and in some cases implemented through intergovernmental administrative arrangements such as a joint board or commission. Another set of relationships, more or less formalised, are those associated with Commonwealth special-purpose payments for specific programs. All of this machinery is sustained by day-to-day contacts between individual officials, 'so informal as to be beyond enumeration' (Warhurst 1987, 261).

The increase in the number and scope of all types of intergovernmental arrangements has accelerated in recent years (Wettenhall 1985; ACIR 1986a; COAG 1993; JCPA 1995). John Warhurst (1983; 1987) has traced the progression in management forms from sectoral linkages between departments to more coherent, centrally coordinated relationships constructed and overseen by intergovernmental managers. The existence by 1990 of well-developed administrative support and co-ordination systems for the intergovernmental relations function in all state and Commonwealth governments was, at the very least, a necessary

THE MACHINERY OF INTERGOVERNMENTAL RELATIONS   93

precondition for the more intensive relations entered into under SPC and COAG, and could well have been a stimulus for those developments. During the same period when these intergovernmental managers became established, the number and variety of intergovernmental agreements, agencies and joint schemes grew significantly, suggesting a process of learning mediated by these officials.

Most of the arrangements that have evolved to handle intergovernmental relations are sub-constitutional in form. Intergovernmental institutions have been crafted case by case for administrative and political convenience. This chapter looks at five particularly striking trends in this gradual process of invention and adaptation, each of them producing more formalised structures of collaboration: first, the trend towards what might best be called the 'managerialisation' of special-purpose payments; second, the proliferation of formal, multilateral, intergovernmental agreements; third, the creation of a number of new, formally constituted intergovernmental executive bodies; fourth, the increasing tendency to transform ministerial councils from non-executive, advisory, consultative bodies into executive-like bodies making decisions that are binding on members; and fifth, an acceleration in the trend towards uniformity in state and Commonwealth legislation, and the use of the various forms of joint executive and legislative action to achieve and maintain such uniformity. First, however, we present a vocabulary for institutional analysis that helps in analysing these trends.

Institutional Analysis

A useful starting point for analysis of problems of coordination and joint action is the paradigmatic case of the 'collective action dilemma'. This has been modelled in various forms: for example, the 'tragedy of the commons' and 'the free rider problem' (Ostrom 1990, 2–7). Self-interested and rational actions are shown to be counter-productive when placed in a social or collective context. In the case of the tragedy of the commons, for example, the goatherd continues to graze goats and the wood-gatherer to gather wood until the common resource is depleted to exhaustion, because refraining unilaterally does not make a difference if others do not take the same action. Game theorists have modelled such situations as the so-called prisoners' dilemma (from the hypothetical case of two partners in crime under separate interrogation, each asked to confess and/or 'dob in' their mate). Applied to the case of the commons, the scenario is as follows: two herders, if they cooperated, would graze five goats each and preserve the common

94   COLLABORATIVE FEDERALISM

resource for the future. But in the absence of cooperation the so-called 'defect' strategy is to herd as many goats as possible. If both chose the cooperative strategy, it would bring some profit; but if both chose the defect strategy, it would bring none because of resource depletion. If one herder tries to cooperate and the other defects, the latter makes a profit at the expense of the 'sucker's' loss. Avoiding the risk that the other will defect if one cooperates makes the defect option the 'dominant strategy': the common is destroyed (Ostrom 1990, 4).

These models are metaphors for a range of situations where the costs of non-coordination may continue to be borne because of uncertainty about the future actions of others in the group. Trust is the essential component to produce cooperation, but mistrust is the rational strategy. The problem of reaching intergovernmental agreement can be modelled in this way. John Taplin (1993) has depicted relations between the participants in the Intergovernmental Agreement on Road Transport in terms of a prisoners' dilemma game: 'defection [non-cooperation] has frequently seemed the safe course for an individual state'. The coordination dilemma in the case of harmonisation of road transport regulations can be presented as a case where agreement was being blocked because of the counter-productive, opportunistic behaviour of some jurisdictions with the support of local road haulage interests (Painter 1992). Doreen Barrie (1992) has applied the prisoners' dilemma metaphor to the problems of inter-jurisdictional management of the Murray–Darling river system, which involves three states and the Commonwealth. Of course, such problems are not federalism's alone. Aynsley Kellow (1992, 11–14) points out that in a 'non-federal' institutional setting the Murray–Darling's policy coordination problems would simply be displaced onto whatever alternative multi-organisational arrangements existed.

Metaphors such as the tragedy of the commons may be deceptively seductive. They take for granted an unequivocal (if unrealised) common interest and a set of actors with similar individual stakes in the issue at hand. The metaphors structure artificial situations in which the counter-productive nature of self-interested action is indisputable, that is where the collective interest unequivocally lies in cooperation. But real-world situations are not that simple. Thus it would be facile, for example, to jump to the conclusion that *all* cases of resistance to coordination involve a hold-out or defector selfishly thwarting the collective good. Most policy disputes in fact are about contested definitions of what constitutes the public good. Arguments about harmonisation and uniformity, for example, involve genuine disputes about sharing the long-term costs and benefits. Complications also arise because different actors have varying levels of intensity of interest in an

THE MACHINERY OF INTERGOVERNMENTAL RELATIONS   95

issue. Even in the simple case of the goats on the common, a crop farmer with one goat has a very different perspective on the nature of the common interest from a goatherd with no other means of support. Further complexities clearly exist where differences in power or capabilities are taken into account (Martin 1994).

Simple models of collective action dilemmas nevertheless provide a starting-point for identifying possible mechanisms of cooperation. They identify structural conditions in which certain counter-productive behavioural outcomes are likely to occur. By focusing on such conditions, the importance of institutional arrangements is highlighted. It is axiomatic in this view that trust and cooperation will not normally arise and persist of its own accord. Any collection of actors intent on solving a coordination problem of the type just discussed will need to engineer an appropriate, workable set of rules so as to provide incentives for cooperation and/or sanctions that prevent defection.

A useful framework and vocabulary for analysing such institutional arrangements has been suggested by Elinor Ostrom (1986). She outlines a more or less exhaustive list of 'working rules' that limit and constrain collective and individual action in joint action arenas, including authority rules which prescribe what actions particular position holders can take; information rules establishing the type and amount of information that actors may or must reveal to others; aggregation rules prescribing the way decisions are taken; and pay-off rules that specify how costs and benefits are to be distributed as the result of a decision. Such a 'checklist' can be a useful descriptive and a diagnostic tool in analysing and comparing the workings of particular intergovernmental institutions (Painter 1991b; 1992). Ostrom (1986, 471–3) also stresses two additional types of variable. The first relates to the nature of the problem itself: for example, are the goods in question divisible or indivisible? and do the conflicts take on a zero-sum character (where there can be no winner without a loser) or are they positive-sum (where some outcomes could bring gains to all)? The second concerns the social, political and cultural contexts of the action arena: for example, is there a basis of community solidarity that might engender a level of trust?

There are particular structural conditions of joint action in a federal system. Perhaps the most important consideration is that the parties to joint action are not identical: the federal government clearly has a special status in that its territory and powers overlap those of all other governments. In some respects this makes joint action more feasible, given the ability of the Commonwealth to tailor the pay-off rules to suit so as to provide a stimulus to reaching agreements. At the same time, fear and distrust has been engendered by the Commonwealth's use of its resources in this way to extend the scope and reach of its powers. Moreover, the default situation following a lack of agreement has commonly not been inaction but rather unilateral, coercive, Commonwealth intervention. Constitutional provisions and their interpretation have shaped outcomes mostly in the Commonwealth's favour over time, although in some cases unilateralism has failed at the constitutional hurdle. If the Commonwealth decides on a cooperative strategy, as Bob Hawke did in 1990, unilateralism still remains an option and a threat.

The special standing of the Commonwealth in the federation, coupled with its extensive financial power, carries the potential for complex combinations of multilateral and bilateral relations in order to deal with joint action problems. What can emerge is a variety of forms of alliance or administrative and financial arrangements between the Commonwealth and one or more of the states and territories, with the recalcitrant or uninterested being excluded. This, too, may increase the chance of agreements being reached (Painter 1991b). The extreme form of joint action in this mode might be a series of separately struck bilateral deals with each state and territory along similar lines, with the Commonwealth setting the perimeters in each case and the states seeking special arrangements within them to suit. As we discuss below, this is often the case with respect to grant programs. It is in such cases that the 'jointness' of the outcome is clearly suspect, and where the Commonwealth's own designs for control are most evident. There is often an element of divide-and-rule in this strategy. A final variant of possible modes of joint action is a purely horizontal form of voluntary multilateral cooperation that excludes the Commonwealth. But there remains the strong possibility of Commonwealth intervention in such arrangements wherever the issue involved can be depicted as having national dimensions.

An important consideration in this analysis is that the actors in intergovernmental relations are governments. As representatives of governments, the actors carry with them a heavy baggage of institutional tradition, culture and interest. 'Reasons of state' are very different to the interests of men and women. The 'national interest' battles with the 'states' rights'. In the light of the history of Commonwealth expansionism, the states often have a strong incentive to cling fiercely to the vestiges of their share of the federally divided sovereignty, the ultimate expression of which is to refuse to cooperate. The inertia of existing uncoordinated arrangements is often considerable because states adopt the most risk-averse strategy. *In extremis*, when an issue has become a matter of joint discussion, the refusal to cooperate is expressed through the exercise of a veto. But this may have less practical relevance than might appear: if there are collective gains to be shared, a veto is an act

THE MACHINERY OF INTERGOVERNMENTAL RELATIONS   97

of self-denial—a deal is often preferred; or if the veto is exercised and results in opting out, all that is demonstrated is that the cooperation of that party was not necessary in the first place. Either way, the credibility of the threat of using a veto is often not very high.

The final complication is that governments are not unitary actors. As Campbell Sharman puts it, they can be like 'teams of more or less unruly players' (1991, 26). Three obvious consequences follow. First, there is a need for each actor to coordinate its decisions as a collectivity (for example providing accurate and sufficiently comprehensive 'riding instructions' to an official delegate and then being able to carry through on the delegate's commitment); second, there is a strong probability of changes in personnel through the succession of office-holders; and third, some actors may have difficulty in ratification of agreements due to the absence of a majority in one or both of the houses of parliament. All of these factors make coordinated joint action highly problematic because each increases the possibility of defection. As we discuss below, ways around some of them have been devised—for example, gaining prior agreement from legislatures to follow a par-ticular process of adoption or ratification that avoids the possibility of amendment, as in the case of the US Congress's 'fast-tracking' pro-cedures for ratifying GATT agreements (Martin 1994).

In the discussion that follows of the evolution of different institutional forms of joint action, these generic and limiting factors in Australian intergovernmental relations will be borne in mind. Discussion begins with a sphere of joint action that exemplifies above all the special status and powers of the Commonwealth—joint schemes stimulated by Com-monwealth financial grants.

Special-purpose Payments and Intergovernmental Relations

The use of Section 96 of the Constitution to attach conditions to Com-monwealth grants has become a central feature of intergovernmental relations in Australia. The proliferation of special-purpose payments in the post-war period has been extraordinary. They received a boost under the Whitlam government (1972–75) and again under the Hawke and Keating governments, rising to in excess of 50 per cent of Com-monwealth grants to and through the states (nine out of every seventeen dollars in a total of $34.2 billion in 1995–96). Ninety-two separate agreements on special-purpose payments were identified in 1995 (JCPA 1995, 10). Here, we are mostly concerned with the special-purpose payments that give grants to the states for expenditure by state agencies, as distinct from grants that go 'through' the states to other bodies, like universities. Grants 'to' the states give rise to programs

98   COLLABORATIVE FEDERALISM

where control and responsibility become, in some form, shared between governments.

The first example of a special-purpose payment occurred in 1923 with the Main Roads Development Act. Funds were provided for main roads on certain conditions, specifying the types of roads on which funds were to be spent, demanding matching state funding and requiring Commonwealth approval of a program of work before funds were handed over (Painter and Dempsey 1992, 55). Further development of road-funding arrangements resulted in the first of what later came to be known as Commonwealth Aid to Roads Agreements with the states in 1926 (in fact 'agreement' was a misnomer, as three states mounted an unsuccessful High Court challenge against the use of Section 96). A pattern was set: the Commonwealth sought to direct its funds to a program of its own choosing through the use of the states as service providers, imposing input controls such as prior program approval, a matching funds requirement, or a maintenance-of-effort clause (to prevent states diverting existing funds following the flow of Commonwealth money).

The states initially resisted the intrusion and the use of the power of Section 96 to direct state funds but, once it was clear that this was permissible, entered agreements to take the money. For a single state, evasion and circumvention of requirements and conditions was not always hard, given the limited resources of the Commonwealth 'in the field'; 'program approval' was often merely a formality; and counter-manding diversions of other funds could thwart Commonwealth program objectives if a state disagreed with priorities (Painter and Dempsey 1992; Parkin 1991). The Commonwealth's controls were blunt and intrusive, often had perverse effects, and became the source of much friction and irritation in the states (particularly within the central agencies). Tacit acknowledgement of the limits of control, along with a degree of commonality of professional or program purpose, frequently resulted in bilateral deals within an overall agreement on a special-purpose payment to accommodate both state and Commonwealth program interests and priorities (Parkin 1991). But the lines of conflict blurred and overlapped: state agencies which depended on the Commonwealth for funds developed close relations with their federal counterparts that enabled them to distance themselves from central agency and ministerial controls in their own government (Warhurst 1983, 2). In turn, state Treasuries sought to limit special-purpose payments in part to rein in their own spending departments' ambitions. Commonwealth central budget managers often voiced similar concerns to their state counterparts.

The political incentives for growth in Commonwealth special-purpose payments were clear. The closer identification of the Commonwealth in

THE MACHINERY OF INTERGOVERNMENTAL RELATIONS   99

a direct-provision program could purchase constituency support. As well, some of these payments were a bribe to the states to come on board in a joint venture. Commonwealth departments had strong reasons to foster such grant programs for the growth in direct program scope and reach they could bring. But from the Commonwealth perspective at least, the structure of incentives and constraints changed in subtle but far-reaching ways in the 1980s with the growth of managerialism. A number of features of special-purpose payments were anathema to the new managerial norms and practices. First, they depended almost entirely on input controls, while output and outcome measures of performance were neglected (JCPA 1995). Second, the controls tended to be intrusive and replete with bureaucratic formalism and ritualism, rather than concerned with substance. Special-purpose payments as an instrument were often ineffective in achieving better strategic direction in policy and enhanced efficiency in resource use because they were so full of loopholes and provided a potential breeding ground for tacit collusion. As we have seen, they enhanced the power and status of functional agencies over their central agency monitors, in a way that placed them beyond strategic direction. Finally, special-purpose payments raised problems of accountability and monitoring which had long been acknowledged by auditors-general, but which gained added edge because of the vital importance in managerialist doctrine of a focus on measurable performance. Special-purpose payments, because they characteristically lacked clear output goals and performance indicators but relied on detailed input controls and administrative approvals, were seen to measure up poorly on the score of accountability.

The Home and Community Care Program introduced in 1985 demonstrated all these problems: unclear program specifications; diversion of funds to existing programs and to new ones 'ready to go', rather than to those supposedly of top priority; confusion caused by the accommodation of conflicting state and Commonwealth agendas and criteria; and so on (Healey 1988; Chapman 1990; Auditor-General 1988). In the case of road grants, the failure of conventional input-based program approval procedures to achieve effective Commonwealth control over a jointly funded program was well documented (Painter and Dempsey 1992, 62–3). Successive Commonwealth Aid to Roads Agreements in the 1980s and 1990s sought to advance three types of reform: first, a clearer delineation of roles and responsibilities to remove over-lap and to target Commonwealth funds more specifically to 'national' priorities; second, a focus on consolidating program categories (referred to in some program areas as 'broad-banding'); and third, the development of general 'quality assurance' and other output-based performance-monitoring mechanisms (Auditor-General 1989). Finally, under an SPC agreement, special-purpose payments for

100   COLLABORATIVE FEDERALISM

non-national roads was ended and the funds transferred to general revenue assistance.

As discussed in Chapter 2, special-purpose payments were targeted by state governments in the new federalism debates as a primary source of overlap and duplication and a core part of the problem of federal fiscal relations. The states objected to being dictated to in areas which they consider their field of responsibility, but at the same time they 'took the money and ran' (Painter and Dempsey 1992, 63–5). Special-purpose payments as an instrument of joint action are first and foremost instruments by which the Commonwealth seeks to exert program control, but characteristically they also entail more accommodative forms of mutuality because the grant relationship places power in the hands of the recipient as well as the donor. The result has been, within a large number of 'national' programs funded by special-purpose payments, a series of bilateral deals and two-person games, resulting in the emergence of local and national programs of mixed parentage and uncertain outcome. Examples of the gamesmanship often observed are provided in Chapter 7 in connection with the funding of vocational education and training.

Intergovernmental Agreements and Joint Action

Formal intergovernmental agreements purporting to bind the parties to specific courses of joint action have become increasingly commonplace. The prototype is generally considered to be the River Murray Waters Agreement of 1914 (Wettenhall 1985; Kellow 1992). The Commonwealth, New South Wales, Victoria and South Australia agreed to parallel legislation to set up a River Murray Commission, which operated from 1917 under an agreed method of joint funding, specified rules of joint decision-making (for example, the need for consent from each state before some actions could be taken), and shared oversight and scrutiny. The agreement thus embodied aspects of each element that goes to make up joint intergovernmental action: parallel legislation; pooling of executive capabilities; rules of financial and administrative reporting and oversight; an agreed funding arrangement; and decision rules for specified actions affecting more than one jurisdiction.

Intergovernmental agreements take many forms: 'The practice followed in relation to agreements varies ... some are scheduled to legislation, some are approved by legislation, some are ratified or authorised by legislation and given the force of law. Some are required to be tabled, in some or all parliaments. Some are never brought before the parliaments at all' (Saunders 1984, 7). Some intergovernmental agreements find expressions directly in joint legislation. The Torres Strait

Fisheries Agreement of 1984 between the Commonwealth and Queensland was an agreement about administrative arrangements for the application of Commonwealth and state law over fishing in the Torres Strait Protected Zone, where both state and Commonwealth had jurisdiction (ACIR 1986). At the more informal end of the scale are 'memoranda of understanding' between ministers and governments. Exchange of ministerial letters is often enough to set in train a joint administrative arrangement, but it has become more and more common to cloak these understandings in greater symbolic formalism. The National Competition Policy, for example, was set in train by formal agreements, solemnly signed in 1995 by all leaders and subsequently appended to acts of parliament, in which reference is made to the agreements.

There are no hard and fast rules about when a formal agreement is necessary or desirable. For example there is no need for such an agreement to fix the annual allocation of financial assistance grants, because the Commonwealth merely disposes. At the same time the Commonwealth, in making public pronouncements about long-term funding commitments, may be entering into as much of a commitment as if it did sign a formal agreement. But formal agreements sometimes suit the parties. A number of agreements are designed to provide a gloss of legitimacy to a Commonwealth scheme that intrudes on state jurisdiction. They then provide a shell within which the Commonwealth and states jostle for control over policy. One such is the Commonwealth–State Housing Agreement, dating back to 1945 and renegotiated every three or four years. Parkin (1991) argues that these agreements, while seeming to tie the states to the implementation of Commonwealth policies and priorities through the medium of special-purpose payments, were

> not in fact ... a major constraint on state housing policies ... Fundamentally, the Agreements need to be understood precisely as 'agreements'. Rarely have they been a vehicle for imposing unacceptable conditions on a reluctant state. Further, the language of the Agreements is characteristically flexible enough for the states to find avenues for pursuing their own objectives. [Parkin 1991, 245]

In this case the existence of a formal agreement, periodically renegotiated, was a reflection of the need on the part of the Commonwealth to create a national political forum for discussing housing policy where none existed before. The states took part because they welcomed the forward commitment of funds. The Commonwealth Aid to Roads Agreements were of a similar character (Painter and Dempsey 1992). As discussed in the previous section, the bilateral nature of special-purpose

102 COLLABORATIVE FEDERALISM

payments, and the game-playing that went on between state spending agencies and Commonwealth monitors, were the crucial factors in shaping outcomes, rather than the statements or commitments embodied in advance in any written agreement.

The kinds of agreement of most interest here are those that affirm broad political commitments and provide a framework for working out the substance of joint action. Most such agreements are in some degree symbolic and 'extra-constitutional' in form. The precise form is less important than the political intent: to bind the parties publicly to a commitment and to prevent defection. Other than in matters where such an agreement results in a constitutional amendment, as in the case of the Financial Agreement of 1927 (ACIR 1986a, 26–32), opting out is always technically possible: such agreements carry largely moral and political weight with, over time, the added weight of inertia due to the many sunk costs of institutionalised joint action, and the disruption costs of disentanglement. The legal significance of an intergovernmental agreement as a binding contract is in itself of little moment, other than possibly in respect to very specific financial or other undertakings (Howard *et al.* 1982, 8–9). The High Court, in a case in which South Australia was seeking to hold the Commonwealth to an agreement to construct a standard-gauge railway line, rejected the state's argument. McTiernan J. described the obligations in such an agreement as follows:

> The promises on either side are of a political nature ... Their performance necessarily requires executive and further parliamentary action. It is a matter for the discretion of the respective governments to take such action if and when they see fit to do so. ... The real nature of the agreements is that they are political arrangements ... [quoted in Howard *et al.* 1982, 8]

Political executives themselves would not wish many agreements to be legally binding, and some agreements contain statements precisely to that effect. They are compromises between the general wish to retain political flexibility and a specific interest in limited cooperation. Certain aspects of an agreement—such as proposed methods for taking joint decisions or amending legislation—may be stated in the legislation required to implement the scheme. But even then, it remains open to any jurisdiction unilaterally to opt out.

Some of the most intractable problems of commitment arise in the case of schemes where a surrender of legislative as well as executive autonomy is envisaged. A formal agreement seeks not only to bind executives to each other but also to help bind others, particularly parliaments. This, of course, it cannot technically do. The political reality is of legislatures that are not always compliant, mostly because

THE MACHINERY OF INTERGOVERNMENTAL RELATIONS   103

upper houses are not controlled by the governing party, but also (and increasingly in the 1980s and 1990s) because of the existence of minority governments in the lower house (Moon 1995). But the symbolic weight of a formal agreement, when taken back to a legislature, is a powerful weapon in the hands of the executive. Faced with proposed legislation implementing such agreements, legislators often complain at being presented with *faits accomplis*. Technically speaking, they need not consider them as such, but the political pressure brought to bear by the publicity and fanfare surrounding a national agreement is often strong.

Thus one reason government leaders adopt formal agreements is in order to buttress each other's power in their relations with parliament. But there may be further parliamentary obstacles: if a contemporary legislature can be coerced or persuaded to agree, future ones may not feel bound. Perhaps more likely is getting out of step by neglect and default. Over time, joint legislative schemes will lose their uniform character and purpose if legislatures do not amend them in step. A formal agreement can bind executives to seek to prevent this by agreeing to pass an act to implement a joint scheme that includes a clause that automatically adopts future amendments if they are decided on by unanimous decision of a ministerial council. These amendments would only need to be passed as detailed legislation in one of the jurisdictions (often Queensland, where there is no upper house to ask awkward questions) in order to have uniform coverage. Even then, no such mechanism can guarantee against future executive or parliamentary rebellion to repeal the original act. But the more such safeguards are formalised and celebrated with symbolic trappings, such as a formal intergovernmental agreement, the stronger is their moral authority and the higher are the costs of defecting. For these reasons, where more or less uniform legislation is required, a formal agreement is also frequently found.

Ministerial Councils

Ministerial councils (Premiers' Conferences included) have been somewhat shadowy bodies, operating almost entirely by unwritten working rules and general understandings. One exception was the Loan Council. Originally established in 1923 as an informal arrangement, it was given statutory status in 1927 as part of the Financial Agreement. A constitutional amendment subsequently affirmed its formal status and legitimacy.

No such formality accompanied the operations of the Premiers' Conferences, which date back to the beginning of federation. That

104 COLLABORATIVE FEDERALISM

institution evolved over the years from a periodic meeting covering a wide range of matters into an annual meeting, the main purpose being for the Commonwealth to announce its decisions on the disbursement of grants to the states. Edwards and Henderson (1995, 38) also point out that conferences called in addition to the annual 'Financial' Premiers' Conference have not been uncommon in recent years. Often the rationale of such special conferences was to sound a political fanfare and to dramatise concern for an issue of the day—drugs, crime, pollution, or whatever. As with the annual conference, one of the main purposes was concerned with political communication between governments and their electorates, with leaders interacting in either a cooperative or adversarial mode depending on the issue and on political tactics. As Campbell Sharman puts it in relation to the annual Premiers' Conference:

> it is clear that the premiers' conferences are not a forum for bargaining let alone an institution having a major coordinative and policy making function. ... Their prime functions are essentially political and educational, in the sense that they alert the participating governments to the implications of their own policies and those of other governments. [1977, 46]

The Loan Council was an exceptional, if not unique, body, not least because of its formal status as a joint decision-making forum. It was initially a device for coordinating the raising of money by Australian governments on the world money markets, but following the 1927 Financial Agreement its role was extended to regulating other aspects of federal fiscal relations. Membership, scope of subject matter and aggregation or voting rules were specified in the legislation formalising the council. Most decisions were taken by majority vote, with the states enjoying one vote each and the Commonwealth two and a casting vote. The Commonwealth and two states could between them thus form a majority.

The case of the Loan Council warns against interpreting any such formal rules literally. The most significant factors were not the formal constitution of the body itself but broader fiscal pressures and political exigencies that have, on the one hand, encouraged the states to exploit loopholes and circumvent the formal procedures and, on the other, enabled the Commonwealth to achieve its fiscal dominance by other means (Saunders 1990; Senate Select Committee 1993). Thus in the early 1930s states circumvented the borrowing rules by creating new semi-government bodies, which were exempt from coverage. The Loan Council at this point proved effective as a collective decision-making entity, recognising the counter-productive consequences and enabling the striking of a gentlemen's agreement to regulate this area of

THE MACHINERY OF INTERGOVERNMENTAL RELATIONS 105

borrowing. Following World War II, the Commonwealth achieved such fiscal dominance over the states that it effectively imposed its own terms and conditions. The states outvoted the Commonwealth in 1951 to achieve a higher borrowing limit, but were unable to raise the funds. The Commonwealth, in agreeing to underwrite their efforts, reimposed its preferred limit. Henceforth the Commonwealth unilaterally made the principal Loan Council determinations. In the 1970s the states found new methods of circumvention through complex financing arrangements for infrastructure projects, and the gentlemen's agreement broke down (Senate Select Committee 1993, 15–20). A system of 'global limits' was instituted, again supposedly as a matter of agreement but in fact by Commonwealth imposition: Queensland was threatened with a reduction in general revenue grants if it exceeded the limits (Saunders 1990, 46–9; Senate Select Committee 1993, 23–4). In 1993 and 1994 the Financial Agreement and the traditional functions of the Loan Council were effectively made redundant with the virtual deregulation of state borrowings and the substitution of other means of overall fiscal control and monitoring.

The first of the functional ministerial councils, the Australian Agricultural Council, was established in 1934 (Bland 1935; Grogan 1958; ACIR 1986a). The Australian Education Council was formed in 1936 (albeit at first as purely an interstate ministerial council) (Spaull 1987, 20–2). These were the forerunners of many more. The Advisory Council for Intergovernment Relations in 1986 counted thirty-seven such bodies, while a review for COAG identified forty-five in 1992 (ACIR 1986a; COAG 1993). Of the forty-five, seven were set up before 1960; seven in the 1960s; fourteen in the 1970s; ten in the 1980s; and seven in 1990–91.

Many of these bodies evolved without fanfare as more or less formal arrangements for communicating and sharing experience. Ministers and governments, while willing to engage in mutual exchange, were wary of closer entanglement. To the extent that ministerial councils performed work of major political importance, ministers were keen to preserve their somewhat shadowy status. Informality, adhockery and secrecy were the norm. Mostly, there was no need for statutory action to enable the kinds of consultation envisaged. In 1986, the Advisory Council for Intergovernment Relations could list only three councils that had been established by statute or by agreement 'appended to statute'. A 1992 survey listed five statutory councils and two that were 'statute-derived'. However, the use of formal intergovernmental agreements to give recognition and legitimacy to a ministerial council's scope and functions has become more common. In 1992 twelve derived their powers from formal Commonwealth–state agreements and nine

106 COLLABORATIVE FEDERALISM

were established by 'other agreement', although seventeen were set up under no formal agreement. A review of ministerial councils by COAG drawing on this survey noted that 'an increasing trend is the striking of an intergovernmental agreement as a means of defining the roles, functions and powers to be exercised by the Ministers in each particular case' (COAG 1993, 18). As discussed below, increasing formalisation has occurred in other ways.

The roles of ministerial councils are many. Most commentaries have tended to assume they were 'consultative' bodies, a view confirmed by many actors and official accounts. A classic statement of this type of role for a ministerial council is to be found in the guidelines of the Australian Education Council, as codified in 1985:

> The function of the Council is to promote the development of Australian education by enabling Ministers of Education to consult on matters of common interest and generally to facilitate the exchange of information and coordination of common programs.
>   Specifically this is achieved in the following ways:
> a by providing a forum ... to discuss policies and procedures
> b by providing a basis for moving towards co-ordinated education policies ...
> c by providing the mechanism for fostering development of collective approaches to education policies which overlap with other portfolios
> d by exchanging information ... [Spaull 1987, 315]

The Commonwealth did not gain an official place at the Australian Education Council until 1972, so its terms of reference might reflect a tradition of interstate, mostly arm's-length cooperation, rather than entanglement in joint administration with the Commonwealth.

By contrast, the Australian Agricultural Council from the beginning dealt with many such matters, foreshadowing a more collaborative model. According to the description by Grogan (1958), it was a body that played a vital role in reaching intergovernmental agreement on a range of policy issues, such as marketing arrangements and stabilisation schemes, involving both state and Commonwealth powers and interests. Several such schemes, at various points in their formulation, were also discussed at Premiers' Conferences. Grogan notes the importance of the standing committee of chief agriculture officials from each jurisdiction, which met more frequently than the council and invariably provided agreed reports and recommendations on items on the council's agenda. The pooling and marshalling of technical expertise and advice provided an important basis for moving issues through the combined processes of intergovernmental and industry consultations and negotiations. The shift in the balance of financial relations after 1942 in favour of the Commonwealth resulted in a subtle change in

THE MACHINERY OF INTERGOVERNMENTAL RELATIONS 107

relationships on the council, with the state representatives more often cast in the role of urging the case for a commitment of Commonwealth funds. Special-purpose payment schemes were the glue that entangled the states in a web of increasing collaboration. The new pay-off rules placed ministerial councils as the hub of an increasingly important sphere of government, largely hidden from view within the interstices of executive and bureaucratic politics. In this circumstance functional ministerial councils acted as powerful influences over central agencies and cabinets: 'General agreement between Commonwealth and state Ministers in the Council on the desirability of a particular course of action is often the prelude to an approach by the Commonwealth Minister to Cabinet for necessary funds' (Grogan 1958, 9). It has also been noted, however, that while they had 'great political suasion' there were 'other occasions when even unanimous decisions in council had failed to influence Cabinets' (ACIR 1986a, 13).

The description provided of the Agricultural Council's decision-making procedures, while stressing the underlying authority rules of a division of powers, suggests that it frequently effectively concluded items of joint policy:

> The decisions of the Council are not, generally speaking, binding on the Governments ... but the ... consistent aim is to reach agreement ... Where such agreement is reached ... recommendations ... will be submitted to the Commonwealth and state Governments concerned and will usually receive favourable consideration and, where appropriate, be implemented. Where majority agreement only is reached in the Council there is never any assumption that a resolution will have binding effect unless it is accepted by all the Governments concerned. [Grogan 1958, 5]

The council's own handbook in 1985 reiterated these comments in very similar phraseology, noting also that 'recommendations are normally made on the basis of the greatest common ground after taking into account special problems of individual states' (ACIR 1986a, 39).

The reference to 'consultation' in most accounts of the work of ministerial councils reflects the necessity for a consensual style of action in the face of possible disagreement. A logical concomitant of the underlying authority rules, namely that each jurisdiction retained the right to make its own decisions regardless of a ministerial council recommendation, was an aggregation rule of unanimity and its accompanying consensual norms. The survey by the Advisory Council for Intergovernment Relations found that some participants were reluctant to talk of 'decision-making' procedures, as this 'conveyed too strong an implication ... observing that progress was more often made through the exchange of information, through discussion and through

108 COLLABORATIVE FEDERALISM

the momentum the council process gave to the ... respective bureaucracies' (ACIR 1986a, 38). One minister made the same point in claiming that 'issues were simply not pushed to the limits of such decisiveness, as no worthwhile outcome could ensue—states had threatened withdrawal' (ACIR 1986a, 40).

Warhurst (1982, 222–4) describes one case where the authority rules led to the use of the veto. A new Commonwealth-inspired scheme for dairy industry assistance was negotiated through the Agricultural Council in 1977, but met opposition from Tasmania and Victoria. The Victorian minister for agriculture rejected a proposal that the Commonwealth minister would act to trigger the assistance scheme on a majority decision of the council, as this would 'enable the majority of states representing the minority of dairy farmers to dictate to the minority of states representing the majority of dairy farmers' (ACIR 1986a, 39). The Commonwealth could not introduce the scheme unilaterally, as Victoria (the largest producer) could block its implementation. Another agreed scheme was substituted.

The proposal for majority voting raised complaints not only that it interfered with the sovereign authority of a state but also (from the other side) that it was an abrogation to a group of state ministers of a Commonwealth minister's responsibility for administering a Commonwealth act (ACIR 1986a, 39). Despite such objections, majority voting was adopted for supervision of the Cooperative National Companies and Securities Scheme in 1980 (see below). A similar provision was put in place in 1984 for some aspects of the work of the National Crime Authority Intergovernmental Committee. In the extensive discussions leading up to the creation of the National Crime Authority, the states were anxious to protect their traditional jurisdiction over criminal investigation and prosecution, and were wary of the Commonwealth Labor government's preference for centralisation. The result was a compromise in which a relatively powerful Commonwealth body was set up, but under the part-supervision of a ministerial council. The National Crime Authority, in conducting investigations and setting up joint task forces with state police, was made subject to requirements for prior approval and reference by the ministerial council. In respect to offences against the law of a particular state, the state minister also had a veto power over the Commonwealth minister's written direction to the authority to undertake an investigation (Wettenhall 1985, 30–1).

Ministerial council supervision of the National Crime Authority was not the preference of the attorney-general, Senator Evans:

> How do you propose to make a success of the ministerial council concept of accountability ... when anybody who has had anything to do with the existing co-operative companies arrangement has been driven practically bonkers by

THE MACHINERY OF INTERGOVERNMENTAL RELATIONS 109

> the difficulty of making it work? ... it gives everyone a role in policy determination ... it is really not all that terrific in practice as a way of sheeting home responsibility when something goes wrong. [NCC 1983, 114, 282]

The South Australian attorney-general, Christopher Sumner, defended the idea: 'I found, at least until the arrival of Senator Evans, that the Ministerial Council was not very much worse than the Cabinet or my local sub-branch, with the controversy and discussion that is involved' (NCC 1983, 303).

The issue at stake was the establishment of continuing supervision and policy oversight of a joint activity, the principles behind which had been settled by exhaustive negotiation and unanimous agreement. The resulting transformation of the ministerial council from a consultative body into an instrument of effective joint executive action was clearly a source of unease. States had reason to oppose the watering down of sovereignty entailed in joint decision rules such as majority voting, while the Commonwealth chafed under the frustration of coming to terms with an often unruly group of state ministers and governments. The best that it could do was to replace unanimity with a majority rule. Collaborative institutions of executive federalism were in the making. While ministerial councils remained political meetings of ministers from separate, arm's-length jurisdictions, the mechanisms now existed by which some of these bodies at least had the appearance—for specified scopes—of being an executive board in the one jurisdiction. Under SPC and COAG, many more cases emerged. Details of some of these bodies, and the variety of decision rules adopted, are provided in later chapters.

Inter-jurisdictional Agencies: The Case of the Murray

The River Murray Commission of 1914 was the first of a number of inter-jurisdictional agencies (Crommelin 1986). Others have included the Joint Coal Board (1944), the Snowy Mountains Commission (1957), and the National Companies and Securities Commission (1980). The problems with the Murray began before federation. The south bank of the river forms part of the boundary between New South Wales and Victoria, leaving the waters in New South Wales but the flood plain divided between both. Its main tributary, the Darling, originates in Queensland, and the waters empty to the sea in South Australia. At federation, South Australia was dependent on the Murray for river trade. Adelaide relies on the river for water supplies, while the other states exploit it for irrigation. The 1914 agreement set up four commissioners, one from each participating government and each with a veto over decisions or recommendations. The agreement specified shares of water normally available to each state, leaving the commission to allocate shares in bad years. The agreement also contained specific proposals for dams, locks and barrages, with the states as constructing authorities. The commission operated the storages and administered the water-sharing arrangements. The commission had to approve new works on the main river, but on the tributaries a state merely had to inform the commission. Detailed provisions were also made for sharing the cost of capital works and the administrative costs of the commission.

The agreement and the commission facilitated the development of a successful irrigation agricultural industry. But its limitations became increasingly obvious. Water quality and salinity became the principal problems from the 1960s, but the commission's powers did not extend either to the tributaries or to the flood plain, so the remedies to the salinity problem were beyond it. Proposals for new powers stemmed from a South Australian initiative in 1973 and finally resulted in a new 1981 agreement. A stumbling-block was the objections of upstream states—New South Wales in particular—to any major limitations on irrigation or proposals for expensive salinity mitigation works (Kellow 1992, 3). The 1981 agreement gave powers to the commission to investigate and propose new works for both quality and quantity measures, including in the tributaries. The consent of the state concerned to such investigations, including water quality measurement, was required. The commission could formulate water-quality standards and objectives and recommend constraints on discharge of saline water into the river, but not execute or enforce them (Clark 1983, 165–7). The institutional framework—including the veto over commission recommendations—was unaltered.

The 1981 agreement was an imperfect and incomplete collective response, but proved significant in helping stimulate further collective action (Kellow 1992). The commission with its new remit began stimulating discussion and publishing authoritative material on the salinity issue. In Victoria the problem was subject to increasing official concern and the topic of a parliamentary inquiry. Both the South Australian and Victorian governments proposed new intergovernmental discussions and reforms. A special ministerial meeting was announced in August 1985, South Australia was asked to present a proposal, and an intergovernmental committee of officials was asked for recommendations. Ministers agreed to set up a Murray–Darling Basin Ministerial Council and a new standing committee. Discussions proceeded in working parties and on the Water Resources Ministerial Council, as well as at a special ministerial meeting in April 1986. The first meeting of the new ministerial council took place in August 1986. Queensland came on board as an observer. Out of these meetings came a proposal for a new

THE MACHINERY OF INTERGOVERNMENTAL RELATIONS 111

Murray–Darling Basin Commission. The voting and other decision rules on matters covered by the existing agreement continued to apply in the new commission, but on the other issues majority voting would apply (each government to have one vote). Membership was to be expanded to include agency chiefs from land, water and environmental agencies in each government (in the end reduced to two representatives from each government). A new agreement was signed in 1987 and, by October 1988, legislation implementing it had been introduced in each parliament. The Murray–Darling Basin Ministerial Council, with three ministers from each participating government from the portfolios of land, water and environment, received statutory status as the overseeing authority for the new commission.

Kellow (1992, 65–6, 70) argues that a key ingredient to the conclusion of the new institutional arrangements was the emergence of a solution to the salinity problems, sponsored by Victoria, that converted the previous zero-sum character of the issue to a positive-sum outcome, thereby removing much of the incentive for New South Wales to exercise a veto. Victoria, from the point of view of the salinity problem, was a victim as much as a perpetrator. The solution was not just to limit upstream discharge but to construct salt interception works in South Australia so that *additional* saline discharge could be permitted, thereby assisting in mitigating saline waterlogging in the irrigation areas. Local political opposition to salt evaporation works in Victoria was also thereby side-stepped. The saline interception works were to be funded by the three states and the Commonwealth equally. An agreed, standard measure of salinity would facilitate monitoring, while a proposed scheme to allow for trading of saline deposit 'quotas' between states also encouraged cooperation. One of the first acts of the ministerial council was to adopt a new Salinity and Drainage Strategy incorporating this set of solutions. The new commission and its attendant Community Advisory Committee provided an important potential focus for mobilising affected groups across state boundaries (Barrie 1992).

In microcosm, these events illustrate the conditions for and chart the emergence of collaborative federal institutional arrangements. A solution to a pressing and inescapable collective action dilemma emerged in parallel with a set of new institutional arrangements that facilitated collective agreement. An important trigger was the evolution of new information rules—the injection of a new, wider, information-gathering role for the original commission in 1981—and an important part of the solution was a new set of authority and aggregation rules—arrangements for inter-jurisdictional joint executive action in an enlarged commission modelled along more 'corporate' lines. The case demonstrates an institutional learning process. A further and even more

112 COLLABORATIVE FEDERALISM

striking illustration of this is provided by the history of companies and securities regulation, the subject of the next section.

Harmonisation of Law and Administration: Companies and Securities Law

Companies law in Australia evolved in each colony and state along separate but similar lines. The demand for greater uniformity resulted in the so-called Uniform Companies Acts of 1961–62. The Standing Committee of Attorneys-General stems from this initiative. An Advisory Committee in 1967 recommended sweeping legislative changes, some of which were embodied in acts passed in the early 1970s (Tasmania excepted). Some steps were taken towards uniform security industry laws by Victoria and New South Wales in 1970, followed by similar acts in Queensland and Western Australia, but major differences were evident in the legislation. The Interstate Corporate Affairs Agreement between New South Wales, Queensland and Victoria in 1974 (with Western Australia signing up in 1975) created virtual uniformity in these states. South Australia fell partly into step in 1979. Under the agreement a ministerial council was empowered to act on harmonisation proposals by majority vote (NCSC 1986). An Interstate Corporate Affairs Commission of the four chief company law administrators and private sector representatives from each state was set up. Both company and securities law were brought under this regime. In spite of it, complete uniformity remained a distant object. The 'conflicting imperatives of reform and uniformity' dogged these efforts at voluntary interstate harmonisation (NCSC 1986, 4). Legislative amendment enacted autonomously by each parliament to remedy defects and to keep up with new technology was a cumbersome and uncertain business, often leading to further inter-jurisdictional disharmony. State administrative bodies retained complete autonomy, resulting in non-uniform administration and interpretation.

Commonwealth interest was sparked in the 1970s by share market booms and busts and accompanying scandals, particularly in the mining industry. The Whitlam government, encouraged by the High Court's intimations of a widened scope of Commonwealth power in the *Rocla Concrete Pipes* case of 1971, was committed to a national scheme (CCH 1991, 13–14). Bills for a national scheme of companies and securities law, including a national commission, were introduced in 1974. They foundered in a hostile Senate. But the Senate's own Rae Committee into securities regulation in 1974 was the trigger for Commonwealth legislative action. It publicised findings of widespread criminality, impropriety and incompetence in the securities industry. The Senate

THE MACHINERY OF INTERGOVERNMENTAL RELATIONS   113

Committee homed in on a lack of effective regulation, specifically the absence of a strong 'national watchdog'. It found a number of deficiencies in state-based regulation, not the least being the loopholes that permitted operators to cover their tracks by jurisdiction-hopping, each transaction being legal but, in combination, amounting to fraud (CCH 1991, 109–10). The findings of the Senate Committee helped to stimulate the states to greater cooperation, but the consensus among most law-reform advocates, peak business groups and financial journalists was for greater centralisation. The principal objectives were to secure a better guarantee of uniformity; to keep legislation under continual review and reform where needed; and to institute a system of uniform administration by a single, national, regulatory body. To achieve these objectives within a framework of cooperation with the states required an elaborate set of institutional arrangements, agreed to under a formal intergovernmental agreement in December 1978. The Cooperative National Companies and Securities Scheme was born, with legislation being enacted finally in 1981 and 1982.

One significant element in the new scheme was a method of law-making and amendment aimed at creating and maintaining uniformity. This had been first used in 1937 to achieve uniform aviation law, following a successful challenge to the Commonwealth's jurisdiction (Howard *et al.* 1982, 11). Known variously as the 'application of laws', 'template', or 'adoptive' legislation, it entails a prior binding commitment by each government to apply in its jurisdiction the laws of another, along with clear procedures for joint decision-making to formulate legislation. In this case, the Commonwealth under its territories power introduced legislation applying to the Australian Capital Territory which, along with later agreed amendments, subsequently became the law of each of the states. Each state passed application of laws legislation to obviate the need to introduce the substantive bills and amendments. Once enacted, the substantive legislation was published separately by each state as the code applicable in its jurisdiction.

The intergovernmental agreement bound signatories to this method of law-making; outlined the creation of a National Companies and Securities Commission (NCSC), the scope of its powers, its relations with existing state regulatory bodies and its funding; and set up a ministerial council, to meet at least four times a year, with clearly specified powers of deliberation and decision-making. Approval of the initial legislation was subject to unanimity, but subsequent amendments could be approved by a simple majority. Each member had one vote. The Commonwealth undertook to submit any amendment approved by a majority of the ministerial council to the Commonwealth parliament and to 'take such steps as are appropriate to secure the passage of the

114 COLLABORATIVE FEDERALISM

Bill' (Clause 44(b)). Each signatory undertook not to introduce any legislation that contradicted the act or its regulations.

The ministerial council had sole oversight of the NCSC, a Commonwealth statutory body, and appointed its members by unanimous vote. Half of the cost of the NCSC was provided by the Commonwealth, the other half by the states, each contributing proportionately to its population. The ministerial council approved the budget. The NCSC, while a national body with specified administrative powers, was enjoined to follow 'the principle of maximum development of a decentralised capacity to interpret and promulgate the uniform policy and administration of the scheme' (Clause 35(2)). The existing state corporate affairs bodies were retained, but in a subordinate relationship exercising delegated powers. These bodies thus were, on the one hand, responsible to their separate state ministers but, on the other, subject to direction by, and responsible to, the NCSC.

The Hawke government was committed to a national, Commonwealth scheme but did not move immediately to bring one in. However, momentum for introducing such a scheme built up. In 1986 a Senate Committee agreed that the Commonwealth should occupy the field. What particularly irked the senators was their perception that they were 'forced' to rubber-stamp legislation approved by a ministerial council (although there was nothing to stop a Senate amendment if there were a deficiency in a proposed bill, with a request for the ministerial council's concurrence). Commonwealth ministers and departments were even more hostile to the cooperative scheme. No attorney-general relished the indignity of having to steer legislation through the parliament on the say of a majority of the states, while the Attorney-General's Department resented not having control over the legislative or administrative processes, and waged continual guerrilla warfare against the NCSC (Bosch 1990; SSCCLA 1986, 275).

The Senate Committee's hearings provided evidence on the operations of the scheme. Business and professional groups concerned with company affairs were divided on the central issues. Some argued that the intergovernmental procedures tended to make the process more opaque and less accessible; others argued that they found access more effective due to their ability to approach state as well as Commonwealth ministers. National organisations like the Business Council of Australia favoured a Commonwealth scheme, while regional groups or national bodies with a more federated structure spoke favourably of the current scheme. The director-general of the Institute of Directors explained: 'one of the reasons why we do not have any difficulty with the present system is that we are well organised in the states. We have little difficulty in negotiating with state or Federal authorities in each state when we are asked to consider something' (SSCCLA 1986, 338).

THE MACHINERY OF INTERGOVERNMENTAL RELATIONS 115

The business communities of Western Australia, South Australia and Queensland were for the most part strongly in favour of keeping a role for the states (Bosch 1990, 214, 223). The ability to influence the 'local interpretation' of the scheme was welcomed. Several witnesses noted that it was easier to get a prompt and consistent ruling from the state Corporate Affairs officials, under delegation from the NCSC, than to get a similar response from the regional office of the Australian Taxation Office. Decentralised administration was also supported because it had encouraged innovation by local stock exchanges and had fostered competition between state registration and regulatory bodies to improve efficiency (SSCCLA 1986, 280, 657). Not surprisingly, the strongest support came from state ministers and corporate affairs officers. The South Australian attorney-general commented: 'there is a concern that a lot of the flexibility that exists in the scheme and the accessibility that people have to the decision makers would be lost if you went to a scheme involving Commonwealth legislation [and] bureaucracy' (SSCCLA 1986, 510).

The ministerial council was a somewhat unwieldy body. Ministers came and went, and their officials tended to run the show. A number of state Corporate Affairs Commissioners were hostile and obstructive, but one by one they moved on. The ministerial council initially had a separate secretariat, located in Sydney as a sop for siting the NCSC in Melbourne. The regular meetings of officials often numbered more than thirty, comprising representatives of six state Corporate Affairs administrations and ministers' offices, the secretariat, the NCSC and the Commonwealth department. A number of reforms in 1985 made the system more effective. The secretariat was scrapped and the NCSC took over its work, while a limit was put on the number of advisers' meetings and the number of representatives attending them.

Under this regime the NCSC had a relatively free hand in its operations. Henry Bosch, its chair from 1985, considered this a principal virtue of the system. His argument was that the corporate regulator had to be politically independent and fearless, while staying in touch with the markets and close to the ground. Under the ministerial council, with no single master to exert political influence, the NCSC effectively had none:

> I reported to eight ministers and the Commission was comprised of eight members who had a collective responsibility. I was therefore able to tell any departmental officer, Commonwealth or state, who let me know his minister's wishes that he was speaking for only one member of the Ministerial Council and that in any case I would have to consult my colleagues. ... The few directions that were given [by the ministerial council] were openly discussed ... in front of ministers from all political parties. ... In practice my term of office was entirely free of political pressure of any kind. [Bosch 1990, 235]

116   COLLABORATIVE FEDERALISM

The NCSC slowly put in place a workable system of delegations with the state bodies, even if it chafed under the limits to its powers and the need to rely on state delegates for much of the investigative work and all prosecutions. Some of this work was delegated back to the NCSC in a new set of more centralised arrangements in 1988 (Bosch 1990, 214). The biggest difficulty faced by the NCSC was lack of funds and staff. The ministerial council was unable to agree to an increase in funding. The states considered fees and charges levied on corporate affairs to be an important part of their meagre general revenue base, not to be earmarked for a 'national' scheme, while the Commonwealth was reluctant to fund a scheme or a regulator that it did not directly control. Each blamed the other.

Attorney-General Nigel Bowen was a strong advocate of a new Commonwealth scheme and seized on the 1986 Senate Committee's recommendations as his chance to forge ahead. The Commonwealth informed the states of its intentions to proceed to institute a national scheme unilaterally. The opinion given by the solicitor-general to the committee was that the Commonwealth did enjoy the constitutional power to proceed alone. The late 1980s were turbulent times in the corporate world, with a growing number of financial collapses and scandals with which the NCSC was hard-pressed to keep up. As the dust began to settle, the calls for reform were buttressed by the requirement to restore 'investor confidence' and 'international reputation'. Bills introduced in 1988 to set up a Commonwealth-controlled scheme were approved by the parliament and received the royal assent in July 1989.

Western Australia, South Australia and New South Wales successfully challenged the scheme in the High Court which, in a judgement of February 1990, interpreted Section 51(xx) of the Constitution to mean that the Commonwealth did not have the power to regulate the formation of corporations (Simmonds 1990). But the states were divided on how to react. Victoria agreed in mid-1989 to refer the corporations power to the Commonwealth and also to hand over its corporate affairs office to the Australian Securities Commission (ASC), the proposed successor to the NCSC. The agreement was assisted by a Commonwealth offer to site the ASC headquarters in Melbourne and by a financial deal that allowed the state government to retain the great bulk of the revenue previously collected under the cooperative scheme. Queensland was induced to withdraw from the High Court challenge and to accept the same financial arrangement, under threat that the offer would not apply to those states party to the challenge (*Australian*, 4 October 1989; *AFR*, 9 February 1990; Bosch 1990, 229). Following the success of the court challenge, the Commonwealth was severely embarrassed and was forced to negotiate. Queensland under the new Goss

THE MACHINERY OF INTERGOVERNMENTAL RELATIONS 117

Labor government reconsidered its position. The deal that was finally struck in June 1990 came about following agreement between the largest states and the Commonwealth, with the other three states joining in reluctantly (Western Australia later had to be given further concessions when its upper house rejected the agreement). Ironically, the ASC chair was now to be located in Sydney, with the deputy in Melbourne.

A new heads of agreement was signed by the states, the Northern Territory and the Commonwealth. A new national scheme was agreed to under an application of laws regime: the Commonwealth acts (as applied in the Australian Capital Territory) 'as in force for the time being' were to be applied by state acts as the law in each jurisdiction. The ASC, with regional offices in each state capital, was to be the sole regulator, reporting exclusively to the Commonwealth minister, and with full powers of investigation. Prosecutions were to be undertaken through the Commonwealth director of public prosecutions. The ministerial council remained in existence, but with reduced functions and powers. It was to be consulted (but no more) on appointments to the ASC and to the new Takeover Panel and Companies and Securities Advisory Committee (with each body to include a member from each state). It was to be consulted also on any proposed new legislation to amend the acts, but that was the limit of its role with respect to legislation covering takeovers, securities, public fundraising and futures. On other matters of legislation the council was given a deliberative function by majority vote, with the Commonwealth having four votes and a casting vote and also enjoying a veto. Thus the states in concert could block any proposal, while the Commonwealth won the principle that it would not be forced to introduce any legislation with which it did not agree. If, in the course of the passage of legislation through the parliament, amendments were moved other than by the government, the government would 'use its best endeavours to ensure adequate consultation with the Ministerial Council', but majority approval on the council would not be required to see them become law (Heads of Agreement, Ss. 22.5–6). A joint standing committee of the Commonwealth parliament was set up to scrutinise the scheme. The Commonwealth took over all collections of fees and charges associated with companies and securities regulation, but agreed to reimburse the states with special-purpose grants in perpetuity to a total of $102 million annually, indexed in line with the consumer price index. A distribution formula was written into the agreement (one-sixth each by population, Grants Commission relativities and number of registered companies, one-half by net state revenue proceeds). As well, having threatened during the negotiations to take over stamp duties, the Commonwealth

118   COLLABORATIVE FEDERALISM

agreed not to interfere with state collections but rather to facilitate them by requiring the ASC to be satisfied that the state stamp duty had been levied prior to registering any charge.

The new national scheme was a considerable step in the direction of complete centralisation. It received the strong support of most of the Sydney and Melbourne business communities, national business organisations and the financial press. It satisfied most of the national parliament's concerns about accountability as well as the Commonwealth executive's wish for effective control and unified administration. The states were left with some influence over parts of the legislation and the right to be consulted on appointments, while they extracted a financial settlement that preserved their revenue. Most of the states had little stomach for a fight to retain a state-based companies regulation regime. The smaller states made some efforts to defend the position of their business communities, who feared domination by the concerns of Sydney and Melbourne. But there was also an element of shadow-boxing even in the High Court challenge, and a financial arrangement that preserved state revenues was sufficient for a final settlement. Only Western Australia raised serious objections of principle, pointing favourably to the example of the decentralised corporate law regime in the United States of America (Simmonds 1990). The domination of the national corporate, legal and financial worlds by Sydney and Melbourne helped to mute a more decentralist point of view. What resistance there was stood to a large degree on the grounds of jurisdiction rather than policy, calling forth a barrage of anti-federal rhetoric in editorialising in the eastern states' press (*Canberra Times*, *Age*, 19 April 1990; *AFR*, 31 May 1990; *Australian* 5 December 1990).

The progressive move through various forms of intergovernmental cooperation to a more centralised scheme provides a case study in institutional experimentation and adaptation. If the received wisdom suggested the 'failure' of the cooperative scheme, it nevertheless showed that a system of intergovernmental joint policy-making and administration could work. From the states' perspective in particular, it provided a model of cooperative forms of national policy in which they could play a significant role. From the Commonwealth's perspective, the experience was less positive, but its transitional nature carried its own lesson— that once the first steps towards collaboration were taken, the process was hard to reverse. The process by which the 1991 national scheme took shape was characterised by adversarial forms of federal politics: Commonwealth unilateralism, state resistance, a High Court challenge, and the exercise of Commonwealth financial power through selective inducements so as to divide and rule. The High Court ruling left the states with a vestige of important formal powers, but they surrendered

THE MACHINERY OF INTERGOVERNMENTAL RELATIONS 119

most of them in a collaborative arrangement in which the Commonwealth was the dominant partner.

Conclusion

The emergence of the more elaborate, formalised structures of co-operation and joint action described in this chapter has occurred as a result of attempts to establish workable arrangements to achieve outcomes that overcome coordination problems. The evolution towards more collaborative arrangements has taken place in a context of the Commonwealth's centralising ambitions, many of which have been realised over time. While a trend is evident, the course taken has been far from smooth and the patterns that have emerged have been highly varied. The indeterminacy of the division of powers and the resulting conflict remain the central point of departure for all these arrangements. The Commonwealth would generally prefer to command rather than to cooperate, but limited resources and constitutional obstacles force it to choose the latter on many occasions. Across different fields of joint action, strategic decisions in a context of wider political demands for particular types of policy response can result in many different forms of arrangement side by side, from the loosely consultative to the tightly constrained and collaborative. The examples given above suggest the latter are becoming more common.

The distinguishing features of these more collaborative forms include a recourse to binding agreements to try to lock in not only the signatories but also other actors, including future legislatures and executives. Such agreements seek to provide a settlement to a set of disputed authority rules arising from overlap and entanglement. The main instrument of such a settlement is new, formalised working rules, the most important of which include decision rules to limit the use of the veto and the power of the hold-out; and authority, information and position rules that give a special place in the decision-making process for jointly mandated, semi-independent intergovernmental administrative bodies. Collaborative norms and procedures run through these arrangements: for example, governments commit themselves not to act unilaterally to contradict joint decisions, and to take these decisions collectively by majority vote in a specifically constituted forum (a ministerial council), but only after receiving the advice of a jointly mandated body. They agree to surrender some autonomy (e.g. to amend uniform legislation) to these joint decision-making bodies. These forms of joint action have departed significantly from more arm's-length, unfettered cooperative forms, in which governments preserved their supposed autonomy of action (and that of their parliaments), severely limited a deliberative role for intergovernmental bodies, and operated purely by consensus and unanimity.

In sum, after ninety years of federal politics and growing administrative entanglement, there was a rich experience of instruments of joint action to hand to assist a national leader calling in 1990 for a more cooperative style of federalism to solve a set of national problems. The remaining ingredients needed to push ahead with an agenda of joint action were common agreement on a range of problems or issues of sufficient significance, and a concerted process of joint decision-making by the heads of government. Chapters 3 and 4 gave an account of the manner in which this political momentum and commitment was created and sustained (with varying levels of success) over the period 1990 to 1997. In Chapters 6 and 7, we continue with the detailed, formal institutional analysis begun in this chapter and look at the instruments and institutions for joint action crafted by SPC and COAG to put flesh on the bones of commitment, and their significance for the underlying character of Australian federalism.

CHAPTER 6

The Institutions of Collaborative Federalism

Many issues considered by the Special Premiers' Conferences and the Council of Australian Governments did not result in new forms of joint action among governments. The most notable failure was fiscal reform, where the Commonwealth refused to accept the demands of the states to provide them with a more secure, guaranteed source of revenue-sharing than was available under the current system. Indeed, this refusal, which meant that the states continued to rely heavily on Commonwealth grants for their basic recurrent expenditures, perpetuated a significant source of entanglement and laid the basis for the Commonwealth to insist on collaborative arrangements in other areas of policy, when some states might have preferred different forms of relationship. As discussed in Chapter 2, the model of federalism underlying the states' demand for more fiscal autonomy was arm's-length, or competitive, not collaborative.

The fiscal reform issue aside, other issues that appeared on the agenda of SPC and COAG did not result in agreement, but only served to remind observers that the federal system, while cooperative in some aspects, remained adversarial in others. Attempts to remove inconsistencies in industrial relations legislation, for example, were doomed so long as it was to the advantage of different governments with markedly different models of such legislation to retain the capacity to pass their own laws. Here, federal politics made it advantageous to heighten difference rather than remove it. Another case was the Mabo issue concerning Aboriginal land rights, which appeared on the agenda of the June 1993 COAG meeting and resulted in heated argument, but no more. The communiqué did not enumerate the deeply divided political views of different governments, but was nonetheless eloquent in drawing attention to them:

122 COLLABORATIVE FEDERALISM

> The Council had a lengthy discussion of the issues which need to be resolved in formulating an appropriate response to the High Court decision in the Mabo Case which recognises a form of native title to land. No course of action was agreed by this meeting and member governments will be considering their positions further.

In other cases, states and the Commonwealth remained at arm's length while agreeing to cooperate. Such agreement sometimes cloaked continuing conflict over specific aspects of policy. A case in point was a series of discussions and statements in SPC and COAG on aspects of environmental policy, where friction was common. The Intergovernmental Agreement on the Environment, considered in more detail later, contained a mix of collaborative elements, such as a relatively weak, jointly mandated national body, and large areas where the states and the Commonwealth retained autonomy to act independently within a set of broad principles.

In this chapter, we look more closely at particular instances of joint schemes and collaborative arrangements arising from SPC and COAG so as to identify how far, in practice, these new areas of cooperation resulted in a more collaborative mode of intergovernmental relations. As we saw in Chapter 5, joint action through a variety of institutional forms was a growing sphere of intergovernmental relations in Australia before SPC and COAG got to work. We pick up from Chapter 5 the same language and framework for institutional analysis, in order to distinguish the nature of different clusters of working rules. Table 6.1 depicts two models of cooperative action, one pure arm's-length and the other pure collaboration. No attempt is made to be exhaustive in the depiction of the array of working rules characterising each model, but illustrative examples of each type are provided. Reading down the columns in Table 6.1, it will be noted that each array of working rules is interrelated, internally consistent and reinforcing. For example, the aggregation rules in the collaborative model take for granted the authority rules; and the aggregation rules under the arm's-length model follow logically from the authority rules. The only element in the arm's-length model that entails any form of joint action at all is an information rule that each government will consult with the others. Some definitions of 'coordination' might not even require that much—for example, the purely self-regulating mode of 'parametric adjustment' (Lindblom 1965, 33). Here, however, we stipulate that cooperation requires at a minimum a prior communication of intention.

In the image of arm's-length federalism, governments not only keep their distance and disagree when it suits them, but also keep their distance when they agree to the need for coordination. That is, the

THE INSTITUTIONS OF COLLABORATIVE FEDERALISM 123

parties agree to cooperate by independent rather than joint action. This model is depicted in column one. When an agreement is reached, it will be in the form of a set of principles or guidelines, leaving it up to the parties to carry through with their commitments to action. Some such agreements 'in principle' are cloaks for lack of commitment; others carry with them strong powers of moral suasion. The common feature is

Table 6.1: Contrasting models of intergovernmental coordination

Rules	Arm's-length cooperation	Collaboration
Scope	Each government's jurisdiction over all or any set of decisions relating to subject matter X is limited only by provisions of the Constitution.	A specific range of decisions about subject matter X is, by agreement, the shared responsibility of all governments party to an agreement.
Authority	Each government can choose whether or not to be bound by any agreement about X arising from any consultative process with other governments.	No policy about X is made in any jurisdiction other than with the approval of a joint ministerial council of all governments.
	Each parliament acts independently in making and amending laws about X.	No parliament can make or amend laws about X other than by a procedure that maintains conformity with the laws of all other jurisdictions.
	Administration of policy and enforcement of laws about X is undertaken by agencies responsible only to each separate government.	Administration of policy and enforcement of laws about X is undertaken and/or monitored by a national commission, which reports to the ministerial council.
Information	Governments will consult with each other and exchange information before determining policy about X.	No decision about X can be taken without considering the advice of a national commission.
Aggregation	No consultative forum can take decisions about X other than by unanimous agreement.	All decisions on policy about X are taken under voting method P (e.g. two-thirds majority).
Pay-off	The Commonwealth and states direct funds independently to X in a manner that mutually supports a unanimous agreement.	Funds for X are pooled by both state and Commonwealth governments, and allocations made by joint agreement under voting method Q (and on recommendation of the national commission).

124   COLLABORATIVE FEDERALISM

that the agreement to act is entirely consensual; nothing in the agreement binds the parties to any external powers of enforcement. One state official aptly labelled this 'unfettered cooperation'. In contrast, the collaborative model depicted in column three of the table has governments entering a range of commitments for joint, coordinated action, binding each other in various ways to avoid defection, and institutionalising mechanisms for subsequent implementation of jointly agreed policy.

Under the auspices of SPC and COAG, officials crafted a variety of institutional arrangements that were variations on those summarised in column three. Table 6.2 lists the agreements and arrangements that reflected all or most of these elements of collaborative federalism. Several other areas of cooperation were discussed at COAG with a view to establishing such arrangements, but the cooperative schemes were not brought to final fruition. Some were in the area of service provision and joint funding, and are discussed in Chapter 7. A number of other agreements were reached in SPC and COAG but are not included in Table 6.2, either because they were in anticipation of or complementary to others, or because the agreement entailed none of the collaborative arrangements identified above. For example, in 1994 COAG agreed to a 'statement of principles' on gas reform and water reform respectively. These both had significant implications for state infrastructure, pricing and resource policies, and committed the states to continuing consultation on a common agenda of microeconomic reform principles. But as discussed below, more binding forms of commitment to joint action on these matters only came with the National Competition Policy Agreement, which subsumed many of these principles as they applied to those industries in a framework that incorporated complementary

Table 6.2: SPC and COAG: Collaborative agreements, 1990–96

Year	Agreement
1991	National Road Transport Commission
1991	National Rail Corporation
1991	Non-Bank Financial Institutions Scheme
1991	National Food Authority
1991	Mutual Recognition Scheme
1992	National Vocational Education and Training Agreement
1992	Intergovernmental Agreement on the Environment
1993	Uniform Credit Laws Agreement
1995	National Competition Policy Agreement
1996	Treaties Council

THE INSTITUTIONS OF COLLABORATIVE FEDERALISM 125

legislation, a national commission and external enforcement. A brief outline of some of the most important features of these arrangements follows. The National Road Transport, National Rail and National Vocational Education and Training Agreements are described in more detail elsewhere.

Non-Bank Financial Institutions

This was an interstate agreement that did not involve the Commonwealth as a formal partner. The agreement was signed by state heads of government on 22 November 1991. It brought uniformity to the regulation of institutions such as credit unions. A national body (the Australian Financial Institutions Commission, AFIC) was set up and uniform legislation was passed during 1992. The formal agreement committed the parties to all the details of the joint arrangements. An agreed template bill was enacted by the Queensland parliament. Regulations under the act, once drafted, were approved by unanimous decision of all governments. This act (with its regulations) was then applied by acts of all other parliaments, with the effect that subsequent amendments to the Queensland act would also apply in each jurisdiction so long as these application acts remained in force. Such amendments (including new regulations) would only be made if approved by a majority of the Ministerial Council for Financial Institutions. Legislation to bring into the scheme the regulation of state-based financial institutions not already covered by the act required a unanimous vote. The board of the commission was appointed by the ministerial council, which also approved its budget. The commission exercised oversight of the scheme, but detailed supervision in each state was undertaken by a 'state supervising authority'. The costs of the scheme were met by industry levies, and industry associations played a major role in self-regulation (Beetham 1993; Waterhouse 1994).

National Food Authority

Efforts to bring uniformity to state food standards legislation had made slow progress to the end of the 1980s, although considerable steps towards harmonisation had been taken (Nelson 1992). Divided and uncertain responsibility and lack of transparency in the federal arrangements for arriving at and implementing standards remained. The Health Ministers' Conference in June 1990 agreed to a joint standard-setting scheme, and this was endorsed by the October SPC. Further details were endorsed in July 1991. Commonwealth legislation set up the National Food Authority in June 1991. The authority was

126   COLLABORATIVE FEDERALISM

made responsible for developing food standards through a process involving extensive consultation with industry. Recommended standards would be approved by the National Food Standards Council (a ministerial council) by majority vote. The states agreed to adopt these standards under their own legislation without variation, such that they came into force upon publication in the Commonwealth *Gazette*. The states passed complementary legislation to this effect, prescribing that food standards as defined in state acts were those gazetted under the Commonwealth act, following the procedures described above. In 1995, New Zealand joined the scheme under a harmonisation treaty. The New Zealand Minister for Health became a member of the Australia New Zealand Food Standards Council, enjoying one vote alongside state and Commonwealth ministers and submitting to the same rules for the automatic adoption of agreed standards. A special clause was inserted to allow New Zealand to opt out of a joint standard, in which case a full justification of the 'exceptional circumstances' leading to this would have to be provided. The National Food Authority was reconstituted as the Australia New Zealand Food Authority.

Mutual Recognition Scheme

The mutual recognition scheme is based on a simple proposition that, in applying standards and other regulations to goods, services and occupations, each state or territory in Australia agrees to recognise the standards determined by another. A good that complies with the regulations of any one jurisdiction can be freely sold in any other; and a person who is registered for an occupation in one can practise it in another without having to satisfy additional requirements. Rather than insisting on uniformity, jurisdictions agree to recognise diversity. At the same time, where diversity is not acceptable (e.g. if one jurisdiction's standards are unacceptably low), procedures are put in place to ease the transition to an acceptable set of agreed standards.

Agreement between the states to proceed with such a scheme was sealed at the November 1991 meeting of premiers, and a formal agreement including the Commonwealth was signed at the May 1992 heads of government meeting. The Commonwealth participated only so as to facilitate what was considered by the officials formulating the scheme to be the most convenient method of implementation. Under the agreement, states and territories were to refer to the Commonwealth, under Section 51(xxxvii) of the Constitution, the power to pass an act to put the scheme into effect. New South Wales, Tasmania and Queensland made that reference, and the Commonwealth act was passed, whereupon it came into effect for those jurisdictions. Victoria and South

THE INSTITUTIONS OF COLLABORATIVE FEDERALISM   127

Australia followed a different method, however, each passing a subsequent act to adopt the Commonwealth act. Any later amendments to the Commonwealth act would have to be separately enacted, and would not apply automatically. Western Australia delayed joining the scheme until 1995, first referring the matter to the Standing Committee on Uniform Legislation of the Legislative Assembly (WA Legislative Assembly, 1994), and then passing its own separate legislation, with a 1998 sunset clause. It called for a review of the scheme at that date, and indicated its preference for a new interstate agreement that would exclude the Commonwealth from any role.

The Commonwealth undertook not to amend its act without unanimous consent of all parties to the agreement. The Commonwealth act provided for temporary, unilaterally declared exemptions, and for a process of uniform standard setting should a state or states object (with or without declaring a temporary exemption) to the implementation in their jurisdiction of any existing standard. The appropriate ministerial council (for example of ministers for the environment, or for consumer protection) would determine an agreed standard within twelve months by a two-thirds majority. If three or more heads of government objected to the new standards within three months, the obligation on jurisdictions to adopt them was nullified. A standing committee of COAG on regulatory reform monitored the scheme, and a COAG agreement in 1995 set out principles and guidelines for ministerial councils and other bodies in the adoption of any new regulatory standards.

Intergovernmental Agreement on the Environment

The environmental agreement is a multi-purpose intergovernmental agreement that includes statements of commitment to broad policy principles. It attempts to clarify agreed divisions of roles and responsibilities and to set out procedures for consultation and clearance in cases of administrative overlap. It agrees to mutual 'accreditation' of each jurisdiction's environmental assessment procedures so as to avoid duplication; and to cooperative, mutually agreed policy frameworks for particular issues (such as climate change and biological diversity) and a commitment to developing additional ones. Under the agreement, a National Environment Protection Authority (later referred to as Council) would be established under Commonwealth legislation, and would take the form of a ministerial council with defined powers and functions. By two-thirds majority, it could determine national environment protection measures. The Commonwealth, on its part, agreed to consult the states before negotiating or ratifying any international treaty with implications for environmental policy. The Commonwealth and

128 COLLABORATIVE FEDERALISM

the states agreed to a procedure to draft and submit legislation to implement the agreement. The specific forms of such legislation, and the method of attaining any desirable uniformity of implementation in national environment protection measures, were left unspecified:

> The Commonwealth and the states agree to develop ... legislation which will enable the Commonwealth and State Parliaments to authorise the Authority to establish any measures. The legislation will also establish mechanisms for the application of measures in the states. The legislation will ensure that any measures established by the Authority—
> (a) will apply ... throughout Australia, as a valid law of each jurisdiction; and
> (b) will ... replace any existing measures dealing with the same matter.

The Commonwealth passed the national Environment Protection Act in October 1994 and all states (other than Western Australia) passed some form of complementary legislation in 1995. This took various forms. In each case, the state legislation fitted the national measures into an existing framework of state environmental law and policies, rather than replicating or adopting a national, uniform measure. The result was a variety of degrees of discretion, in some cases purely through executive action, in incorporating and implementing national measures in state environmental administration. The spirit of the agreement appeared to commit the signatories to uniform, self-enforcing outcomes for agreed national measures (although wording such as that above left plenty of room for doubt on this point). Western Australia at first declined to participate in the implementation of the agreement, but subsequently introduced legislation that contained a specific 'local exception' clause, namely that the Western Australian parliament could disallow a national measure that did not, in its view, take account of Western Australian 'regional difference' (WA Legislative Assembly, 1996).

Uniform Credit Laws

The intergovernmental agreement on uniform credit laws was negotiated by the ministerial council, not COAG. It was an agreement among states and territories to enact similar consumer credit legislation. The agreement provided for an agreed 'template' consumer credit bill to be passed by the Queensland parliament, and for each other jurisdiction to apply the Consumer Credit Code as a law of that particular jurisdiction. Queensland, as the only unicameral parliament, was favoured as the source of such legislation. On the insistence of Western Australia, an alternative method of achieving uniformity was agreed to, known as 'alternative consistent legislation', under which a state or territory could choose to achieve consistency by passing its own legislation mirroring

THE INSTITUTIONS OF COLLABORATIVE FEDERALISM 129

the template bill. Instead of agreeing automatically to apply amendments to the template bill (as approved by a two-thirds majority of the ministerial council), the state or territory adopting this second method agreed to pass its own amendments. The agreement specifically exempted a state or territory adopting the 'alternative consistent' method from having to obtain the approval of the ministerial council to any amendments. At the same time, the agreement stipulated that a state would cease to be party to the agreement if its legislation ceased to be 'uniform or consistent' as a result of any amendment.

National Competition Policy Agreement

This agreement is in fact three agreements: a Conduct Code Agreement, a Competition Principles Agreement, and an Agreement to Implement the National Competition Policy and Related Reforms. The Conduct Code Agreement deals with the enactment of template legislation by the Commonwealth, which the states and territories undertook to apply in their own jurisdictions. The form of this legislation had been agreed before the agreement was signed. Amendments are agreed to by a majority vote, with the Commonwealth having two votes and a casting vote. The members of the Australian Competition and Consumer Commission (set up under the agreement to replace the Trade Practices Commission as the regulatory authority to police the competition rules) were appointed by the Commonwealth following a prescribed process of consultation with the other signatories, and approval by a majority. The agreement was said to commence once the Commonwealth and at least three other jurisdictions had executed it through the agreed legislation (a device to protect the scheme from the disruptive effects of a laggard or hold-out).

The second element was the Competition Principles Agreement, which set out agreed principles about government enterprise pricing policy, competitive neutrality policy, structural reform of public monopolies, review of regulatory legislation, access rules for essential infrastructure, and application of the principles to local government. The principles left the states with considerable discretion as to the pace and method of applying them. Appointments to the National Competition Council (set up to advise on policy and administration in relation to the principles) were made by consultation and majority vote.

The third agreement was on financial matters, and was the key to the final deal (see Chapter 4). The real per capita value of the financial assistance grants pool would be maintained on a three-year rolling basis, and from 1997 special payments would be made to the states and territories so long as they met certain conditions. For the first tranche of

130   COLLABORATIVE FEDERALISM

$200 million in 1997–98, states and territories had to meet the deadlines for review of legislation and implementation of competitive neutrality policy in the terms set out in the Competition Principles Agreement, and to achieve 'effective implementation of all COAG agreements' on electricity reform and the national framework for free and fair trade in gas and 'effective observance' of road transport reforms. In 1999–2000 a second tranche of $400 million would be paid, subject to continuing progress on the implementation of the same set of reforms, plus water industry reforms agreed to by COAG; and the third tranche, by 2001–02 of $600 million, would depend on 'having fully implemented, and continu[ing] to observe fully, all COAG agreements with regard to electricity, gas, water and road transport'.

The implementation commitments were in some cases quite specific, relating to policies and timetables agreed to in the Competition Principles Agreement and in earlier COAG decisions. For example, the February 1994 COAG agreement on trade in gas contained twelve specific points of agreement which, until this financial agreement, contained no external means of enforcement, but depended on voluntary compliance by those signing the communiqué. Among the twelve points were agreements to remove all legislative and regulatory barriers to the free trade of gas by July 1996; complementary legislation to implement a nationally uniform third-party access regime both between and within jurisdictions, and a list of points of principles to be incorporated in this legislation; agreement on corporatising gas utilities by July 1996; and legislation to 'ring fence' all transmission and distribution activities in the public and private sectors.

The water reform proposals that were to be fully implemented by 2001 for the payment of the third tranche had also been discussed at the February 1994 meeting, but agreement in principle to aspects of the proposals for recommended methods of charging, asset refurbishment and institutional reform was qualified by some jurisdictions by riders and reservations. In any case, the principles and policies for charging, conservation and usage of rural and urban water, while quite detailed and specific, were only statements of intent accompanied by implementation timetables, with no enforcement mechanisms. Typical of the statements in the 1994 agreement was the following:

the Council agreed:
4. in relation to institutional reform:
    . . .
    (f) that the arrangements in respect of service delivery organisations in metropolitan areas in particular should have a commercial focus, and whether achieved by contracting out, corporatised entities or privatised bodies this be a matter for each jurisdiction to determine in the light of its own circumstances.

THE INSTITUTIONS OF COLLABORATIVE FEDERALISM   131

The tying of payments to progress added an enforcement mechanism to these earlier COAG agreements, but holding the states and territories to the implementation of policies such as that above (particularly when, in the case of water policy, three states announced at the time their reservations to some aspects) would clearly leave room for disputes over compliance. In the final analysis, the choice by the Commonwealth to meet the financial obligations would in any case be a political one for the government of the day. In that regard, one of the first statements made in the agreement was that 'the financial arrangements would have to be reviewed if Australia experiences a major deterioration in its economic circumstances'. Indeed, this did happen in 1996, when the real per capita guarantee was broken on the excuse of correcting a Commonwealth budget deficit.

Treaties Council

The states had long sought a means of influencing treaty-making and implementation, thereby hopefully preventing the Commonwealth from acting unilaterally with the effect of significantly invading trad-itional areas of state jurisdiction. This had occurred, under the external affairs power of the Constitution, in areas such as labour laws, the en-vironment and the criminal law. At the June 1996 COAG, an agreement was reached on a new procedure for consultation with the states on international treaties and other instruments, such as UN Draft Dec-larations. The agreement involved a formal set of procedures for consultation through a Standing Committee on Treaties (a committee of officials) and a Treaties Council of first ministers, which would meet at least once a year. The Treaties Council had only an 'advisory function'. Information rules were closely specified to allow for early state and territory input, including providing the states every six months with a list of current and forthcoming negotiations. The Common-wealth agreed to undertake and publish a 'national interest analysis' of every future treaty, including statements about methods of implemen-tation and the extent and results of consultations. The Commonwealth did not concede to the states in this new set of any arrangements any of its prerogatives to make or sign treaties, nor to implement them under heads of power available to it in the Constitution (notably, the external affairs power). However, the formalisation of consultation and information exchange acknowledged the need for joint decision-making. The Treaties Council was accompanied by cognate procedures for the tabling of treaties in parliament before being ratified, and the setting up of a joint parliamentary committee (COAG communiqué, 14 June 1996).

132 COLLABORATIVE FEDERALISM

Collaborative Arrangements in Context

The establishment of these collaborative institutions occurred in a context that retained underlying features characteristic of arm's-length federalism. They were negotiated in a context where the parties retained their autonomy, and from that starting-point agreed to (bargained and negotiated) a specific set of interlocking, joint actions and arrangements. In the National Competition Policy Agreement, a set of other agreements on gas, water and electricity, which had originally contained no enforcement mechanisms and no binding institutional commitments, were locked in to a timetable of implementation by a set of financial inducements and penalties. It might be argued that these were not so much imposed by the collectivity on its members, as imposed by the Commonwealth on the states and territories. But the states were not just passive recipients of a take-it-or-leave-it financial offer. They made their compliance subject to receiving such an offer from the Commonwealth, which made a considerable concession in tying itself to a committed level of funding so far into the future. The Competition Principles Agreement was—without this set of inducements and sanctions—a statement of intent by autonomous parties to a voluntary agreement. With the financial agreement in place, it became a set of jointly made commitments with penalties for defection. Other aspects of the National Competition Policy Agreement, such as the joint decision rules for legislative amendment and appointment of commissioners, also demonstrated the kinds of interlocking institutional arrangements that characterise collaborative federalism. The package as a whole carried great weight as a binding agreement that locked in future coordinated action under a uniform legislative regime and a national regulatory body. The very fact that it was so long in the making, and had involved so much conflict, made the final settlement a powerful, defining event. Such agreements generate their own force by building up expectations and commitments beyond those that can be specified on paper as formal enforcement mechanisms.

It is worth recalling in this context that SPC and COAG were not themselves collaborative institutions, although (as described in Chapter 4) they clearly provided a framework conducive to collaborative initiatives. SPC and COAG were meeting places of autonomous heads of government, and worked by consensus and unanimity. They provided a forum for pressing towards joint action and agreement when it suited the mutual political interests of the leaders, but they were also a forum for more adversarial forms of federal politics. As we saw in Chapter 4, one means of reaching agreement in a context of conflicting political positions was to craft elaborate and detailed collaborative working rules (such as the zonal authority and aggregation rules in the agreement on

THE INSTITUTIONS OF COLLABORATIVE FEDERALISM   133

the National Road Transport Commission, or the insertion of a voting arrangement in the process of amending the Conduct Code of the National Competition Policy). But the nesting of these collaborative arrangements within the wider context of the federal political system gave some of them a precarious status, and made them subject to continuing contestation. Indeed, their survival in some cases depended on a degree of flexibility in the interpretation of the rules, and a willingness to reconsider the basis of an initial settlement when defection threatened the survival of a scheme. Nowhere is this better illustrated than in the case of the National Rail Corporation.

National Rail Corporation

Discussions about creating an integrated, national interstate rail freight system connecting the mainland capital cities resulted in the setting up in September 1989 of a National Rail Freight Initiative Committee, comprising a representative of the Commonwealth Minister for Transport, the state railways, the Australian Council of Trade Unions (ACTU), Broken Hill Proprietary Ltd, and three major freight companies—TNT, Mayne Nickless and Brambles. Following consultants' feasibility studies, the committee recommended establishing a National Rail Corporation as a public company owned by the participating governments. This was a novel proposal, bringing governments together in a joint commercial venture, and creating a unique hybrid commercial entity. In September 1990 the Australian Transport Advisory Council agreed to set up a task force of state and Commonwealth officials (plus a representative of the ACTU) to put together detailed proposals. The task force began work in October, supported by a heads of agreement signed at the October SPC setting out eight broad conditions, including the requirement of commercial viability, a 'clean-sheet' industrial agreement, rights of access to state assets, and a 'no-disadvantage' provision to safeguard state rail systems during a transitional period. The task force reported to ATAC in April 1991, noting some unresolved disagreements about equity participation and funding. A further committee was set up to draft a shareholders' agreement and articles of association. Following further discussion at the July ATAC meeting, the July 1991 SPC saw four shareholder governments—the Commonwealth, NSW, Victoria and Western Australia—plus Queensland as a non-shareholder participant sign an agreement to support the establishment and operation of the National Rail Corporation. South Australia did not sign the agreement but indicated it might sign up later.

Under the agreement, the signatories undertook to 'take all practicable steps' to enact legislation to implement the agreement. Legislation

134 COLLABORATIVE FEDERALISM

was needed to permit the vesting and transfer of assets, to empower the corporation to act, and to refer to the Commonwealth under Section 51 of the Constitution the power that would enable it to hold shares in the new company when it was to be engaged in intrastate as well as interstate rail transport services. Five hundred ordinary shares were to be issued, of which the Commonwealth would hold 270, New South Wales 140, Victoria 65 and Western Australia 25. Provision was made for additional share issues if a fifth and sixth state became shareholders. Nine directors were appointed. The Commonwealth nominated three, including the chair and one representative of the ACTU. New South Wales and Victoria nominated two each and Western Australia one. The Commonwealth was to provide equity funds over a five-year period amounting to $295.8 million, with New South Wales, Victoria and Western Australia providing $75.6 million, $35.1 million and $8 million respectively. The states planned to fund their contributions from operating savings arising from the transfer of assets and operations, and from transfer of assets themselves. Provision was made for the transfer or vesting of assets in return for share equity. The National Rail Corporation was to prepare a corporate plan setting out its requirements for asset transfers by the end of the five-year establishment period. Under the agreement, the states agreed to comply with its subsequent request for such asset transfers, but could choose between transferring ownership, leasing or entering into a contract granting access. After five years, the shares could be disposed of as governments saw fit, an option that opened the possibility of privatisation.

Each party agreed also to fund the losses incurred by its part of the network during the establishment period. Clearly, however, the viability of the agreement depended on the National Rail Corporation turning the loss-making interstate rail freight business into a profit-making commercial venture. Losses in 1989–90 were estimated at $377 million. The corporation was expected to break even within three years and be fully self-sufficient by the end of the establishment period. A new enterprise agreement with railway workers was a key element in this planned turnaround, as were operating efficiencies arising from integration, and from planned new public investment. In February 1992, as part of *One Nation*, Paul Keating announced the expenditure of $454 million over two years on the national rail network, including completing the standard-gauge conversion between Melbourne and Adelaide and upgrading other sections.

Special provision in the agreement applied in the case of Western Australia, which guaranteed compensation to that state for any 'detrimental effect on the financial position of the rail authority of Western Australia, because of a reduction in revenues not matched by a

THE INSTITUTIONS OF COLLABORATIVE FEDERALISM   135

commensurate reduction in costs'. The assessment of the extent of compensation (if any) due was to be done by an 'independent expert', and the schedule of payments was to be agreed between the company, the Commonwealth and the states. Under Part VII of the agreement, disputes over this and any other such matters (the valuation of assets being transferred, the payments to the company to cover operating losses, the terms and conditions of any service contract between a state rail authority and the new company) were made subject to conciliation and arbitration, except that in the case of the special compensation payments to Western Australia, final agreement would 'if necessary, be negotiated at Heads of Government level'.

The Commonwealth government put a high priority on creating a more effective national rail system from the separate state-owned systems. Victoria and New South Wales saw the chance to use this commitment to extract a favourable deal. For their part, the creation of a national freight system provided the opportunity to extract significant financial benefit, and to win plaudits from the business community for a reform that promised major efficiency gains for industry. Effectively, they were offered the chance to off-load a loss-making asset on very favourable terms. The New South Wales Minister for Transport, in introducing the bill, could hardly restrain his glee:

> It is expected that by 1996–97 ... the benefit to New South Wales through savings ... will be about $140m, after allowing for both redundancy payments and the New South Wales cash contributions with ongoing savings of perhaps $100 million or more in each subsequent year. The financial gains will far outweigh the level of investment required of this state and there is potential for New South Wales to reap a dividend stream and capital gain from its investment. Even if the corporation were only to break even, New South Wales would still be better off than if the present situation remained and the SRA's planned cost containment programs were fully implemented. [NSW *PD*, 13 November 1991]

Victoria was primarily concerned about the costs of redundancies arising from the transfer of assets, and also about the financial commitments it was entering into at a time when its budgetary position was precarious. It was not happy about taking equity unless the risks were widely spread, or the Commonwealth carried the bulk of them, and it was keen to achieve the full participation of Western Australia, Queensland and South Australia. Despite these reservations, Victoria would gain similar benefits to New South Wales in the longer term from offloading a loss-making business.

In Queensland, there was less at stake, as the national rail system as defined for the purpose of integrated operations extended only to Brisbane, a relatively short distance across the New South Wales border.

136 COLLABORATIVE FEDERALISM

The Queensland government chose to become a 'participating' rather than a shareholder state. The rail link between the main freight terminal and the New South Wales border, and a portion of the terminal itself, would be leased to the National Rail Corporation. The Queensland cabinet felt the benefits flowing to the state from the creation of the corporation could be attained without sharing any of the commercial risk as a shareholder. Moreover, the procedures for joining as a shareholder at a later date within the three-year transitional period were not disadvantageous. The safest option was to sign the agreement but to decide about any further commitment as a shareholder until the corporation's track record was clearer. Apart from off-loading the $13 million losses currently borne by the interstate freight business, a significant side-benefit was the termination of a financially unfavourable border agreement with New South Wales, under which the latter's State Rail Authority operated the interstate standard-gauge line to the border.

South Australia's position was complicated by the fact that the Commonwealth already owned all non-metropolitan railways in that state (as it did in Tasmania) through Australian National. The South Australian government was anxious about the fate of Australian National and of railway workers in the state, and did not want the Commonwealth's new railway venture to distract it from maintaining the South Australian non-trunk operations of Australian National, once the bulk of its freight interests had been taken over by the new corporation. Following a series of deals about the Commonwealth's continuing support for Australian National, such as new investment in workshops and other assets, South Australia finally signed the agreement as a non-shareholder in August 1992.

The National Rail Corporation came into existence in September 1991. By mid-1992 Victoria, New South Wales, the Commonwealth and Queensland had all passed the legislation required under the agreement. Western Australia was left in the not unusual position of disrupting its implementation. Premier Carmen Lawrence in October 1990, when signing the initial agreement with other heads of government, had insisted on an explicit condition that Western Australia would not be financially disadvantaged. She experienced continuing strong pressure to sign from her Labor colleagues in Victoria and the Commonwealth, but extracted major concessions as the price of agreeing to become a full equity shareholder. Western Australia's insistence on a special deal was a source of friction on the ATAC task force and committee in 1991. The amount of cash equity to be contributed, $8 million, was considerably less than originally suggested and, as described above, compensation was payable for any financial loss by Western Australia experienced as a result of the operations of the

THE INSTITUTIONS OF COLLABORATIVE FEDERALISM   137

National Rail Corporation. Westrail's interstate business was a large proportion of its revenue (some 20 per cent); moreover, it was 'profitable', in the sense that (unlike the other states) revenue exceeded operating and capital replacement costs, giving a contribution to fixed overheads of $14.1 million. Along with the payments that would be due to the National Rail Corporation as a result of becoming a full shareholder, the total 'loss' to the state over five years was calculated at $105 million. The premier objected to any agreement that would 'effectively involve, in the short term at least, Western Australia's subsidising the other states' (WA *PD*, Ministerial Statement by the Premier, 28 March 1991).

The Western Australian Labor government under Carmen Lawrence was under siege due to the scandals of 'WA Inc.' By April 1992, following defections and by-elections, it held only twenty-eight out of fifty-seven seats in the Legislative Assembly (albeit supported in office by a handful of independents) and sixteen out of thirty-four in the Legislative Council. Opinion polls showed the government to be very unpopular, and an election was due by early 1993. The opposition was in no mood for anything other than opposition. The bill to implement the intergovernmental agreement was introduced in the Legislative Assembly in November 1991, but in the face of these parliamentary uncertainties its second reading was delayed until September 1992. The Liberal Party argued that Western Australia should have followed Queensland and become a non-shareholder participant, but the government argued that as a shareholder it was in a better position to influence the way National Rail Corporation operated and hence the final impact on the state's railway assets and financial position. The government only succeeded in getting the lower house to approve the bill by striking a deal with the National Party, to the effect that new clauses were inserted that gave parliament a veto over any decision to transfer assets to the National Rail Corporation, and required the tabling of information in parliament on aspects of the corporation's operations under the agreement (including the tabling of a proposed report on the impact on country towns of redundancies).

The upper house was a more difficult proposition. The Liberal Party gave notice that it would refer the bill to the Standing Committee on Legislation. The effect of this would be yet further delay. By November 1992, the delay in implementing the agreement was becoming a critical issue. Opposition speakers in the parliamentary debates made repeated mention of the pressure they were under from transport industry interests, the Business Council of Australia and party colleagues in other states to expedite passage of the legislation. Aside from the serious inconvenience of delay for the operations of the NRC, under the terms

138   COLLABORATIVE FEDERALISM

of the July 1991 agreement, it was a case of 'all in or none in'. This was a common feature of such agreements in order to lock everyone in (although it carried the cost of putting the agreement at the mercy of a hold-out). Each state had to implement its part of the agreement, or the signatories wishing to press ahead would be forced back to the drawing board to put together a new agreement, and then pass new legislation in each parliament, in order to make the national scheme effective.

The Commonwealth, New South Wales and Victoria looked on in dismay as the process of ratification in Western Australia faltered. It was by now clear that the Labor government in Western Australia was in its last weeks or months of office. Over a weekend in late November, the four governments agreed to a process which would allow Western Australia to reconsider its status as a shareholder within six months of passage of the bill. Western Australia would sit on the board of the National Rail Corporation as if it were a shareholder until 30 June. If in the meantime it chose to become a non-shareholder participating state, the other shareholders would cancel Western Australia's shares, and they would not be reissued. The National Rail Corporation would not transfer any assets from Westrail before that date. These undertakings were given in the form of identical letters to the Western Australian government from each of the other shareholder governments. The Liberal Party opposition received legal advice that these undertakings would allow a new government to withdraw without penalty before 30 June.

The opposition was not opposed to the National Rail Corporation in itself, but rather to the participation of Western Australia as a shareholder. But if the agreement was not ratified, the same terms and conditions for participating as a non-shareholder state might not exist—the same generosity might not be shown again. In other words, in order to change Western Australia's status as a partner without risk of penalty, the agreement had first to be ratified. The government insisted on joining as a shareholder. The undertakings were a way of escaping this dilemma, and the opposition allowed the bill to pass. After being elected to office in February, it proceeded in April to extricate Western Australia from its shareholder status. The corporation commenced revenue-earning operations on 5 April 1993. As stated in its annual report for 1992–93, 'this change of status will have minimal impact on operations, due to continuing involvement of Western Australia as an "other state"'. After difficult negotiations, the National Rail Corporation reached final agreement on its operations in Western Australia in August 1994.

The significance of this case lies in the manner in which the parties

THE INSTITUTIONS OF COLLABORATIVE FEDERALISM   139

to a joint arrangement set up working rules in a formal agreement that permitted the achievement of a jointly desired outcome, but promptly turned around and modified them to accommodate a changed political circumstance. The initial agreement allowed for various forms of participation in the joint venture, but bound the signatories to a set of commitments for implementing it. When these threatened to unravel because of a possible defection, a new rule was invented on the run. This allowed the agreement to be implemented and the National Rail Corporation to begin operations, while preserving the fundamental interests of the major shareholders and meeting the reform objectives so keenly sought by major business and labour interests across Australia. Western Australia's inability to meet its terms of the agreement in 1992 was due to the Labor government's lack of control of the parliament. The Western Australian parliament was the most hostile of the nine in Australia to the growth of collaborative intergovernmental arrangements, seeing them as direct threats to the sovereignty of state parliaments. Despite this, the remaining parties to the agreement were able to find a formula that brought about the desired result, intervening in the local political situation so as to produce an outcome amenable to both sides in Western Australia. It is significant, however, that both sides saw the benefits of a national rail system and that, in those circumstances, the unifying interests of system-wide economic reform won the day over assertions of local exceptionalism.

From a vantage point six years after the initial agreement was signed, it seems clear that the National Rail Corporation was, in any case, a transitional arrangement in a wider process of rail reform. Its major significance may well have lain in its facilitation of a major investment program in the interstate track system. The access rules of the National Competition Policy, and the increasing attractiveness to all governments of privatisation, transformed the policy settings of rail reform. The new Commonwealth government in 1996 showed a singular lack of enthusiasm for the National Rail Corporation, and withheld a major cash injection that was due under the shareholders' agreement. It blamed the previous government for entering a set of arrangements that (it claimed) effectively condemned the Commonwealth's other rail corporation, Australian National, to being a non-viable commercial entity. Australian National had been created in 1974 out of the takeover of the Tasmanian railway system and South Australia's non-metropolitan railways. With the creation of the National Rail Corporation, a large portion of its assets and business was lost to the new body. During the course of 1996, the coalition government announced its preference for privatising all of its rail businesses.

140 COLLABORATIVE FEDERALISM

Joint Schemes in Practice: Road Transport Reform

The products of collaborative arrangements and agreements were new institutions, arenas and other frameworks of action. Interactions within these settings created new interests, issues and responses, but they took place in a context of an existing, embedded set of institutions and relationships. The National Rail Corporation, for example, had to compete for attention and resources with existing railway authorities and had to suffer the buffetings of evolving fiscal and political circumstances in the respective governments. The question is whether the new arrangements really made a difference, or whether they were swamped by other agendas of arm's-length politics and policy. In some measure, the new institutions were alien implants, hybrid experiments in a system more accustomed to other norms and routines of conflict and co-operation. Nevertheless, considerable effort went into the detailed elaboration of these new institutional arrangements. As we saw in several cases in Chapter 4, the nature of the decision rules for implementing collaborative schemes was a matter that preoccupied the negotiators in hammering out a number of SPC and COAG agreements, and the rules agreed to were as much a product of the search for a temporary political settlement as they were a well-thought-out prescription for an operating administrative arrangement. If the rules, however elaborate, were only a means to an end—that is, to solve a particular political deadlock—then why should they remain sacrosanct if the political circumstances changed, and as administrative and policy exigencies emerged on the agenda?

The case of the National Road Transport Commission (NRTC) is instructive. Here, we describe some aspects of its operations up to 1997. The negotiations over the establishment of the commission as part of an intergovernmental agreement were described in Chapter 4. They centred on resolving the differences between the more heavily populated states, and the rest. New South Wales and Victoria, for example, had high road costs and sought maximum recovery of the costs of heavy-vehicle damage, along with tight regulations over mass and dimension limits and driver behaviour. Western Australia and the Northern Territory, on the other hand, had lower per-kilometre road costs and less congestion, and the local transport industries were used to lower registration costs and weaker regulation. Primary producers were especially sensitive to road transport costs and spoke out strongly against increases in charges. All states supported a clause in the agreement allowing for concessions and rebates to primary producers who owned heavy vehicles. Queensland finally lined up with the low cost states in a 'zonal' arrangement under the new agreement, which allowed for differential application of charges and regulations. The incentive for

THE INSTITUTIONS OF COLLABORATIVE FEDERALISM   141

Zone A states (New South Wales, Victoria and Tasmania) to relax heavy-vehicle limits was the possibility of higher mass-distance charges to cover their higher road costs, while Zone B governments avoided having to contribute to these costs by imposing significantly higher charges on their transport operators. The Commonwealth, however, carried some of the burden via the inclusion of a fuel tax component in the proposed charging system. An additional pay-off agreed to at the July 1991 Premiers' Conference was the 'untying' of a minimum of $350 million of Commonwealth special-purpose road grants, although the details, including the distribution between the states, were left to be determined later. The Northern Territory did not sign the agreement, but indicated a commitment to harmonisation and promised a review of its position following the initial stages of implementation.

The NRTC came into existence as an interim body in late 1991. Commonwealth legislation establishing it formally, and incorporating the agreement as a schedule, came into effect in January 1992. The NRTC was given a pivotal role in the formulation and implementation of uniform national charges and regulations for heavy vehicles. In May 1992, the scope rules were changed by a further intergovernmental agreement adding responsibilities for bringing uniformity to regulations relating to light vehicles. Decisions were formally the preserve of a newly named Ministerial Council for Road Transport. However, most decisions could be made only after recommendation by the NRTC. With authority rules limiting the ministerial council to a power of disapproval of such recommendations, the NRTC occupied a crucial position. One of its major tasks was to recommend any new legislation for road transport regulation to bring about 'uniform or consistent' regulations (Parliament 1991, 15). At this point, a set of new authority rules took over. So long as such a recommendation was not disapproved by a majority of the ministerial council, it would first be enacted by the Commonwealth to apply within the Australian Capital Territory. The states undertook to pass legislation that would apply this act and repeal or amend any existing state legislation in so far as it was inconsistent with it, and also undertook not to introduce any separate legislation that would conflict with such an act. Regulations under the act adopted as a result of ministerial council agreement would also automatically apply in all jurisdictions. A state or territory could make an 'application order' which varied the uniform legislation, but such an order had to be recommended by the commission and was made subject to disapproval by a majority of the ministerial council.

The aggregation rules varied according to the nature of the decision taken by the ministerial council: recommended new legislation and application orders were subject to disapproval within two months by a

142 COLLABORATIVE FEDERALISM

simple majority; changes to the decision rules, along with agreement on funding of the commission, required unanimity; the mass-distance charges to apply in the separate zones could be disapproved by majorities in those zones; the level of the road-use charge, comprising a portion of the Commonwealth excise tax on fuel, was subject to approval by a simple majority of the full council; charging principles could only be changed by a two-thirds majority of the full council; appointment and dismissal of the three members of the national commission were also subject to a two-thirds majority; and changes to the boundaries of the zones required a three-quarters majority. Any other resolution of the council could be carried by a simple majority.

Uniform Charges

The NRTC was required to produce a quick answer to the vexatious issue of heavy-vehicle charges. In January 1992, it released a paper arguing that 'there is little to be gained from the implementation of a two-zone charging system' (NRTC 1992a, 21). In April, a further report rejected the methodology for road-use charges that had formed the basis for earlier calculations, including those used in framing the 'indicative' charges in the report of the Overarching Group on Transport to SPC in 1991 (NRTC 1992b). The uniform charges recommended by the NRTC were considerably lower—indeed, New South Wales would be required to decrease its existing charges, resulting in a significant loss of revenue. The NRTC argued that the level of taxation on road transport was already high, and expressed a preference for a high road-use charge (comprising a portion of fuel taxes) over a high mass-distance registration charge. It placed the onus on the Commonwealth to contribute more of fuel tax revenue to road expenditures (NRTC 1992b, 20). If New South Wales was, to put it mildly, disconcerted by the NRTC report (*Sydney Morning Herald*, 17 April 1992), the Northern Territory government now felt able to sign the agreement (on 15 May 1992).

The NRTC's rejection of a zonal system effectively made the zonal decision rules on the ministerial council redundant. The recommended uniform charges were adopted by the council in August 1992, with Western Australia and New South Wales voting against them. Although lower than anticipated, the new charges would still represent a significant increase in the Zone B states. The Western Australian government came under strong pressure to avoid this increase from its intrastate road haulage industry. The smaller local interstate sector would have preferred uniformity, as operators would be subject to the higher charge when they crossed the border, but their voice was swamped. New South Wales opposed the new charges purely on revenue

THE INSTITUTIONS OF COLLABORATIVE FEDERALISM 143

grounds, claiming a loss of revenue as high as $75 million (Deputy Premier, press release, 22 June 1992). Notwithstanding the opposition of these two states, the NRTC proceeded with draft legislation, which was approved by a majority of the ministerial council. The legislation, introduced by the Commonwealth to apply within the Australian Capital Territory, became law in May 1993. The commencement date for the new charges was set at 1 July 1995.

The next step was for the states to pass the necessary legislation. Western Australia and New South Wales proclaimed their intention to defy the majority. In the meantime, other states showed varying levels of enthusiasm. Queensland proved to be the most enthusiastic and met the July 1995 deadline in full, while Victoria and the Northern Territory also came close. South Australia proclaimed an 'all in or none in' position, that is, they would comply once all the others did. South Australia had low charges and loose regulations, and for that reason attracted a number of interstate operators to register from across the border. The New South Wales minister for transport dubbed South Australia 'the Liberia of the trucking industry' (NSW *PD* 22 November 1995, 3799). Tasmania had customary difficulties with its upper house, and struggled to reach a settlement in the face of demands for concessions from transport operators.

In New South Wales, the initial refusal to adopt the lower charges was coupled with a bid for more Commonwealth road funds by way of compensation. The Commonwealth steadfastly refused to tie fuel tax revenue directly to any formula for road funds or their distribution, despite the NRTC's inclusion of this revenue as part of its calculations on road cost recovery. However, part of the 1991 agreement was to untie a portion of special-purpose road funds and to take full responsibility for funding an expanded network of national highways. The latter brought a potential bonus to New South Wales, in that the allocation of these funds on economic criteria to particular projects, as distinct from their allocation on a historic shares basis to the states, would lead to a significant increase in the amount spent on roads in that state, so long as overall expenditure was maintained. As a consequence, the state was effectively (if indirectly) compensated for lowering its charges. However, until 1995 the New South Wales government continued to oppose the new charges. A further strategy was adopted of seeking to tie their possible introduction to a set of national driver and vehicle regulatory reforms which New South Wales favoured. This strategy met with no success.

In Western Australia, the other hold-out, the newly elected conservative government also focused on road funding, waging a fierce war of words with the Commonwealth and demanding a larger allocation of

144 COLLABORATIVE FEDERALISM

fuel taxes to roads and a 'fair return' on these taxes to the state. The Commonwealth would not concede that any part of these revenues was earmarked for roads, and treated the proceeds as part of consolidated revenue (Painter and Dempsey 1992). As a result of the untying of road funding, Western Australia was faced with a cut in Commonwealth funding for national highways as Commonwealth funds were allocated to projects with higher benefit–cost ratios in the eastern states. The state government claimed that Commonwealth road funds overall for Western Australia from 1994 were reduced by 33 per cent (WA *PD* LC, 4 August 1993, 1765). In this climate, Western Australia continued to resist the imposition of uniform vehicle charges.

The 1995 National Competition Policy Agreement, which included reference to 'already agreed' road transport reforms, brought these two states and the laggards elsewhere into line. The first 'competition policy payment' in 1997–98 was tied to, among other things, the implementation of agreed road transport reforms, including the uniform charges. As discussed in Chapter 4, Western Australia was placed under enormous pressure to end its opposition to the National Competition Policy Agreement during the early months of 1995, and implementation of the new charges was simply part of that package. In New South Wales, the Fahey coalition government also, reluctantly, agreed to come on board. In the lead-up to the 1995 election in that state, Labor won support from the trucking industry with a promise to go along with the national charging scheme. But in introducing legislation implementing the national charges in November 1995, the new Labor government was reluctant to specify a commencement date. A cat-and-mouse game ensued. New South Wales wanted to wait until South Australia (along with Western Australia) committed to a date before doing the same—as the minister put it 'one in, all in' (NSW *PD*, 22 November 1995, 3799). Discussions took place between the states, and at the Australian Transport Council meeting a commencement date of 1 July 1996 was agreed. Full compliance was finally achieved in October 1996. In Tasmania, the threat of withholding competition payments was used by the government as a weapon to help overcome upper house obstruction. However, even though the minister introducing the bill remarked that 'it is not a matter of doing some of the reforms, it is a matter of completing all of those reforms' (Tas. *PD* LA, 20 June 1996), the upper house insisted on amendments to exempt certain classes of vehicle owners from the full impact of the new charges.

Uniform Regulations

The role of the NRTC was crucial in the achievement of uniform charges, but perhaps not entirely in the way envisaged. Its determin-

THE INSTITUTIONS OF COLLABORATIVE FEDERALISM   145

ation of charges in 1992 was in itself a challenge to some of the presumptions of the agreement, and showed the NRTC to have an independent voice. In speaking up for the industry in the argument that road users were already over-taxed, it presaged a wider role for itself, seeking to mediate and integrate the conflicting private and public interests evident in the tangled world of road transport politics. The NRTC viewed the charging issue to be less significant than the achievement of reforms in vehicle and driver regulations (*Annual Report*, 1992, p. 2). Here, the passage of uniform legislation according to the 1991 agreement proved an elusive goal, but significant progress was made notwithstanding.

The NRTC had the formidable task of drafting new legislation to cover all aspects of road transport regulation and charging. It established its own legal and drafting division, set up a Legislative Advisory Committee of government officials from all jurisdictions, and consulted regularly with parliamentary counsel. This was only one part of its elaborate consultative machinery, and it took other measures to integrate itself into the existing network of actors and relationships in the road transport policy sector. In the first year, it set up a Transport Agency Chief Executives Committee; an Industry Advisory Group; a Bus Industry Advisory Group; and a Technical Liaison Group. The last was constituted jointly with the federal Office of Road Safety to deal with Australian Design Rules, and brought together more than twenty experts from government and industry. A memorandum of understanding was signed with the Office of Road Safety about joint procedures for developing Australian Design Rules, which would eventually rely on any new legislation proposed by NRTC for their implementation. NRTC clearly overlapped with the functions and role of Austroads, the combined association of Commonwealth, state and territory road authorities, which (under other names over the years) had been responsible for many initiatives in road regulation reform (see Chapter 4). It was a delicate matter to sort out complementary roles, and joint working arrangements were agreed in April 1993 (Hurlstone 1995). For example, Austroads entered into consultancy relationships with NRTC to design and refine a number of the packages of regulations that NRTC ultimately recommended to the ministerial council. Austroads operated by assigning items of work to road authorities or to joint working parties that drew on these agencies for staff and other resources.

Among the networks of relationships, those with the private sector of the industry were critical for the NRTC's success. Successive chairs of the commission had private-sector backgrounds. The formal committees referred to above were augmented in 1996 by a Remote Areas Project Group, with industry representatives from remote parts of

146 COLLABORATIVE FEDERALISM

Australia to give them 'a stronger voice in the development and implementation of national reforms' (NRTC *Reformer*, December 1996). The NRTC published copious technical papers and consultative documents, distributing them widely in the industry and calling for feedback and submissions. In 1996, it began to distribute a newsletter on its program and its achievements. It provided the peak bodies of the industry with a national forum to press demands for uniformity and for regulatory reform generally. It was also intent on shaping industry opinion and attitudes towards reform and regulation. Its findings on charges won it many industry friends. Its views on 'alternative compliance', and its preference for light-handed regulation over by-the-book policing and enforcement, found a sympathetic ear with the industry as a least-cost means of public-interest regulation, at a time when several states were under strong pressure from road users and parliamentary road safety committees to throw the book at bus and truck operators in response to a few dramatic—and fatal—transgressions. The NRTC also produced research which showed the wider economic benefits of specific reforms which the industry favoured, such as higher mass and dimension limits (NRTC 1996). The commission and peak industry bodies had much in common, and the development of a shared agenda of reform (albeit with disagreements over some matters) produced a new force in the transport policy sector.

The NRTC was formally responsible to the Ministerial Council for Road Transport, and was subject to its direction and to no other. In managing this relationship, the commissioners soon became acquainted with the untidy nature of Australian federalism. Comments in successive annual reports chart a steep learning curve:

> In October 1992 it was decided to segment the development of road transport legislation into a number of separate bills with distinct sets of regulations. This modular approach was endorsed by Ministerial Council. ... Jurisdictions can adopt regulations as they are approved, permitting sizeable blocks of policies and rules to be developed in stages. [NRTC, *Annual Report*, 1993, p. 6]

These six modules were: heavy-vehicle charges; vehicle operations; dangerous goods; vehicle registration; driver licensing; and compliance and enforcement. The modular approach was seen to provide for a manageable work program. New South Wales for one objected to the approach, refusing to approve any one of the modules until the whole package was completed.

> The original concept of progressive adoption of regulations by states and Territories to allow early reforms is proving elusive as several Governments now wish to see the complete National Law before submitting it to their

THE INSTITUTIONS OF COLLABORATIVE FEDERALISM   147

Parliaments. Nevertheless, it is pleasing to note more recent cooperative moves by jurisdictions that have been approved by Council. These have provided an avenue for adoption of many reforms ahead of the formal passing of National Law. [NRTC, *Annual Report*, 1994, 1]

The difficulties of some jurisdictions in adopting legislation, when approved as modules, have become clearer over the past year. The Commission intends to maintain the modular approach because it does allow for earlier implementation by those jurisdictions who wish to do so. However, it is recognised that some will await either the completion of all the modules or the availability of the full package of road transport legislation. This remains an issue for individual government. [NRTC, *Annual Report*, 1995, 2]

The original conception of working in an orderly and logical fashion through a supposedly pre-agreed reform agenda was in 1995 supplemented with a more piecemeal and opportunistic approach. Instead of six modules, the flag-bearer of reform was now a 'ten-point plan', otherwise known as the Heavy Vehicle Reform Package. Significantly, this package was developed by the Transport Agency Chief Executives' Committee, and represented a list of specific, achievable innovations from across the 'modules'. A number of state ministers and governments committed themselves publicly to the ten-point plan and projected it as their own. In Victoria, it appeared as a full-page government advertisement in the *Herald Sun* (15 September 1995). The ministerial council gave it the imprint of a national strategy, and several governments introduced legislative amendments or changes to existing regulations in order to conform. There was more than a hint here of a reversion to lowest-common-denominator styles of consensual decision-making, and to conventional arm's-length authority rules under which the states chose their own method and pace of enactment. In 1996, a second Heavy Vehicle Reform Package (the 'second ten-point plan') was agreed to,

following several months' work by the NRTC with help from the Road Transport Forum and transport agencies. The idea behind the reform packages is simple: identify initiatives which will deliver big gains to the road transport industry in terms of cost savings, improved road safety or other benefits, and get them in place quickly. Most of these initiatives pick-up or extend some aspect of the Commission's major reforms. [NRTC, *Reformer*, March 1997]

The 1995 annual report reiterated the difficulties and alluded to the new strategy:

Virtually all legislation submitted by the Commission to date has received clear majority support. However, often jurisdictions have indicated concern over specific issues and either sought further investigations or advised that variations to the template legislation would be made. ...

148   COLLABORATIVE FEDERALISM

> There has been a discernible impetus to deliver tangible benefits in anticipation of the national law by bilateral agreements, mutual recognition and stand-alone amendments to existing legislation. The temptation to stop there will be real. However, unless the rigour of the establishment of national law is maintained, the benefits achieved by such agreements are at risk of dilution over time. [NRTC, *Annual Report*, 1995, 3]

The 1996 annual report reflected further on these difficulties:

> The deliberative voting process of the Ministerial Council is available for resolving disagreement, but the Commission would prefer to obtain consensus as far as is practicable. This has led, for example, to revisiting the approved truck driving policy, causing a delay. . . .
> We have learnt a few important lessons in the past 12 months. One of these is not to get too far in front of the field in case one or two controversial elements of a proposal might bring down the whole. [NRTC, *Annual Report*, 1996, 2–3]

The ministerial council, although provided with decision rules that supposedly overcame the problems of the laggard and the hold-out, seemingly produced results much like any other: that is, it reverted to operating in large measure by consensus. Its operations on the face of it were different—it made majority decisions; it processed formal business put in front of it by an executive agency, often out of session; and its decisions provided a trigger for legislation. But its distinctiveness as a new type of ministerial forum was blunted in 1993 due (somewhat ironically) to a COAG-inspired restructuring of all ministerial councils. The Ministerial Council for Road Transport, while retaining its separate formal status for voting purposes, was absorbed into ATAC to produce the Australian Transport Council. To some extent, this only formalised the original position of common membership and meeting dates, but it nevertheless reinforced the tendency for conventional consensus norms to reassert themselves, and for ministers and governments to treat these decisions as no more binding than any others taken by the Australian Transport Council.

By 1996, three pieces of legislation reflecting the first three modules—charges, vehicle operations and dangerous goods—had been enacted by the Commonwealth as a result of the formal decision processes. But what happened next was nothing like the agreement's prescribed procedures. State and territories proceeded unevenly and at their own pace. As we saw, it took until October 1996 for all jurisdictions to pass laws adopting the heavy-vehicle charges embodied in the 1993 act, and then not all did so using the agreed procedures. Queensland in 1995 passed its Transport Operations (Road Use Management) Act, providing the first instance of a state passing legislation to allow for automatic application of the modules for heavy vehicle charges, vehicle

THE INSTITUTIONS OF COLLABORATIVE FEDERALISM   149

operations, driver licensing and vehicle registration as and when agreed by the ministerial council. The Northern Territory was next, but insisted on delaying final implementation until all other states had implemented their charges as well. Victoria in 1995 passed application laws to implement the charges and the dangerous goods legislation. New South Wales declined to pass application of laws legislation until all the modules were complete. In the meantime, it would 'give effect to the evolving national law by normal legislative processes' (NSW *PD*, 15 November 1995, 3207). Tasmania took the same position. Western Australia, in adopting the uniform charges, refused on principle to use the application-of-laws technique and merely altered its charges under existing state legislation by regulation.

During this period, state governments continued to hold their own parliamentary inquiries on road safety, to amend their own legislation, and to respond piecemeal to pressures and demands from road users and the transport industry. For example, in 1993, Queensland acted unilaterally to bring its regulations on truck and bus driving hours into line with those of New South Wales and Victoria. The changes were welcomed by the NRTC, but did not result from the adoption of an agreed national policy or set of uniform regulations. The NRTC, as we saw, learnt to take advantage of these separate, state-by-state processes of reform. It also tried to shape these processes. With the prospect of legislation for heavy-vehicle charges in 1995 and 1996 in all states, the NRTC achieved agreement among the states and territories to pass at the same time any legislation necessary to implement the ten-point plan. In Tasmania, for example, the bill introduced in 1996 included not only the new charges but also the adoption of national vehicle mass, dimension and loading rules; common national standards for vehicles and trailers and mutual recognition of inspections and defect notices; and a uniform over-mass vehicle permit system.

The NRTC also learnt to be flexible. As it made efforts to develop a package of regulations covering driving hours and related matters, the Northern Territory and Western Australia insisted on special measures to cater for the long-haul conditions of uncongested roads in the outback. Tasmania also stuck to its guns and refused to insist that drivers in that state keep logbooks. The national package on driving hours that was developed and approved by a majority vote in December 1995 contained options for jurisdictions to pick up, comprising a conventional regulated hours regime and an optional 'fatigue management' regime which relied on self-enforcement and monitoring rather than on-road reporting and inspection. The NRTC made a virtue of this, supporting a 'pilot project' on fatigue management in Queensland. Western Australia and the Northern Territory were excluded from coverage, but

150 COLLABORATIVE FEDERALISM

drivers from those jurisdictions would be able to choose which of the options to comply with when driving interstate (NRTC 1996, 62–3).

Summary

Despite the difficulty and frustration, the NRTC remained optimistic in its projections for achieving substantial reforms to road vehicle and driver regulations. It learnt very soon that the deadline envisaged in 1991 for the adoption of uniform legislation—January 1993—was hopelessly optimistic. Leaving aside conflicts over policy, the sheer volume of work required, for example in overcoming drafting and other technical difficulties across all jurisdictions, had been underestimated. By the end of 1997, by various means, uniformity had been achieved in relation to important aspects of vehicle operations, vehicle standards, charges, and (with Western Australia and the Northern Territory being allowed to opt out) driving hours. Uniform arrangements for the carriage of dangerous goods were in the process of being adopted, and a national registration scheme for heavy vehicles and a national driver licensing scheme, rather than state-by-state registration and licensing, were near to finalisation. At the February 1997 meeting of transport ministers, the life of the NRTC was extended beyond 1998 for at least five more years and a new set of deadlines for the next series of reforms was agreed to. The NRTC had established itself as a legitimate, respected and significant player in the transport policy sector, adopting the role of 'independent catalyst for broad-ranging road transport reform in Australia' (NRTC, *Reformer*, March 1997). This form of words, drawn from the communiqué issued after the February meeting, reflected the lowering of expectations that had occurred as a result of the experience of implementing reform. The steadier, less dramatic and more piecemeal approach that the NRTC came to adopt in the face of implementation difficulties was one that the states felt comfortable with, and their continued support was forthcoming precisely because the NRTC recognised the practical limits to the lock-step, collaborative procedures set out in the original agreement. The February 1997 meeting of the Australian Transport Council agreed to proceed with the next phase of reforms without waiting for the passage of template Commonwealth legislation, in effect reverting to the more traditional method of passing mirror legislation, to be based on model legislation drawn up by the NRTC and approved by the ministerial council.

Conclusion

Intergovernmental agreements are not considered to be legally binding on governments, and compliance by the parties depends on political

THE INSTITUTIONS OF COLLABORATIVE FEDERALISM   151

rather than legal or constitutional factors. To some extent, these factors are situational and circumstantial, as the chair of the NRTC (for example) emphasised:

> Commitment to reform is required from governments, transport ministers, bureaucrats and road users. The change in governments and ministers since the SPC has not assisted in this respect. There have also been changes to personnel in the road and transport authorities leading to a loss of collective memory about why the Agreements were signed and what they were intended to achieve. The Agreements were themselves the result of compromises by governments and individuals. With the change in personnel, the danger is that compromises are forgotten and the same issues often become stumbling blocks to implementation. [Hurlstone 1995, 10]

On the other hand, important questions are raised about the binding nature of rules and of the factors which shape institutional arrangements in this particular setting. Were the understandings and conventions associated with arm's-length federalism so powerful as to override the written rules of newly crafted collaborative arrangements? As we have seen, the fine print of the 1991 Road Transport Agreement, with its detail about aggregation and authority rules, was not fully observed. The new collaborative arrangements existed in a wider political and institutional context where other conventions for dealing with inter-governmental relations had normally been applied. The political dynamics of arm's-length federalism, including political pressures and evolving policy issues peculiar to each jurisdiction, were a source of continual tension for the smooth operation of the new collaborative arrangements. The two sets of rules were fundamentally inconsistent, and the newer ones, although they were solemnly signed and sealed, proved the more precarious.

But rules do not become irrelevant because compliance is weak, nor do they necessarily lose their significance because they are inconsistent with others. Two features of the case we have just discussed highlight the continuing significance of the new collaborative arrangements, despite the apparent breaches and departures present in the process by which the new national measures were implemented. First, the competition policy agreements saw the parties implicitly but effectively recommit themselves to the rules, albeit within a framework that admitted more flexibility as to methods of implementation. Part of this reaffirmation was the acceptance of a set of external sanctions in the form of the competition payments. Second, the rules acquired effective advocates in the form of national bodies such as the NRTC. The setting up of the NRTC as a part of the new arrangements in itself transformed the conditions and circumstances in which policy was made in the sector.

The commission acquired support and legitimacy, and it focused attention and resources on a national approach. While continuing to advocate strict application of the rules as the preferred method of implementing national reform, it adopted a more flexible approach as time passed, taking advantage where possible of other avenues for achieving change. This more piecemeal, pragmatic and incremental approach filled a vacuum left by the delay in implementing the agreed packages, and served to maintain momentum and to justify the NRTC's existence. The approach was not, in itself, inconsistent with pursuing the long-term comprehensive reform strategy.

In sum, this brief experience of a new set of collaborative working rules in one sector of policy allows for no simple conclusion about the extent to which systemic changes were in train. On the one hand, the National Competition Policy Agreement in 1995 was significant in reaffirming and strengthening the recent history of collaboration, while prodding the backsliders to conform. Collaborative arrangements were part of the landscape and a key part of the machinery of ongoing microeconomic reform. In the case of the NRTC, the information and aggregation rules still operated in a way that facilitated significant collaborative outcomes, but the application-of-laws method of implementing uniform legislation proved unworkable. The practical difficulties of achieving national reform through this device threatened to undermine other elements of the collaborative arrangements, and the NRTC found other means of implementing change. The suspension of this method of law-making in 1997 prompts the conclusion that a well-developed collaborative system in any one sector faced an uphill struggle against the reassertion of the traditional conventions of arm's-length cooperation that continued to apply in other sectors. The traditional patterns of consensual executive decision-making, along with law-making according to each parliament's own methods and timetable, were backed up by constitutionally grounded authority rules. Political leaders continued to prefer cooperation by more consensual, piecemeal means, and continued to assert their autonomy and to resist pressures towards uniformity to the extent that such behaviour won them votes, protected the revenue, or achieved whatever other end was considered at the time to be paramount. But before coming to any general conclusions about the overall impact of the new institutions on the underlying character of Australian federalism, we look in the next chapter at a set of further attempts to rationalise intergovernmental relations in the field of social expenditures and service provision.

CHAPTER 7

Duplication and Overlap: New Roles, Old Battles

The tensions and dilemmas of intergovernmental financial relations have been highlighted at a number of points in this book. The states' vision of competitive, arm's-length federalism highlighted the need for wholesale reform to financial relations so as to guarantee the future viability of state governments as partners in the federation. The states called for a realignment of roles and responsibilities so as to reverse the incursion by the Commonwealth into state jurisdiction. They particularly wished to see a marked reduction in special-purpose payments (amounting to about 50 per cent of all transfers) and the absorption of these payments into general revenue-sharing arrangements. To them, the problem of duplication and overlap comprised the unnecessary involvement of the Commonwealth, through its financial muscle, in detailed program administration in areas of service delivery already adequately covered by state jurisdiction. The solution was disentanglement, through Commonwealth disengagement from major service sectors, conversion of special-purpose payments to block grants, or to untied revenue payments, and a 'clean lines' division of functions. They sought to reverse and unravel an already existing set of arrangements that had built up over many years around the plethora of special-purpose payment programs.

The Commonwealth had a different perspective. So long as the Commonwealth retained political interests in directly shaping education, housing, health, transport and other programs, it needed to retain the financial capacity to assert those interests. Essentially, the Commonwealth's purpose in addressing the reform of roles and responsibilities was to achieve greater value for its financial and political investments in these programs. Far from disentangling direct program relations with the states, this objective required more effective collaborative

154   COLLABORATIVE FEDERALISM

arrangements so as to improve service effectiveness, efficiency and responsiveness according to Commonwealth policy objectives (Fletcher and Walsh 1992). In the minds of many Commonwealth officials, joint decision-making arrangements in areas of service overlap and duplication had to set out the methods by which Commonwealth funds and priorities would more effectively be translated into service outcomes through restructured state administrative arrangements. Thus, the elaboration of models of COAG-style collaborative federalism as part of a solution to the problem of shared roles and responsibilities was mostly identified in the states' eyes with the growing assertion of Commonwealth power.

Despite these conflicting views, based on traditional patterns of intergovernmental financial relations, possibilities were explored during the life of the Special Premiers' Conferences and the Council of Australian Governments for new sets of funding arrangements within a collaborative framework. In an arm's-length federal arrangement, the existence of extreme vertical fiscal imbalance creates a situation where apparent collaboration in a field of joint jurisdiction masks a high level of adversarialism. The interdependencies created by fiscal transfers, including those that have strings attached, create as many differences as commonalities. The states play games of evasion, substitution and concealment in the effort to pocket the money while escaping inconvenient conditions, and the Commonwealth in its turn seeks new sanctions and methods of control. In the attempt to link fiscal transfers to collaborative arrangements, it can prove difficult to escape these dynamics. In modelling such arrangements, a minimum condition would require funds to be pooled and their disbursement made subject to the aggregation rules applicable to other joint decisions. Any conditions attached to their allocation to particular governments or agencies would also be determined collectively, and sanctions for noncompliance might be administered by a jointly mandated national body. In Table 6.1, such pay-off rules were included as part of the institutional arrangements of collaborative federalism. Such models were developed in COAG working parties and elsewhere in the search for new ways of administering service delivery where roles and responsibilities overlapped. The experience of one such an arrangement—the National Vocational Education and Training Agreement, which established the Australian National Training Authority—is discussed later in this chapter.

Discussion of duplication of services, or roles and responsibilities as it came to be referred to in COAG, appeared on the agenda of all but one SPC and COAG meetings from 1990 to 1996. The aim initially was to undertake a wholesale review of all functional areas so as to arrive at

DUPLICATION AND OVERLAP

better arrangements. Funding arrangements and tied grants were closely related issues on the agenda. In the initial stages, the states' definition of the problems enjoyed the ascendancy. A number of general principles were set out in the October 1990 SPC communiqué, with a preference being stated for a 'clean lines' division of functions, giving one sphere of government 'full responsibility' when possible:

4. Where full responsibility ... is assigned to one sphere of government, it would then fully determine program priorities and delivery mechanisms without interference and would be held fully accountable for performance. Funding would have a simple relationship to responsibility and adjustments to Financial Assistance Grants would follow as appropriate.
5. Where shared responsibility is the outcome, in addition to their policy interests, the States would generally have the dominant role in managing service delivery ...
6. In these cases, the principle should be that that the Commonwealth involvement in the operational management of the program is reduced to the greatest degree possible consistent with ensuring that national objectives are met.

Even where a 'shared responsibility program' was identified, 'the clearest model ... would involve defining the outcome required and assigning responsibility for delivery to one level of government'. Whatever the model, there should be agreed 'strategic plans'; 'simple administrative arrangements which ... clearly delineate the roles and responsibilities, including funding responsibility, of the respective levels'; 'agreed consultative arrangements'; and 'accountability measures that focus on results achieved'. The best arrangement would be in the form of an 'agreement' negotiated for a specific period of time, with 'the government not having responsibility for service delivery stepping back from involvement' until the time for its renewal.

At the October 1990 meeting, a working party of central agency officials was set up to look at the issue of tied grants, while specific functional reviews of areas of duplication were handed over to ministerial councils and line agency officials, to report back to SPC. Specific areas referred to included the Home and Community Care Program, health, aged care, housing, training and labour market programs, child care, and the Supported Accommodation Assistance Program. As well, work already under way within particular sectors was brought under the umbrella: technical education, road funding and disability services. The last had virtually been concluded, and final negotiations continued outside the framework of this review process. The July 1991 meeting rubber-stamped the new disability services agreement. As well, as part of the agreement on heavy-vehicle charges and regulation, full responsibility for national roads was accepted by

156 COLLABORATIVE FEDERALISM

the Commonwealth, and remaining road funds were untied and incorporated in general revenue assistance (see Chapter 6).

The Commonwealth–State Disability Agreement, 1991

Despite the apparent acceptance of much of the states' reform agenda in these early general pronouncements, it was something of an omen that the only new comprehensive agreement actually reached by the end of 1991 was seen by the states to be in breach of the 'agreed principles'. On the insistence of the states, SPC's approval of the disability agreement in July 1991 carried the rider that 'these specific arrangements should in no way be viewed as a precedent for reforms that may be developed through the processes of the special Premiers' Conferences'. The disability agreement was negotiated through a working party set up by the Social Welfare Ministers' Conference in 1989, which considered two broad options: a block grant model accompanied by total devolution to the states, and a functional split and shared responsibility. The latter was supported by the Commonwealth, which insisted on retaining employment-related services because of their linkages with the Commonwealth Employment Service and with the social security system. The states preferred a model in which total responsibility for distributing funds and administering all services lay with the states, with the Commonwealth participating in the establishment of national objectives and broad service priorities (Ernst & Young 1996, 1011).The outcome was that the Commonwealth took full responsibility for employment, training and placement services for people with disabilities, and the states took responsibility for accommodation support, information services, independent living training, recreation services, and respite care. Previously, 70 per cent of the Commonwealth's funds for its own programs had gone to accommodation services (Yeatman 1996, 56). These programs and funds were now to be fully devolved. Joint responsibility was accepted for planning, priority-setting and program evaluation. Each state and territory agreed to pass complementary legislation adopting the principles and objectives in the Commonwealth Disability Services Act (Lindsay 1996). Funding arrangements were critical. Each government committed itself to maintain effort in the area of disability services over the life of the agreement. Approximately $200 million per annum was committed by the Commonwealth to funding the services transferred to the states, and in addition the Commonwealth agreed to approximately $250 million in 'transition' and growth funds. These funds were provided though special-purpose payments, not for specific programs, but on condition that they be devoted to disability services in accord with the principles of the agreement.

DUPLICATION AND OVERLAP

Transition and growth funds were conditional on the states' adoption of the act.

The states were not happy with this agreement as a model, for a number of reasons. They preferred their own full devolution model, which would obviate the need for any special-purpose payments; they objected to the need to comply with the Commonwealth act; and they suspected that the Commonwealth would use the agreement as an opportunity to devolve expensive obligations without adequate funds, while giving its own area of responsibility generous attention. Despite these objections, the agreement did embody some principles consistent with those set out in the October 1990 SPC statement. The Commonwealth had for some time been in agreement with the states on the need to remove intrusive controls over program funds and management (largely because they believed other forms of control were more effective, not because they were no longer interested in control). In this respect, the disability agreement was an improvement on other agreements, such as the Home and Community Care Program, in which funding conditions were detailed at the program level, complex approval and consultation procedures were mandated, and there were requirements for matching funding. In the disability case, the special-purpose payment was not a specific program grant with detailed conditions attached, but a block grant for the whole area of disability services for which the states were made responsible. While the states were required to maintain overall effort, they were not required to match Commonwealth funds devoted to specific programs. They could use Commonwealth funds to build on and develop their own programs, so long as these developments were in line with the principles of the act that they were required to adopt.

However, the functional split embodied in the agreement did perpetuate a number of problems that the SPC review of functions was designed to remedy. Although on the face of it clean and logical, it was still a recipe for demarcation disputes, cost-shifting (the redefinition of a client's service needs so as to shift the burden of meeting them to another program, agency, or level of government) and client confusion. The states accused the Commonwealth of 'creaming' by leaving the states with the most difficult and expensive services, and of shifting costs by adopting a narrow definition of 'employment services' while transferring clients and their problems into state programs (Ernst & Young 1996, 29–30). Clients and consumers continued to complain about the confusion of roles and the lack of integration, particularly as other closely related services in the Home and Community Care Program and in state and Commonwealth health programs remained subject to their own complex divisions of roles and responsibilities (Yeatman 1996).

158   COLLABORATIVE FEDERALISM

The disability agreement was reviewed by an outside consultant in 1996. One of the principal conclusions was that the system should be restructured so as to facilitate a true 'partnership' among all the players: 'The CSDA was a multilateral Agreement, that is one which involved all participating governments ... In operational practice, however, the CSDA was less of a multilateral initiative and more one where each level of government got on with its role in the CSDA division of roles and responsibilities' (Yeatman 1996, 99). The vision was a 'national strategic approach' to 'open up the system to networked delivery through public, community and private service arrangements'. In focusing on the intergovernmental dimensions, Yeatman identified three potential models. The first was based on the status quo, designed to 'articulate a division of labour' between different operational areas. Cooperation in limited spheres remained necessary, in particular to ensure account-ability and to monitor performance. The second option was to identify a joint intergovernmental 'funder role', with delegation of operational management to states. The planning and policy role would be under-taken jointly, but all areas of operations (including the role of pur-chaser) would be delegated to the states. The states as purchasers would develop contractual relationships with an array of community, government and private providers. The third model considered was the Australian National Training Authority (ANTA) model (discussed in detail below), that is a new joint funder-purchaser agency with industry involvement at the national level. Yeatman dismissed this option as too 'complex and unwieldy' (1996, 105), and recommended that under a new agreement the aim should be to progress from the first to the second option. This would involve, at some point, setting up a new 'National Management Agency'.

The distinctions between options two and three were less important than the similarities, as both emphasised the importance of new collaborative relationships for joint planning at a national level. Both also drew on a more general language of public-sector restructuring that was having a widespread impact on the reshaping of service delivery in all governments. The emergence of these themes as guiding principles in dealing with the issue of roles and responsibilities was an important development in the way COAG approached the issue. Before turning to this, however, we consider the experience of ANTA.

The ANTA Agreement, 1992–97

As described in Chapter 4, the establishment of the Australian National Training Authority was a political settlement, stimulated by a Common-wealth offer to step in and take over full funding responsibility for

DUPLICATION AND OVERLAP

vocational education and training. It had been preceded by a series of major inquiries and reports, which had identified a need for reforms and for greater levels of investment in the vocational sector. That sector had long been dominated by state-owned Technical and Further Education (TAFE) systems, with each state system autonomously managed. The Commonwealth's involvement had been relatively minor until the mid-1980s, except that it assumed full responsibility for labour-market training programs as part of its overall responsibility for unemployment policy. It also had a major interest in the question of accreditation of overseas qualifications and in aspects of vocational training for newly landed migrants as part of its immigration portfolio. In the case of the first, the injection of large amounts of Commonwealth funds into the training system through special labour-market programs to cope with high unemployment continued to occur as a separate policy enterprise, even after ANTA was in place.

ANTA's establishment in late 1992 had been preceded by a phase of active intergovernmental cooperation through existing, arm's-length institutions. A heightened Commonwealth interest led to a series of inquiries which stimulated new thinking and gave rise to a series of agreements between state and Commonwealth training ministers: Training Cost Review Committee, 1990 (Deveson Report); Australian Education Council Review Committee, 1991 (Finn Report); Employment and Skills Formation Council, 1992 (Carmichael Report). The Commonwealth—and later ANTA itself—liked to refer to the outcomes of these agreements as the 'National Training Reform Agenda'. Vince Fitzgerald identified eight elements, each of them endorsed or acknowledged by decisions of governments: competency-based training, competency standards, national recognition of training, national curricula, a standardised system of entry level training, the development of a training market, access and equity principles, and a nationally coordinated system of funding (Allen Consulting Group 1994, 18–19).

One result of this activity was some new ad hoc intergovernmental agencies. For example, a Special Conference of Ministers for Training in 1989 set up a National Training Board and a National Office of Overseas Skills Recognition. The National Training Board was charged with framing a new set of competency-based standards. The Council of Ministers of Vocational Education, Employment and Training in 1990 and 1991 approved the introduction of a system of competency-based training across the sector, and from 1992 all new training programs were designed in competency-based terms. This system rests on a set of competency standards, both generic and vocation-specific, agreed to in cooperation with industry. The National Training Board was incorporated as a public company in 1990, in which each government was a

160 COLLABORATIVE FEDERALISM

shareholder, with funding for its operations coming from the Commonwealth (50 per cent) and the states and territories in proportion to population (50 per cent). The board of directors was made up of nominees from each government, plus two nominated by the Australian Council of Trade Unions (ACTU), two employer representatives and an independent chair. The National Training Board developed the Australian Standards Framework, consisting of eight competency levels, and approved industry-specific competency standards which were tied to this generic framework, on the basis of submissions and advice from industry competency standards bodies. By 1994, training for over 60 per cent of the workforce was covered by competency standards approved by the National Training Board.

The 1990 agreement on national competency standards was complemented in 1992 by the adoption of the National Framework for the Recognition of Training, which states and territories all agreed to implement through their separate frameworks of legislation and regulation. The national framework was the product of recommendations from the Vocational Education and Training Advisory Committee, which reported to the ministerial council. Henceforth, all state-based accreditation and registration processes replicated those set out in the national framework. National curriculum development was agreed upon at a 1990 Special Ministerial Conference, when the Australian Committee for Training Curriculum was set up. It oversaw the development of standard materials for both workplace and institutional training, channelling funding for curriculum development projects to TAFE and to industry bodies or enterprises, and issuing approved standard curricula when completed.

To this point, implementation of this emerging national agenda remained principally at the behest of the states and territories. Funding issues provided the trigger for the establishment of ANTA. Before 1992, public funding was provided in conventional ways through state budgets topped up by Commonwealth special-purpose payments. In 1991, the Commonwealth provided 17 per cent of recurrent vocational funding through grants (Taylor 1996, 93). A central issue raised by several of the reports referred to earlier was the relatively low level of funding for vocational education in Australia. Compared with higher education, which was directly funded by the Commonwealth, vocational education was a neglected sector. The Commonwealth, as the major source of any future growth in funds, was prompted for many reasons to view the sector in national terms, and was reluctant simply to hand funds over to the states. Up to 1992, the trend towards a more concerted national effort had come about through conventional ministerial council structures and had focused on standardising and harmonising state-based systems. The Commonwealth, in announcing in October 1991 its intention to provide \$720 million in additional funds over a four-year period, tied the announcement to the need for a new national strategy, and to effect this offered to take over full funding responsibility. The outcome, after protracted negotiations, was a formal agreement for joint decision-making.

ANTA and the States

The National Vocational Education and Training System established under the agreement, with ANTA at its core, is a collaborative arrangement of the kind modelled in Table 6.1, including a national authority and a ministerial council with special voting rules. The arrangement under which state and Commonwealth governments jointly applied funds to vocational education also embodied collaborative elements, although (as might be expected) they were a source of constant tension. Familiar arguments and conflicts were played out, with the states highly suspicious of the Commonwealth's motives and actions. The states characteristically depict any arrangement that places constraints on their use of funds as a case of the assertion of Commonwealth power. In this case, however, the constraints were part of a jointly signed agreement. The principle was adopted that all funds for vocational education, including state own-source funds, existing Commonwealth grants and new Commonwealth growth funds, were to be pooled, and subsequently disbursed through ANTA. Commonwealth labour-market training programs were deliberately excluded, as were vocational education and training programs for groups 'for which the Commonwealth has a special responsibility', such as Aboriginals. The agreement attached strings to the disbursement of funds. States undertook to 'maintain effort', and the Commonwealth undertook to maintain its existing and committed funding levels, while also adding the growth funds. State-sourced revenue would be handed back to each of the states along with Commonwealth grants in line with current arrangements, while growth funds would be delivered on a population basis, other than 20 per cent from 1994 on that would be delivered on the basis of performance as assessed by agreed measures. ANTA and the ministerial council were charged with agreeing on such outcome measures. Growth funds were made conditional on agreement by the ministerial council to an annual 'state training profile' setting out planned programs and activities.

ANTA was constituted as a board, under Commonwealth legislation, with five members chosen by the ministerial council. Priority was given to industry representation. It was charged with developing a draft national strategic plan. It also would advise the ministerial council on

162   COLLABORATIVE FEDERALISM

policy matters and on the principles to be applied in the allocation of funding between states. ANTA would both receive and disburse the pooled funds referred to in the sections on funding. State training agencies were specified in the agreement to be 'distinct bodies in the context of a national training system … accountable to State Ministers and parliaments for the operational responsibilities of their agencies and accountable to the ministerial council on matters of national policy'. Legislation would be passed by the Commonwealth (to set up ANTA) and by the states to constitute the state training agencies and define the new roles and relationships.

The ANTA ministerial council set up under the agreement comprised all state, territory and Commonwealth training ministers and was chaired by the Commonwealth. It remained a separate body in the 1993 reorganisation and consolidation of ministerial councils undertaken by COAG, although it was expected that it would meet 'back to back' with the renamed Ministerial Council for Employment, Education, Training and Youth Affairs. On the ANTA ministerial council, each state and territory minister had one vote, and the Commonwealth two, with a casting vote from the chair. All matters could be decided by a simple majority. The council was charged with wide-ranging responsibilities: agreeing to the necessary legislation to set up the national system; appointing the ANTA board and its chair; determining the ANTA budget; determining goals and priorities for the national system, the national strategic plan, the principles to be applied in allocation of funding between states for any national programs, and planning parameters to be included in the guidelines issued by ANTA for state training profiles. It also agreed to state and national profiles setting out a plan for the following year for each state and nationally; advised the Commonwealth minister on Commonwealth decisions about growth funding requirements; and generally oversaw the operations of ANTA. As stated in the agreement, the ministerial council was 'to be accountable to state and Commonwealth Parliaments for the operation of ANTA and the expenditure of funds'.

The states did not show any enthusiasm in passing legislation to designate or set up state training agencies in the form required, and to define their relationship with ANTA. By the end of 1993 only Queensland had fully complied. New South Wales acted early in 1994, and Victoria and Tasmania followed suit soon after. South Australia and Western Australia were dragging their feet. South Australia complied in 1995, but Western Australia was in the midst of a major review of its vocational education, with a report delivered in late 1993. Legislation implementing reforms, and incorporating provisions agreed to under the ANTA agreement, came into effect in 1996. This reluctance and

DUPLICATION AND OVERLAP   163

delay were symptomatic of more deep-seated problems in the collaborative relationship. The pooling of funds was never more than a convenient fiction. Most states resisted the measure, and no state actually transferred any funds to ANTA (Taylor 1996, 34–6). Instead, they agreed at the May 1994 ministerial council to an alternative recommended by ANTA, under which they established and maintained identified accounts in their own budgets for vocational education funds, with ANTA being provided with written notice of the actual transfer of funds to these accounts and with an annual audit certificate. Several states entered reservations about these arrangements, and three did not comply.

The collaborative arrangements were also placed in question when the Commonwealth in April 1994 unilaterally amended provisions in the Vocational Education and Training Funding Act, one of two acts that gave effect to the ANTA agreement. This amendment allowed the Commonwealth minister to refuse or delay payment of growth funds without waiting for majority approval by the ministerial council. The amendment was presented as a temporary 'precautionary measure' on the grounds that some states were not complying with the arrangements, including the legislative changes. Its main effect was to strengthen the Commonwealth's hand in enforcing compliance with the clauses regarding maintenance of effort. The amendment expired in December 1995. Letters of objection from state ministers were tabled in the Senate, claiming that it 'strongly conflicts with the spirit of the ANTA Agreement' (Cwlth *PD*, Senate, 16 December 1993, 4910). Effectively, the amendment supplanted the collaborative funding arrangements with a model more akin to a conventional Commonwealth special-purpose payment with conditions attached, enforced by the Commonwealth.

In December 1994, the Commonwealth minister used the amended section of the act to delay payments of growth funds to Western Australia, Victoria and South Australia. In these states, recently elected Liberal governments had introduced severe budget cuts to cope with fiscal crises, and the impact of some of these cuts was felt in vocational education. Victoria argued that, despite lower funding, the level of activity was not being reduced because efficiency was improving. In 1995, ANTA advised the minister that these states had complied with the maintenance-of-effort provisions, and growth funds were retrospectively restored. Disputes over the maintenance of effort by South Australia and Victoria continued into 1996. South Australia at one point was accused by the Commonwealth minister of seeking to channel funds from the Commonwealth-funded Better Cities Program through the TAFE budget in order to boost its 'effort' (Cwlth *PD* HoR, 30 March

1995). It is not surprising that some states, faced with budget problems, were resorting to time-worn tactics of substituting Commonwealth funds in the search for economies. For this purpose, they viewed the growth funds no differently from any other tied grant from the Commonwealth. Dual funding sources and maintenance-of-effort clauses create incentives for such behaviour, particularly in the context of continuing Commonwealth restraint in general revenue funding. Whether a state was evading a Commonwealth control or defecting from a collective agreement was something of a technical nicety. The states concerned did restore some of the funding when faced with ANTA's reports on their performance and the consequent Commonwealth threats. Victoria, however, succeeded in reducing its financial effort in 1995–96 by demonstrating to ANTA that it was meeting activity targets (Senate Employment, Education and Training References Committee 1995, *Minority Report*, 11). Victoria and other states argued strongly that efficiency gains should allow them to reap a dividend for the state budget.

A fundamental problem with the clause regarding maintenance of effort was inadequate definition. The ministerial council developed its own interpretation of what constituted maintenance of effort, drawing together information on expenditure, activity (hours of student contact, derisively labelled 'ANTA hours'), enrolments, and module load completion (an output measure). The ministerial council gave most weight to activity measures. But basic measurement problems made it a simple task to evade effective scrutiny. The measures were open to gross misreporting due to the state of records in some TAFE systems (for example unreliable figures for enrolments and completion dates). When better data became available in later years, ANTA discovered over-reporting of activity measures of up to 40 per cent. Moreover, the activity measures alone merely encouraged faster throughput, perhaps at the expense of quality, and may have biased resources towards programs promising quicker, more certain results at the expense of others that might produce more valuable outcomes (Taylor 1996, 96–7). ANTA was charged with coming up with appropriate performance measures, but this proved impracticable in the short term. The provision that 20 per cent of growth funds should be distributed on the basis of performance using such measures was as a result not implemented; instead, the ministerial council agreed to distribute all funds on a population basis.

Other familiar patterns of conflict were evident in the ANTA arrangements. Turf issues arose from the very existence of ANTA, which effectively supplanted the role formerly fulfilled by the group of state training authority chief executive officers (CEOs) advising the ministerial council. The CEOs wanted to have an input to ANTA board

DUPLICATION AND OVERLAP

business, and to advise their ministers in relation to ANTA ministerial council matters, rather than have them rely solely on ANTA advice. The relationship between the CEOs and ANTA was handled by setting up a separate ad hoc ANTA CEOs body, to allow for ANTA recommendations to be discussed and the views of CEOs communicated. It was stressed in the formal reporting of this arrangement that 'the CEOs' advice does not intervene between the advice of the ANTA Board to [the ministerial council] but "sits behind" the ANTA Board in the hierarchy' (Auditor-General 1996, 5). The body also served as a communication channel to assist in implementation. Complaints persisted that ANTA had a 'privileged' position in the policy-making chain, and that state ministers in particular were not always well served. This attempt to locate the states' administrative agencies in a national system of joint decision-making, where a separate national agency played a key role, highlighted underlying contradictions in lines of accountability that are invariably faced in such arrangements.

The submission of state training profiles required by the agreement was another source of irritation. State officials viewed this as an unnecessary form of detailed administrative interference, particularly when ANTA made demands for data, or complained about the quality and detail of the submissions—'dogmatic uniform requirements' as one state official put it. In Western Australia, a familiar complaint was the amount of resources that had to be devoted to compliance and reporting. One Queensland state training agency official, while making similar points, also saw a benefit:

> via ANTA, we as a sector have been able to put pressure on our Government for funding under the maintenance of effort provisions—as part of the deal, the Government has had to boost its effort, so from the [vocational] sector's perspective in this state, it's been a good thing to be tied into the central system. [personal communication]

A familiar paradox was evident, expressed by one ANTA official as follows: 'state and territory training agencies want to keep ANTA so as to shield themselves from their Treasuries, and at the same time they don't want accountability to ANTA'.

Another grievance of the states was the exclusion of the Commonwealth's labour-market programs. The Commonwealth Department of Employment, Education and Training (DEET, or DEETYA when Youth Affairs was added in 1996) directly funded a network of training coordinators and providers through these programs, and built up its own system of regional and local coordination through community, industry and other groups. NETTFORCE (National Task Force on Employment and Training) programs were directed at stimulating

166   COLLABORATIVE FEDERALISM

industry uptake of traineeships, for example, but their activities were not taken account of in the state training profiles. Industry complained of confusion and duplication of effort as both ANTA and DEET sponsored partnership and consultative arrangements, which offered separate training products and services to industry:

> There is a high level of confusion over the definitions of, and difference between, Programs and Funding (for example, Apprenticeship/Trainee-ship/Job Start/Job Compact/Job Guarantee) ... there is some confusion between labour market programs and the AVTS ... few understand the role of NETTFORCE and how it fits in ... there is a high level of competition and antipathy ... [Business Council of Australia, Submission to the Review of the ANTA Agreement, 1996]

DEET's view of ANTA was unwelcoming from the outset, as the alternative scenarios for enhanced Commonwealth involvement would have put DEET in control. DEET viewed ANTA as an unwelcome trespasser on their territory. The Commonwealth's Taylor Review into ANTA in 1996 found that 'DEET has failed to take the necessary steps to ensure coordination of labour market programs with [vocational] programs', despite a section of the agreement specifically requiring this to be done. From the states' perspective, the more fundamental prob-lem was the 'dual standards' of the Commonwealth in not submitting its own array of training programs to the same collaborative constraints as were required of the states, but continuing to use those programs unilaterally to pursue its own agenda.

Creating a National System

Despite the criticisms, ANTA in 1995 was strengthened by transferring the functions of the National Training Board, the Australian Committee for Training Curriculum and the National Staff Development Com-mittee to a new body, the Standards and Curriculum Council, under the wing of ANTA and the ministerial council. This was an important step, bringing under ANTA some of the most important policy instruments for creating a national system, such as competency standards, national recognition, national curriculum, and assessment. ANTA officials and the board developed a set of priorities for future directions, and became an influential voice. They sympathised with some of the complaints of the states about the way the agreement was working. While main-tenance-of-effort provisions were important in some form to maintain commitment to growth in the system, the disputes over their imple-mentation had become a distraction—a 'monkey on our backs', as one official put it. Similarly, the level of detailed involvement with state

DUPLICATION AND OVERLAP 167

planning and profiles was on balance becoming counter-productive. ANTA's role should be more at a strategic level, pursuing the national reform agenda.

ANTA's chief officials were increasingly critical of the TAFE systems as being dominated by providers and, in some states, bureaucratically managed. The need for a more responsive, industry-led system was becoming the prominent issue. Here, ANTA's funding role had an impact only at the margins, and hardly touched the core of the state systems. One of ANTA's strategies was to use a portion of Commonwealth funds for 'national projects', such as a set of pilot schemes to stimulate a more competitive training market. ANTA officials placed increasing emphasis on its role in coordinating data and monitoring outcomes. In 1996, ANTA coordinated a major exercise in developing a set of key performance indicators, through a Performance Review Committee. These data, it was felt, could have major strategic value as a lever over the system at large. As one ANTA official put it, 'Will the Commonwealth continue to provide growth funds for a state that makes no effort to clean up its act once agreed indicators have showed that its system is inefficient?' The newly elected Liberal government announced there would be no more 'growth funds' in the current form, but that 'the government's proposed new funding arrangements allow for future growth to be derived from increased efficiencies' (Cwlth *PD* Senate, 17 June 1997).

The ANTA board was close to industry, where the message was that the system, including the national reforms already agreed on, provided as much disincentive as encouragement to industry. It was over-regulated, provider-dominated, complex and inaccessible. Existing forms of industry participation through state and national Industry Training Advisory Boards led to duplication and were unsuited to many new industries. Some complained about trade union domination. Industry submissions to the Taylor Review articulated many of these concerns:

> significant cross sections of industry are unaware that they are expected to drive the process, while other enterprises have consciously chosen not to get involved ... much of industry remains unclear about how ITABs work, who is accountable to whom. The structure and calibre of representation on ITABs has been raised as a concern. [Business Council of Australia]

> The Council is of the view that competing industrial relations interests have considerably impeded progress ... Also, the processes involved have been such as to make it very difficult to have and maintain broad industry involvement ... Industry remains confused about the training system and the various State and federal bodies [with] ... different agendas. [Council of Textile and Fashion Industries of Australia]

168   COLLABORATIVE FEDERALISM

Union domination was an issue taken up strongly by the Liberal opposition in framing its training policy platform: 'many small businesses are concerned that under Labor's tripartite training arrangements, taking on a trainee may bring trade unions into formerly non-unionised workplaces' (Liberal Party of Australia 1995, 32).

The ANTA board and chief officials were strong advocates of the creation of an 'open training market'. The concept of user choice had been stressed in a report commissioned by ANTA and written by Vince Fitzgerald, who emphasised the need to refocus policy on the 'demand side' away from the 'supply side' (Allen Consulting Group 1994). Industry and employers should be the dominant voice in the system because the training system's principal objective was to improve productive efficiency. Only by responding flexibly and promptly to industry needs and demands would this objective be met. Industry should be the major voice in the national standards-setting and regulatory processes (which must be quick and simple), and there must be a competitive market of providers, both public and private, with a demand-driven system of funding at the local level.

Fitzgerald was critical of the 'management system' currently in place for implementing the national agenda, lamenting the lack of strategic capacity, the difficulty in cementing collective commitment, the fragmentation between vocational and labour-market programs, and the ambivalent views of state governments and training agencies to the creation of a competitive training market:

> A key to the management of the system is that ANTA must enlist the States/Territories and the Commonwealth to explicit commitment to the same strategic goals which it makes itself accountable for and which it publishes as the common set of objectives through its annual report ... Ideally this should encompass all training, including that funded by DEET under labour market or other programs, to avoid having dual national strategic planning and outcome monitoring systems. [Allen Consulting Group 1994, 76]

The Fitzgerald Report, the Senate Committee inquiry in 1995 and the Taylor Review in 1996 documented numerous criticisms, but few of the major participants argued in favour of winding back the national system and abolishing ANTA. In their submission to the National Commission of Audit (NCOA) in 1996, the states called for a much-diminished role for ANTA, but not the end of the cooperative arrangement. They feared the revival of the Commonwealth's more aggressive takeover tactics. ANTA should adopt 'an advisory, non-operational role ... facilitating broad strategic direction setting', with no involvement in direct funding or service provision. Funds should be devolved in a block grant, linked

DUPLICATION AND OVERLAP

to 'broad strategic directions approved by the ministerial council, which States and Territories would address in ways appropriate to local priorities and circumstances' (States and Territories Joint Submission to NCOA 1996, 28–9). The NCOA came down on the side of a 'clean lines' division of powers and a Commonwealth takeover, along the lines of higher education. This recommendation was ignored. New 'business arrangements' between ANTA and the states in 1996 dropped the requirement for state training profiles, but called on state ministers to consult with ANTA before approving annual state plans and to report on outcomes using key performance indicators.

The new government retained ANTA and enthusiastically endorsed the major directions in which its board and officials had been moving. The Fitzgerald Report had been the source of a number of ideas for the Liberal Party policy platform on training. The new minister, David Kemp, was an energetic and enthusiastic advocate of the reform agenda. The principle of industry leadership and involvement was adopted wholeheartedly, with strong support for a user-buys system. Legislation was introduced to expand the ANTA board by adding two new industry representatives. Labour-market training programs were severely cut in the 1996 budget, and a new enterprise-focused Modern Apprenticeship and Training System was announced, to be administered by ANTA.

The ANTA ministerial council meetings in November 1996 and May 1997 (ANTA 1997b) gave strong endorsement to most of the new government's policies, albeit with reservations from New South Wales (the only Labor government in Australia). The coincidence of Liberal leaders in all but one jurisdiction assisted in creating the right climate. In addition, several states were in the midst of implementing a series of reforms to vocational education on their own account. Victoria had been moving towards a restructured, decentralised TAFE system for a number of years, and Western Australia had just completed implementing the findings of a major review which embodied many of the same elements. Industry was acquiring a more prominent role in a number of jurisdictions. In other words, the majority of states were not averse to the thrust of the reforms, and for partisan reasons were sympathetic to rhetoric about mending the damage of the Labor legacy. At the November 1996 meeting of the ministerial council, ministers agreed to national and state consultative processes to move ahead with the new agenda. The separate state consultations were conducted by state training agencies. A user-choice task force was set up to report to ANTA. The resulting new National Training Framework thus bore the stamp not only of the new government and the ANTA board, but also of most of the states.

170   COLLABORATIVE FEDERALISM

The Modern Apprenticeship and Training System was given the endorsement of all governments under the new name of 'New Apprenticeships', to commence in January 1998. Enterprises or group training companies (local bodies seeded with public funds, which acted as training brokers between enterprises and the public system) would choose 'the provider who can most effectively adapt a training package to meet its needs'. A training agreement would be drawn up with the enterprise or group training company, and public funds would then flow to the chosen provider, whether public or private. The ministerial council agreed to the principle that access to publicly funded school-to-work training was an individual entitlement for all Australians—in effect, trainees had access to training 'vouchers'. The states (other than New South Wales) committed themselves to the user-choice principle when allocating their own-source, as well as Commonwealth, funds under the scheme. The states would set the unit costs of training programs, and these would form the basis of the level of funding to the provider selected by the client. There would be no barriers to prevent a training provider (including TAFE colleges themselves) from offering a program in another state. The Commonwealth minister claimed the total in Commonwealth, state and territory funding committed under the user-choice principle would amount to 'more than $500 million a year' (Cwlth *PD* HoR, 4 June 1997).

Industry needs for training, both on and off the job, would be met by the development of new National Training Packages. Industry groups would play the central role in designing their own training requirements, with a national system of accreditation endorsing them. This national accreditation system would be developed by the National Training Framework Committee of ANTA, and approved by the ministerial council. So-called National Training Packages (i.e. courses of training) would be endorsed by the framework committee if they satisfied requirements for broadly based competency standards determined appropriate for each industry; contained adequate assessment guidelines; and offered standardised national qualifications related to the Australian Qualifications Framework. The details of course content were not made part of the requirements for endorsement (a deliberate ploy to diminish the influence of existing provider groups). The second element in the new national regulatory system involved the registration of providers of particular packages. The registration process itself would be handled by state training agencies, but under protocols and standards agreed to by the ministerial council. With adequate quality assurance measures in place, registered training organisations could be delegated accreditation powers, and allowed to extend their training activities without further registration. The ministerial council also

DUPLICATION AND OVERLAP

agreed to mutual recognition. All national qualifications issued under the Australian Qualifications Framework (or Statements of Attainment) by a registered training organisation, along with all provider-registration decisions taken by state registration authorities, would be recognised equally in all jurisdictions. The existence of agreed minimum standards in the national framework would underpin mutual recognition.

These decisions brought the idea of a national system much closer to reality. A coherent policy framework and a series of collective commitments existed by mid-1997, with implementation to be negotiated through a series of bilateral arrangements so as to accommodate specific states' needs and interests. At various points in the policy framework, it was stressed that implementation details were being left to the states. This was consistent with the states' general position on the need for ANTA and the Commonwealth to keep their hands off detailed operational matters, a view that ANTA was happy to support. Other than New South Wales, states undertook to incorporate the provisions of the new National Training Framework in legislation.

A point insisted upon by all states was the right to declare particular regions and occupations exempt from the user-choice regime, if they could show that there was a 'thin market' of providers. These exemptions had to be justified annually at the ministerial council. User-choice was not viewed with universal enthusiasm, and state ministers remained cautious about exposing their TAFE systems to open competition. The South Australian Minister for Employment, Training and Youth Affairs, speaking at the ANTA national conference in July 1996, entered a caveat:

> I welcome the coming of a liberalised training market ... I also welcome the freedom of choice which that presupposes, but *not* if that is to come at the expense of a robust public sector training provider ... TAFE, which has a stable and dedicated workforce, and the capacity to look ahead and plan ... offers the very mechanism on which any national strategy will depend for its implementation and success.

All state governments asserted their right to continue to recognise the existence of training courses other than the National Training Packages. However, if the latter succeeded in stimulating demand by meeting the needs of industry, the only way to meet this commitment of universal access through the voucher entitlement, while remaining true to the commitment on user choice, would be to transfer funds from state-accredited courses and activities.

The acceptance of the principle of user choice and a national training market brought the National Competition Policy into play. States agreed to review their TAFE systems with a view to opening their infrastructure

172 COLLABORATIVE FEDERALISM

to access by other providers. In some states, this already happened to a limited extent. The success of user choice depends heavily on structural reforms within the TAFE system because, in the short run at least, the scope for the rapid transfer of resources from the dominant public providers to new private competitors is limited. In 1996, private providers accounted for only 2.2 per cent of vocational training (NCVER 1997). ANTA sought to gain agreement on uniform structural reforms, such as full separation of purchaser and provider roles, but the states insisted that 'separation of roles is a "structure of government" matter to be dealt with by State/Territory governments' (ANTA 1997a, 21). This is an area where states have different approaches. For example, in Victoria and Western Australia, the creation of autonomous colleges, the removal of bureaucratic controls and the separation of a decentralised system of providers from the state training agency as regulator and purchaser were already in place, but New South Wales retained a more centralised TAFE system.

But not all was sweetness and light, and in mid-1997 a bitter dispute blew up over funding. Vocational education was not immune from the Commonwealth's budget-tightening program, which was justified by the minister as 'an incentive to achieve efficiency gains' (Cwlth *PD*, 4 June 1997). The creation of what was effectively an entitlement or voucher system under the new schemes would have the effect of squeezing the existing TAFE systems in favour of directing funding to alternative providers. These issues came to a head during discussions over a new ANTA agreement, in which Commonwealth funding would be tied to the achievement of efficiency improvements in TAFE based on benchmarking. The projected extra places in TAFE programs arising from the new training initiatives would have to be funded from this source, not from additional Commonwealth funds. In September, Kemp wrote to the states threatening to withdraw the five-year financial commitment under the new agreement, and to proceed unilaterally (*Age*, 18, 19 September 1997).

In sum, under the ANTA agreement the collaborative arrangements setting up a new national system showed both the possibilities of, and the obstacles to, new federal arrangements. The initial model implemented under the 1992 agreement was found wanting in two respects. First, the funding arrangements brought into play a set of counter-productive responses typical of the adversarialism of arm's-length fiscal politics; and second, ANTA's role aroused familiar resentment about duplication of administrative functions. In the model of provision underlying the new 1997 schemes, collaborative funding rules that attempted to channel tied funds to the states' service provision systems gave way to a collectively agreed set of client access rules so as to direct these funds to the customer's chosen provider. Pay-off rules styled on

DUPLICATION AND OVERLAP 173

the norms and practices of a command bureaucracy (that is, conditions tied to growth funds or to special-purpose payments) were to be replaced by those of the market. The Commonwealth and ANTA hoped to achieve their objectives by enlisting industry users to exercise market power through the use of these funds. ANTA's detailed oversight of state training profiles was, by the same device, also made redundant. The ministerial council and the ANTA board, both advised by ANTA officials, would be the key decision-makers in setting and maintaining the rules of access for providers in the market.

The national standards-setting framework, coupled with a market-driven model of provision, carried the seeds of a transformation of the respective roles and responsibilities of state and Commonwealth governments, and of their agencies. The states' regulatory roles exercised on the input side through the bureaucratic accreditation of staff and courses, and their near-monopoly of the provider role through centrally funded systems of TAFE colleges, would each be undermined by new sets of relationships constructed collaboratively in a new quasi-market of service provision. The states in their regulatory roles were cast as agents of the national system rather than as independent regulators.

However, the dispute that flared up over funding in 1997 brought the underlying issues of jurisdiction and autonomy to the surface. The states' first priority remained the funding of their TAFE establishments and programs, but the Commonwealth was intent on undermining this 'provider dominance' of the system. Here, the Commonwealth was in a weak position, as the capacity for private providers to move quickly into the field and weaken the dominant role of the TAFE systems was at best untested. The market was not going to bring quick results, so the Commonwealth reverted to command and control. Improved responsiveness and efficiency in the TAFE system was sought by more conventional methods—squeezing more productivity out of the bureaucratic system by demanding best-practice efficiency improvements on pain of withdrawal of funding. A key tool in the hands of the Commonwealth was a new, agreed set of ANTA performance indicators that promised to overcome the earlier information deficits. Faced with this strategy, the states, having agreed to a set of cooperative program reforms, baulked at the last hurdle. This Commonwealth government was as aggressive, punitive and centralist as any other. Federal politics reverted to type— adversarial thrust and riposte, and a familiar squabble over funding.

COAG, Roles and Responsibilities

The disability agreement and ANTA were two cases of efforts to restructure roles and responsibilities during the lifetime of SPC and COAG, but neither was the direct product of any progress on the wider,

174   COLLABORATIVE FEDERALISM

general reform agenda by COAG's working parties. Indeed, SPC and COAG produced very little in the way of concrete reform in this area. Work on the functional reviews set up in October 1990 by SPC proceeded with varying levels of commitment and enthusiasm during 1991. The collapse of SPC itself in November 1991 was in no small part due to the fear of Commonwealth ministers that the outcome of a reallocation of roles and responsibilities would be the surrender of Commonwealth program control. With the revival of interest in cooperative federalism and the establishment of COAG in May 1992, the fiscal reform agenda was dropped, and with it was lost much of the enthusiasm and momentum for comprehensively addressing overlap and duplication.

Interest in a general review of overlap and duplication was revived at the June 1993 COAG, when a new working group was set up 'to identify those functional areas which exhibit inefficiencies in existing inter-governmental arrangements and where there is scope for clarification of roles and responsibilities'. The terms of reference listed the 'relevant issues' for identifying areas for priority attention:

- problems of duplication and overlap
- inefficiencies in delivery of services to clients
- incentives to cost-shifting between governments
- lack of transparency and clear accountability and unnecessary duplication in program monitoring.

Cost shifting was identified as a particularly acute problem in health, where the states faced budgetary pressures in containing public hospital costs. The medical and pharmaceutical benefits schemes were indi-vidual entitlement schemes, and there was a strong incentive for the states to induce or force patients to obtain funds for their hospital treatment through that channel. The mix across different jurisdictions of budget-capped programs and directly linked, entitlement-driven, uncapped programs was a recipe for expenditure distortions and unintended outcomes.

The February 1994 COAG reported that it 'did not have the oppor-tunity to conclude its consideration of the report from the Working Group', but agreed to put it at the top of the agenda for the next meeting. However, specific priority areas for review were highlighted, and the work being undertaken on them was brought under the umbrella of COAG. They included public housing, child care, health, community services (where a Commonwealth–State Steering Com-mittee reviewing the Home and Community Care Program was asked to report progress to the next scheduled COAG meeting) and labour market programs. But the August 1994 meeting in Darwin, where the

DUPLICATION AND OVERLAP 175

states and the Commonwealth were at each other's throats about competition policy, also failed to discuss the item.

Nevertheless, work was going on, under the auspices of the working group, through a number of other task groups and working parties. Central agency officials as well as the line agencies were involved, and a number of broad general themes were emerging. The processes had acquired a life and legitimacy of their own, even if the political leaders attending COAG itself were preoccupied with other matters. In the field of Health and Community Services, COAG set up a task force, while the ministerial council in March 1994 took up the COAG reference and set up its own working group of officials on 'The Attainment of National Objectives in Community Services'. Its report of June 1994 outlined six options, five for further consideration and one for immediate implementation as an interim measure. The aim was a 'single, national policy framework for a cohesive, coordinated community service that minimises gaps, removes duplication and clarifies roles and responsibilities'. Among the issues to be resolved was the 'skewing of resources' across the sector as a whole as a result of the impact of tied grants on state community service budgets. The ambition was for a national framework to encompass twelve existing programs: Home and Community Care, Supported Accommodation Assistance, Commonwealth child care and state children's services, state and Commonwealth disability services, substitute care, child protection, community and family support, aged care, community services, and personal financial assistance. The six options were:

1. State-only responsibility (with the exception of the aged care residential program), with no tied grants or reporting on expenditure.
2. State-only responsibility, with national agreements, entailing a process to agree on national objectives and a monitoring and reporting system on outputs and outcomes.
3. Shared responsibility, with national agreements for all services; a 'broadbanded' specific-purpose payment for all community services; joint determination of national policy objectives for all programs; state-only responsibility for planning, administration and delivery of services; and joint planning on broad priority issues, service models and equitable distribution of resources.
4. Shared responsibility, with national agreements for joint programs, a 'broadbanded' specific-purpose payment for joint programs, and as for option 3 except for the exclusion of some state-only and Commonwealth-only programs from the national agreements.
5. Shared responsibility for all services, with national agreements and divisions of functional responsibility, with arrangements as for

176 COLLABORATIVE FEDERALISM

option 3, except that either level of government could have responsibility for planning, administration and delivery of a program
6. Existing arrangements with national agreements and other reforms, with specific-purpose payments to the states for existing joint programs, and otherwise as for option 3.

The enumeration of these options served most of all to highlight the complexities of the situation and to accentuate what was at stake. Option 1 was infeasible, option 5 lacked coherence, and option 6 was effectively the status quo. The remaining options uneasily combined both Commonwealth and state agendas, with an insistence on national agreements and joint decision-making on the one hand, and strong elements of the states' aims of devolution along 'clean lines' principles and removal of all financial strings.

COAG's own Task Force on Health and Community Services released a discussion paper in January 1995. Its approach was different, in part because it was dominated by central agency officials. It had a different starting point, namely the fundamentals of the service itself rather than its organisational structure as a system of roles and responsibilities. Three 'streams of care' were identified, on the basis of three categories of individual need: general care (requiring a range of community and preventive health and welfare services); acute care (requiring, for instance, hospitalisation and a complex medical procedure, followed by rehabilitation and possibly a need for a long-term disability service); and coordinated care (e.g. a range of specialised services required by a frail, aged person with a mental illness). Restructuring services around these different types of need would, it was claimed 'help shift the focus from providing inputs to discrete service providers to emphasising the outcomes of the services provided for the person'. The aim should be to:

improve consumer outcomes by:
- making individual needs more important than discrete services and institutions as the basis for planning and funding the system;
- providing, over time, a funding mechanism which supports better outcomes ...
- facilitating better integration and linkages between services ...
- shifting the focus from individuals' medical needs to their total health and community care needs. [COAG Task Force 1995, 11–12]

As to the organisational framework for such a system, the paper suggested 'multilateral arrangements' at the national level for plan-ning policy, setting outcomes and monitoring performance (based on the development of agreed performance indicators), plus 'bilateral'

DUPLICATION AND OVERLAP

Commonwealth–state arrangements to reflect broader national agreements and to allow for differences between states. These bilateral arrangements would incorporate 'multi-year agreements based on states meeting defined access and performance standards, with appropriate incentives and penalties'. New funding arrangements would accompany the changes, based on 'baseline funding and performance levels' for the three care streams. Existing programs would each be assigned to a care stream, and programs would no longer be separately funded, but managed and funded across the care stream as a whole. 'Output-based' funding would be introduced, on the model of case-mix hospital funding, where a fixed price for an item or episode of care is set in advance. In the case of coordinated care, the model of 'care managers' was advanced, a role that could be filled by a general practitioner, a private insurance fund, a community health service, or other service providers. The care manager would assist a client to package and 'purchase' a mix of services specific to their needs, providing a single point of entry rather than leaving the client to seek out services at a series of distinct access points. The care manager would have to work within a budget constraint, for example a standard fee, a fee negotiated between a health insurance fund and a group of providers, or a Medicare entitlement. In introducing such a system, new and improved national databases on individual care episodes and service items would need to be developed to allow for tracking and monitoring of outcomes.

It is no accident that these proposals mirrored the model advanced for vocational education and training, because both drew on the same ideas and experience of broader public-sector reform. Edwards and Henderson (1995, 27–8) describe how the COAG proposals represented a major 'change in approach'. The key question became how to improve services for clients, by providing them with greater choice and by focusing the mind of service planners on access and outcomes, rather than on organisational roles and responsibilities. Concepts such as the purchaser–provider split and competitive service provision placed the proposals squarely in the context of wider public-sector reforms. They were heavily influenced by the 'new public economics' and by other strands of thought that emphasised the benefits of mimicking the market in the provision of public services (Painter 1997). The key question was not a political or constitutional one of how to divide powers or allocate functions, but a managerial one of how best to deliver a service. The necessary elements included mechanisms for monitoring performance (outputs and outcomes), and incentives and sanctions that rewarded efficiency and effectiveness. One approach was to place 'purchasing power' in the hands of consumers or their agents, and to allow them to discriminate on price and quality between providers. The

178   COLLABORATIVE FEDERALISM

key roles in this system were those of funder, purchaser, provider and customer. As in the case of ANTA and the new 'national system', roles were defined through the actualisation of a quasi-market for a particular industry. The recategorisation of the roles of government and public agencies in these terms sought to side-step the jurisdictional questions that had bogged down previous attempts at dealing with the problems of overlap.

At the April 1995 COAG meeting, agreement was reached in principle on the model outlined in the task force's January discussion paper. The working group was charged with refining it and recommending an implementation strategy, but the process would be overseen by the Council of Health and Community Services Ministers. A task force of line agency officials assisted the working group. At the June 1996 COAG (that is, following the change of Commonwealth government) support for the model was reaffirmed, along with further details on implementation. The communiqué was blunt and reflected the new way of thinking:

> There has been too great a focus by governments on financing and intergovernmental tensions at the expense of improvements in the health of Australians. ... As a result ... there is insufficient control of costs; and there are inefficiencies between levels of government. ... The Council agreed that there is an urgent need to shift the focus of health and community services from programmes to people, through a partnership between the Commonwealth and the States.

All health and related community services, including the medical benefits scheme and pharmaceutical benefits scheme, would be under the umbrella of a single multilateral agreement, with bilateral agreements covering funding and outcome measures. Gone was the hankering after 'clean lines' divisions of functions:

> Such reforms would involve sharing responsibility ... across health and related community services by both levels of government rather than a separation of responsibilities. This would entail significant changes to the current delineation of roles, and a greatly increased separation between funders, purchasers and providers.
>
> A significant realignment of roles and responsibilities could flow from this approach, involving both levels of government in jointly setting objectives, priorities and performance standards, and funding the system; with the Commonwealth taking a leadership role in relation to public health standards and health research and the States primarily responsible for managing and coordinating the provision of services and for maintaining direct relationships with most providers. [COAG communiqué, April 1996]

DUPLICATION AND OVERLAP

A 'nationally consistent information and payments system' would be explored as an option; and a range of options for interim reform would be followed up, including converting current special-purpose payments into identified grants within the stream of general-purpose payments, with 'bilateral agreements defining broad objectives and specifying access and measures of output and outcome for broad functional areas' across groups of related programs. This is an ambitious blueprint and, at the time of writing, it remains little more than something to which heads of government have committed themselves in principle, and around which officials have begun to plan and draft proposals for service reorganisation. The model may be clear in outline, but there is uncertainty on a number of matters and room for sharp conflict. The precise definition of the 'streams of care' contains many unresolved complexities, as do the pricing principles. The idea of a 'national payments agency', disbursing a Commonwealth–state pool of funds to be drawn on by the purchasers of items of service, would bring to the surface fundamental jurisdictional issues.

Similar issues arise in connection with an agreement on reforms to roles and responsibilities in the housing sector, also adopted in principle at the 1996 COAG meeting. These followed a similar model, with the bulk of Commonwealth funds in future to be allocated through rental assistance to individuals ('housing vouchers') rather than as direct grants to the states for public housing construction and rental subsidy. The public housing authorities would receive their funding through charging market rents to tenants, and would compete with private rental housing providers for access to the Commonwealth funds. The implementation of this agreement bogged down in a dispute over the costs of extending the same level of rental assistance to existing private renters as would need to be given to public housing tenants to prevent them being worse off.

Conclusion

Each of the cases discussed in this chapter, and the broader review undertaken by COAG, are unfinished chapters. The potential for a structural transformation of intergovernmental relations can be highlighted, but the likely outcomes are not clear. In the ANTA case, states were careful to express reservations and to make bottom-line claims about jurisdictional issues, such as the insistence that a state can proceed with its own training programs and schemes alongside the national system, and that the pace and direction of structural reform will be entirely a local decision. The redefinition of intergovernmental roles in terms that mimic the market does not, in itself, lead to constitutional restructuring, but it has become a tool in the hands of those who wish to assert a much stronger role for national policy-making machinery. Most of those who have advanced these models of reform are also committed to collaborative forms of national planning, funding and standards-setting. Many advocate privatised systems of provision, or at least a mix of private, community and public providers, the main requirement being that they are decentralised and not tied closely to any government. As a result, bureaucratic and political empires in the states are certainly under threat. The states are faced with the prospect that their basic, traditional business, that is the provision of public services of various kinds, might be subsumed under a market-mimicking set of jointly mandated purchasing arrangements, and exposed to the whims and uncertainties of consumer demand in a competitive environment of service provision. State governments may play a major role as purchasers, that is in writing contracts and monitoring them, but many of their policy roles in relation to levels and standards of service and regulatory frameworks would become part of a jointly managed national system. In such a model, the question of how these systems of management would distribute powers between governments restates the underlying federal question, and its answer must lie in the political forces that shape them in the long run.

CHAPTER 8

The Future of Collaborative Federalism

This book has been concerned with the way in which federal arrangements were reshaped by the efforts of state and Commonwealth governments to implement an economic reform agenda. The initiative launched by Bob Hawke in 1990 carried with it the high hopes of advocates of fundamental federal reform. Federalism was accused of many faults, most of all of retarding economic modernisation. Some federal critics eager to see progress on an agenda of microeconomic reform revived arguments about the frustrations of federalism, bewailing the costs of parochialism. But as, outlined in Chapter 2, there was deep disagreement among the protagonists in federal politics about the priorities for federal reform. Thus, some critics highlighted the costs of centralism rather than parochialism, particularly the centralisation of fiscal power. Looking back, we cannot say federalism was reshaped during this period according to any clearly articulated model set down at the outset. However, if the prospect of wholesale reform became bogged down in familiar federal debates and in struggles over turf, the movement gathered pace towards new federal arrangements through less dramatic means. If answers to some of the big questions could not be found, agreement was reached on many smaller ones through a spate of institution-building in and around the Special Premiers' Conferences and the Council of Australian Governments. Attention moved swiftly from seeing federalism as the problem, to seeing federal institutions as part of the solution. The result was a set of institutions and practices that I have labelled collaborative federalism.

The Reform Record

How well did these institutions cope with the microeconomic reform agenda? Did federalism 'pass the test'? Any answer to this question that

182 COLLABORATIVE FEDERALISM

reiterated the customary complaints about federalism itself—delay, lowest-common-denominator outcomes, the abuse of the power to obstruct, and so on—and contrasted the outcomes of this process with some imaginary ideal of swift, rational comprehensive planning and decision-making, would miss the point. Any political process that produces policy answers to complex, highly contested problems will be slow, will require compromises, and will provide opportunities for obstruction. That is, it will produce outcomes that dissatisfy nearly everyone in some measure. A federal process introduces extra complexities to the political process and further limits the possibility of any one view prevailing over others. That is one of federalism's justifications.

Perhaps a more constructive question would ask whether the institutional changes that accompanied SPC and COAG succeeded in their own terms in advancing the agenda of economic reform. The answer would be yes. Issues that might otherwise have languished for lack of interest or commitment were provided with a new federal forum, and a set of processes were put in place that provided incentives for the parties to make progress. The institutionalisation of cooperative forms was important. When adversarial politics took over the agenda, the existence of new collaborative institutions provided a parallel set of processes operating under different working rules, where discussion and negotiations could proceed or be revived. However, these institutions coexisted uneasily with existing elements of the federal system, adding to rather than reducing complexity, and creating new or heightened tensions as well as providing ways of smoothing the path to agreement. The result was not at all like the neat and tidy solutions that some of the initial reformers envisaged.

This assessment probably provides cold comfort to many advocates of economic modernisation, who envisaged a concerted national effort involving all governments working speedily towards common goals and uniform outcomes. One response to them might be to focus on some of the positive federal aspects of the new arrangements. Where national, collaboratively determined reform schemes have been agreed to, we see the federal factor still at play, perhaps to the national benefit. For example in many agreements, clauses were written so as to permit different approaches and local variations in implementation. In other cases, state governments dragged their feet and insisted on being different regardless of an agreement, arguing for the right to proceed at their own pace or in their own way. State governments objected to uniform, national schemes in many cases not because they disagreed in principle with a program, but because they believed they had a better understanding of the principles and a better way of implementing them. They may often have been right, given the local circumstances. For

THE FUTURE OF COLLABORATIVE FEDERALISM   183

example, the Kennett government in Victoria firmly believed it was at the forefront of microeconomic reform. Attempts to make it conform with a national scheme for an open-access electricity supply and distribution market, or a national system of regulation for the price of water, were treated not just with hostility but with scorn. Meanwhile, the Court government in Western Australia (for example) worked through its own agenda of reform in transport services and regulation, or vocational education and training, and saw no particular reason why it should be diverted from that agenda by demands to conform with another set of priorities, or with a timetable set by a national body.

In sum, intertwined with a growing area of collaborative policy-making was an evolving patchwork of state and Commonwealth reform initiatives and responses. Collaborative policy-making occurred in discrete areas, but economic reform also proceeded by unilateral action of separate governments. Commonwealth and state leaders continued to pursue their own political and policy agendas. Some state governments moved faster than others, and faster than the Commonwealth, on microeconomic reform. The Commonwealth pursued its own policies in industrial relations, labour-market training and so on. Differences in pace and enthusiasm reflected community divisions over the costs and benefits of many of these reforms, while states had divergent interests over economic reform strategy as a result of markedly different economic bases and prospects. Thus, from the standpoint of an economic reform agenda, SPC and COAG were valuable and useful additions to existing patterns of federal policy-making, which otherwise continued much as before.

A New Federal Departure?

Perhaps we are jumping the gun. What was new about this New Federalism? None of the institutional developments we have described in this book was without its precedent in Australia's federal experience. The very style of problem-solving itself, entailing the design of new forms of executive cooperation and program coordination, was a familiar one. Australian governments turned to old habits—building new bureaus and designing new machinery—when faced with new policy challenges. They called on a wealth of experience in inter-governmental cooperation, added some new embellishments to some familiar machinery, and put it to new uses. For example, ministerial councils where decisions were made other than by unanimity were not new (although they were rare); neither were jointly mandated executive agencies and schemes for uniform legislation entirely novel. Some of the adaptations were strange-looking new beasts, but they were mutations from existing stock rather than entirely new creations.

184 COLLABORATIVE FEDERALISM

COAG itself was perhaps the least novel of the innovations. Albeit a symbol of the importance of a contemporary agenda of cooperative reform, it entailed no sharp break with traditional ways of conducting the business of intergovernmental high politics. It brought into focus an existing set of resources and practices, and allowed them to develop to a new level. The central agency club was provided with new opportunities to assert its interests and impose its style, and in this way SPC and COAG became more than usually efficient instruments for processing intergovernmental joint decision-making. Without the constant grind of financial friction to dominate the agenda or the tenor of its business, the achievements were considerable. At the same time, COAG showed all the signs of the conventional pattern of adversarial politics between state and Commonwealth leaders. When it suited them, leaders used COAG as a forum for political theatre to make political points for home consumption.

However, although the bits and pieces of this cooperative machinery were quite familiar, it has been suggested at various points in this book that the sum of these parts represented the potential for a new departure. We have styled this 'collaborative federalism'. The consistent application of collaborative rather than arm's-length solutions to problems of cooperative joint action could, it was suggested, usher in a fundamental change to the federal system. The cumulative effect might be unintentional, but were states and the Commonwealth to find themselves locked in to more and more jointly agreed courses of action via collaborative institutional arrangements, traditional forms of arm's-length federalism in Australia could wither away. This process would involve a further reduction in the states' claims to be distinctive, autonomous political units.

Creeping centralisation followed by a withering away of the states has been the prediction of most observers of institutional change in the federal system since 1901. So far, the results have confounded most of their predictions. It is undeniable that the uniform trend for most of the twentieth century has been towards the enlargement of the capacity of the Commonwealth to act on what it defines as a national agenda, and that the states have been in large degree on the defensive in developing and asserting their own, distinct jurisdictions. But this enlarged capacity of the Commonwealth, through its lion's share of total revenue and through generous interpretations by the High Court of the Commonwealth's constitutional powers, has not necessarily been at the direct expense of the states. The relative power of state and Commonwealth is not always a zero-sum game. State capacities have also enlarged in some areas where the Commonwealth has not been strong or willing, and in others where the Commonwealth has also been active. In the latter,

THE FUTURE OF COLLABORATIVE FEDERALISM   185

overlap has sometimes brought cooperation that has further enhanced each government's powers and capacities, through dividing the field in new ways and through taking advantage of mutual interdependencies. Such outcomes have often emerged where friction and lack of co-operation have become self-defeating and mutually debilitating, leading to various sorts of cooperative institutions. SPC and COAG are part of that tradition of mutual adjustment of the respective and changing powers of state and Commonwealth governments, perhaps with the effect of enlarging the capacity of each.

Collaboration with the Commonwealth: Centralism in New Clothes?

We must take seriously the kind of objection to collaboration expressed by one Western Australian official:

> COAG succeeds in reaching outcomes where the Commonwealth wants the cooperation of the states for its purposes, but not vice versa. If the Commonwealth is not prepared to talk about an issue, it won't get anywhere. The Commonwealth should acknowledge that when we cooperate, it means we are being compliant—they should recognise this, but not exploit it. [personal communication]

The example mentioned to confirm this view was the states' experience with fiscal reform, and the Commonwealth's unwillingness to consider seriously the states' agenda. In contrast, the states' agreement to the National Competition Policy was an acknowledgement on their part that economic reform affected the national interest, even though some states (Western Australia prominent among them) challenged some of the presumptions behind the need for a national, uniform approach. As argued above, SPC and COAG did not achieve fundamental federal reform of the kind that would be required to correct vertical fiscal imbalance, because the presumption that there was some common ground on that agenda was false. What it did achieve was to bring together under a national umbrella a number of issues on which there was at least sufficient common ground to reach partial agreement. It is not surprising that most of these issues (albeit not all) were of the Commonwealth's making, because the Commonwealth by and large has the greatest political incentive to raise such matters and pursue solutions to them. Issues like obstacles to interstate transport, barriers to the free flow of goods and services, or deficiencies in the system of vocational training that are claimed to affect international competitiveness are first and foremost of 'national', and hence Commonwealth, interest.

186   COLLABORATIVE FEDERALISM

Collaborative decision-making is not, however, simply a matter of centralisation. In replacing unanimity with a majority aggregation rule in matters of joint action, it submerges individual state identities, not beneath a Commonwealth identity, but beneath one that is the outcome of negotiation and discussion among all parties. In some cases, it reduces the capacity of the Commonwealth to act unilaterally across all jurisdictions. It can be argued that this is the principal innovation in the spread of collaborative forms of decision-making. The states gain a deliberative vote in national policy-making and, depending on the voting formula for particular decisions, can impose this view on any parties that dissent, including the Commonwealth.

The Persistence of Arm's-length Federalism

The cleavage of Commonwealth versus states (either individually or collectively) remained the most persistent and obvious one in Australian federal politics throughout the life of SPC and COAG. Collaborative institutions did little if anything to transform such underlying cleavages or, for that matter, many other enduring characteristics of federal politics. In observing negotiations and decisions on COAG and on other institutions of collaboration, the traditional patterns of conflict were evident: partisanship; small versus large states; specific interstate rivalries depending on the nature of the issue; and individual states, groups of states, or often all states, versus the Commonwealth. Adversarial, arm's-length politics remained much in evidence. So too did familiar patterns of political and bureaucratic opportunism that accompanied the interdependencies that sat side by side with these political cleavages—shifting costs, substituting and diverting funds, fudging the figures and so on.

In other words, the new collaborative institutions were nested in others that operated by very different rules and principles. The disharmonious coexistence of institutions is nothing new in Australia's federal system. Campbell Sharman (1990) highlighted the incoherence of federalism and Westminster-style parliamentary majoritarianism. Some of this incoherence looks less problematic if we focus attention on the real-world character of modern executive federalism, rather than the historical or philosophical roots of either federal theory or the Westminster model (Painter 1996). Federal checks and balances and the benefits of dual government come about in Australia as much through the adversarial relations of strong executives as through constitutionalised checks on the institutions of limited government, such as the separation of powers. To reiterate a point made in Chapter 1 of this book, just as significant, but less remarked on in discussions of

THE FUTURE OF COLLABORATIVE FEDERALISM   187

Australia's federal model, are the difficulties of reconciling the overlap of functional responsibilities with the division of sovereignty into two distinct parts with equal claims on the use of the public power (within the limits of the Constitution). Parliamentary sovereignty and executive prerogative as principles apply equally in state and Commonwealth governments, but these governments are constrained to cooperate because they share functions. Both their essential separateness and their ineluctable interdependency are asserted simultaneously.

Not surprisingly, then, cooperation and adversarial thrust and riposte have always coexisted. Recent emphasis on collaborative forms of cooperation has merely highlighted this, because such forms require attention to institutionalised authority-sharing, such as majority decision-making, the surrender of legislative freedom to amend agreed uniform legislation, and agreement on external enforcement mechanisms to punish recalcitrant or defecting parties. Collaborative institutions place fetters on parliamentary sovereignty and executive prerogative. However, our investigation of the establishment and operations of these forms of joint decision-making has tended to highlight their limits. Even where collaborative institutions were clearly specified and seemingly in operation, in several cases we noted their subversion or circumvention. Traditional forms of more unfettered cooperation and conflict reasserted themselves. The National Road Transport Agreement was written as a tightly constrained set of collaborative institutions, but worked in a much looser form. In the face of obstacles presented by reluctant governments, obstructive parliaments, inconvenient changes of government and so on, those charged with seeking agreement on uniform measures looked to other strategies of cooperation. The National Road Transport Commission was a new political force set down in an existing federal system, using the new rules of the game when it could do so to advantage, but having to learn their limits. The new institutions did not supplant more deep-rooted sets of constitutional rules and conventions, but became one among many factors in the political process.

The durability of pre-existing forms of conflict and coordination was highlighted as well by the case of National Competition Policy. The final piece of the jigsaw in creating a national agreement was the decision by the Commonwealth to open the financial coffers and meet some of the demands of the states for access to the promised fiscal dividend. At the same time, the Commonwealth could not pass up the opportunity to impose conditions. Not only payment of the competition dividend, but also access to growth funds in the general revenue-sharing arrangements, were made conditional upon passing milestones in microeconomic reform. These agreements were a sign of the extent to which interlocking, collaborative forms of joint action had become a part of the landscape, and even absorbed as familiar features. Performance on a series of collective agreements about energy, transport and regulatory reform were tied together with an external enforcement mechanism. At the same time, the agreement was a finely balanced financial deal, in which the states locked the Commonwealth into a commitment to growth funds and specific payments, while the Commonwealth in turn demanded some leverage via these funds over the states' implementation of economic reform. Questions were left hanging: how firm was the commitment (for example, if there were a change of government)? In 1996 a new Commonwealth government managed to get all but one of the states to agree to a 'postponement' of the growth funds as part of a contribution to reducing the Commonwealth deficit. Of course, whether or not the states agreed with the measure was beside the point. How high were the hurdles of compliance, and was the threat of withholding competition payments a plausible one? Doubts exist about what actually constitutes non-compliance with the implementation of various agreements (Harman and Harman 1996). Not uncharacteristically, reporting on compliance will be the task of a non-political entity, the National Competition Council, but any subsequent decisions about funds will remain with the Commonwealth.

In sum, the answers to the questions just posed will unfold as part of the politics of intergovernmental relations. The terms and conditions of intergovernmental agreements are an important constraint to be considered in a government's political strategy, but these agreements are far removed from being legally binding documents. On the other hand, the institutions that flow from them do have the potential to exert a strong influence. It was pointed out in Chapter 6 that the National Road Transport Commission achieved considerable movement in road transport reform, even if it did not do so in the way set out in the letter of the agreement, and even if the progress remained slow and uneven.

A similar conclusion can be drawn concerning the potential for reforms to service delivery roles and responsibilities. The states were potentially surrendering territory to new national regulatory bodies, and agreeing to embark on a reform process that was driven by a national agenda not entirely in their control. Industry representatives and the Commonwealth played significant roles in shaping reforms within the terms of the ANTA agreement. The ministerial council during 1996 and 1997 emerged as the centre of executive action and initiative, driven by a reform strategy that was the joint creation of ANTA and the Commonwealth minister. Again, though, the kinds of agreement reached, particularly in the fine print, expressed in equal measure the commitment to collective action on an agreed agenda and the

THE FUTURE OF COLLABORATIVE FEDERALISM   189

'sovereign' right of the states and territories to exercise discretion. Room was left for a state to proceed at a different pace to others and for the details of implementation to be decided locally. Again, the collaborative element in policy and implementation was patched on to an existing set of political and administrative arrangements that are not in themselves immediately compromised. However, the potential exists in the user-choice process for new forces to be let loose that will transform the state systems from within, but in a manner that is being determined by the national bodies (Painter 1997).

Collaboration and Competition: A New Federal Tension

In contrast to the collaborative model of cooperative federalism, an alternative vision, that of competitive federalism, has been advocated by the states. These models are not in all respects mutually exclusive, neither do they represent the only options. As pointed out in Chapter 2, the states' rhetoric of competitive federalism hides some inconsistencies and tensions. It is not clear always what is the object of 'competition' (whether it is more diversity, or one best-practice model); who is competing with whom (state versus state, or states versus Commonwealth, or states and/or Commonwealth versus external competitors); and which 'restraints on trade' are good and bad (for example, whether fiscal equalisation might be 'anti-competitive').

These problems aside, the basic flaw in the states' model of competitive federalism is that it requires wholesale reform. Fiscal reform and the restructuring of roles and responsibilities along the lines advocated by the states would entail a major upheaval. In particular, they require the Commonwealth to surrender some discretion over the distribution of revenue, and both Commonwealth and state governments to vacate fields of jurisdiction. In the context of historical trends and contemporary tendencies, the states' agenda is a radical one and for that reason alone is unlikely to be realised. Collaborative institutions, on the other hand, have emerged as natural extensions of or amendments to existing institutional forms in the course of resolving substantive problems of joint action. The pattern is a familiar one in the history of Australian federalism: constitutional reform fails, but constitutional evolution proceeds apace.

At the same time, the emergent model of collaborative federalism is battling against entrenched conventions that assert unfettered forms of federal conflict, competition and cooperation. The outcomes are not shaped so much by interpretations or applications of competing models, but by the politics of intergovernmental relations that are being fought out in various arenas, where collaborative forms may or may not emerge as possible solutions to the limits of competition and the need for cooperation. Here, the shape and form of institutional developments will vary according to a host of ever-changing political factors. The most dramatic case of intergovernmental cooperation for many years, the introduction of uniform gun laws in 1996, was introduced without recourse to any new collaborative institutions. To some extent, the relegation of COAG in this case to the role of bystander was a matter of personal style and preference. COAG was not John Howard's creation, and he preferred to leave most matters of policy detail to portfolio ministers. More generally, ministerial councils rose to greater prominence, and COAG lost standing, during 1996 and 1997. At the same time, as in the case of the ANTA ministerial council, developments in some sectors were proceeding through a set of collaborative institutions inherited from the COAG legacy.

The decision to employ one strategy rather than another, or one piece of machinery in preference to another, is a political one. Prime ministers and premiers will continue to choose adversarial or co-operative approaches for political reasons, and will adopt unfettered or collaborative styles of cooperation according to their judgement about political advantage at the time. However, such choices are always within a range of what is possible and acceptable, that is, they are strongly influenced by an institutional inheritance. In the period after 1990, a set of institutional arrangements was established that expanded this range. Tensions between collaborative and arm's-length federalism have not been resolved, but the inheritance of federal institutions that future decision-makers can draw on now includes a wide range of collaborative arrangements. Whether or not they come to occupy a bigger or even dominant place in Australia's federal system will be determined by the same pragmatic, evolutionary processes of adaptation that have shaped most of the other transformations in Australia's federal history.

References

Advisory Council for Inter-government Relations (ACIR) (1984). *Register of Commonwealth–State Co-operative Arrangements.* Hobart: ACIR.

——(1986a). *Compendium of Intergovernmental Agreements.* Hobart: ACIR.

——(1986b). *Operational Procedures of Inter-jurisdictional Ministerial Councils.* Information paper No. 13. Hobart: ACIR.

Alford, John, and Deirdre O'Neill (eds) (1994). *The Contract State: Public Management and the Kennett Government.* Geelong: Centre for Applied Social Research, Deakin University.

Allen Consulting Group (1994). *Successful Reform. Report to the Australian National Training Authority.* Melbourne: Allen Consulting Group.

Auditor-General (1988). *Efficiency Audit Report on the Home and Community Care Program.* Canberra: AGPS.

——(1989). *Efficiency Audit Report, Department of Transport and Communications: Commonwealth Road Funding Programs: The National Highway.* Canberra: AGPS.

——(1996). *The Administration of the Australian National Training Authority, Performance Audit Report No. 2, 1996–7.* Canberra: AGPS.

Australian Education Council Review Committee (1991). *Young People's Participation in Post-Compulsory Education and Training.* Canberra: AGPS.

Australian National Training Authority (ANTA) (1997a). *The Report of the ANTA Board on the Implementation of New Apprenticeships.* http://www.anta.gov.au/pubs/minco.html

——(1997b). 'Landmark Ministerial Council Meeting.' *Australian Training,* June 1997.

Axelrod, R. (1984). *The Evolution of Cooperation.* New York: Basic Books.

Bannon, J. C. (1987). 'Overcoming the Unintended Consequences of Federation.' *Australian Journal of Public Administration,* 46(1), 1–9.

——(1992). 'Cooperative Federalism. Good Policy and Good Government.' *Discussion Paper No. 16.* Canberra: Federalism Research Centre, Australian National University.

Barrie, Doreen (1992), 'Environmental Protection in Federal States: Inter-jurisdictional Cooperation in Canada and Australia.' *Discussion Paper No. 18.* Canberra: Federalism Research Centre, Australian National University.

192   REFERENCES

Beetham, Richard M. (1993). *A Review of the Structure, Efficiency and Effectiveness of the Financial Institutions Scheme.* Canberra: Access Economics.

Bland, F. A. (1935). 'Inventing Constitutional Machinery: A Study of Dr. Earle Page's Proposal for National Councils.' *Australian Quarterly,* 9 (December), 10–21.

Bosch, Henry (1990). *The Workings of a Watchdog.* Melbourne: William Heinemann.

Breton, Albert (1985). 'Supplementary Statement'. In Royal Commission on the Economic Union and Development Prospects for Canada, *Report, Volume Three.* Ottawa: Supply and Services Canada, 485–526.

——(1996). *Competitive Governments: An Economic Theory of Politics and Public Finance.* Cambridge: Cambridge University Press.

Bryce, J. (1888). *The American Commonwealth.* London: Macmillan.

Bureau of Industry Economics (BIE) (1995). *Issues in Infrastructure Pricing.* Research Report No. 69. Canberra: AGPS.

Business Council of Australia (BCA) (1991). *Government in Australia in the 1990s: A Business Perspective.* Melbourne: Business Council of Australia.

Butlin, N. G., A. Barnard and J. J. Pincus (1982). *Government and Capitalism.* Sydney: Allen & Unwin.

Carroll, John (ed.) (1993). *Rationalisation of Occupations and Markets.* Brisbane: Royal Australian Institute of Public Administration, Queensland Branch.

Carroll, Peter (1995). 'Federalism, Microeconomic Reform and the Industry Commission.' In Carroll and Painter (eds).

——and Martin Painter (eds) (1995). *Microeconomic Reform and Federalism.* Canberra: Federalism Research Centre, Australian National University.

CCH Corporation Law Editors (1991). *Australian Corporations Law Guide.* North Ryde, NSW: CCH Australia.

Chapman, Ralph (1990). 'Australian Public Policy, Federalism and Intergovernmental Relations: The Federal Factor.' *Publius: The Journal of Federalism,* 20 (Fall), 69–84.

Charles, Christine (1995). 'COAG and Competition Policy—A South Australian Perspective.' In Carroll and Painter (eds).

Churchman, Susan (1996). 'NCP—Its Evolution and Implementation: A Study in Intergovernmental Relations.' *Australian Journal of Public Administration,* 55(2), 97–9.

Clark, Sandford D. (1983). 'Inter-Governmental Quangos: The River Murray Commission.' *Australian Journal of Public Administration,* 42(1), 154–72.

Commonwealth–State Overarching Group on Land Transport (OAG) (1991). *Report on Road Transport Reform.*

Coper, Michael (1989). 'The Second Coming of the Fourth Arm: The Present Role and Future Potential of the Inter-State Commission.' Canberra: Centre for Research on Federal Financial Relations, Australian National University.

Council of Australian Governments (COAG) (1993). *Review of Ministerial Councils.*

——Task Force on Health and Community Services (1995). *Health and Community Services: Meeting People's Needs Better—A Discussion Paper.*

Crommelin, Michael (1986). *Federal–Provincial Cooperation on Natural Resources: A Comparative Discussion of Problems and Solutions.* Papers on Federalism No. 5. Intergovernmental Relations in Victoria Program. Melbourne: Law School, University of Melbourne.

Davis, Glynn (1995). *A Government of Routines: Executive Coordination in an Australian State.* Melbourne: Macmillan.

REFERENCES

——(1997). 'Toward a Hollow State? Managerialism and its Critics.' In Mark Considine and Martin Painter (eds), *Managerialism and its Critics.* Melbourne: Melbourne University Press.

Davis, S. Rufus (1995). *Theory and Reality: Federal Ideas in Australia, England and Europe.* St Lucia: University of Queensland Press.

Department of Prime Minister and Cabinet (DPMC) (1994). *Commonwealth–State Ministerial Councils: A Compendium.* Canberra: Commonwealth–State Relations Secretariat.

Dollery, Brian, and Andrew Worthington (1995). 'Federal Expenditure and Fiscal Illusion: A Test of the Flypaper Hypothesis in Australia.' *Publius: The Journal of Federalism,* 25(1), 23–34.

Downs, Anthony (1967). *Inside Bureaucracy.* Boston: Little Brown.

Economic Planning Advisory Council (EPAC) (1995). Private Infrastructure Task Force. *Interim Report.* Canberra: AGPS.

Edwards, Meredith, and Alan Henderson (1995). 'COAG: A Vehicle for Reform.' In Carroll and Painter (eds).

Employment and Skills Formation Council (1992). *The Australian Vocational Certificate Training System.* Canberra: AGPS.

Ernst & Young (1996). *Commonwealth–State Disability Agreement Evaluation. The Implementation Study.* Canberra: AGPS.

Fitzgerald Report, *see* Allen Consulting Group (1994).

Fletcher, Christine, and Cliff Walsh (1992). 'Reform of Intergovernmental Relations in Australia: The Politics of Federalism and the Non-politics of Managerialism.' *Public Administration,* 70 (Winter), 591–616.

Forsyth, Peter (1995). 'Microeconomic Reform in a Federal System: Constraints and Incentives.' In Carroll and Painter (eds).

Galligan, Brian (ed.) (1989). *Australian Federalism.* Melbourne: Longman Cheshire.

——(1995). *A Federal Republic: Australia's Constitutional System of Government.* Cambridge: Cambridge University Press.

——, Owen Hughes and Cliff Walsh (1991). 'Perspectives and Issues.' In Galligan, Hughes and Walsh (eds), *Intergovernmental Relations and Public Policy.* Sydney: Allen & Unwin.

Goss, Wayne (1995). 'Restoring the Balance: The Future of the Australian Federation.' Canberra: Federalism Research Centre, Australian National University.

Greiner, Nick (1990). 'Physician Heal Thyself: Microeconomic Reform of Australian Government.' Address to the National Press Club, 25 July.

Grogan, F. O. (1958). 'The Australian Agricultural Council.' *Public Administration, (Sydney),* 17(1), 1–21.

Halligan, John, and John Power (1992). *Political Management in the 1990s.* Melbourne: Oxford University Press.

Harman, E. (1996). 'The National Competition Policy: A Study of the Policy Process and Network.' *Australian Journal of Political Science,* 31(2), 205–24.

——and F. Harman (1996). 'The Potential for Local Diversity in Implementation of the National Competition Policy.' *Australian Journal of Public Administration,* 55(2), 12–25.

Haward, Marcus (1991). 'The Offshore.' In Brian Galligan, Owen Hughes and Cliff Walsh (eds), *Intergovernmental Relations and Public Policy.* Sydney: Allen & Unwin.

Healey, Judith (1988). 'Packaging the Human Services.' *Australian Journal of Public Administration,* 47(4), 321–31.

194 REFERENCES

Henderson, David (1995). 'The Revival of Economic Liberalism: Australia in an International Perspective.' *Australian Economic Review*, 58 (1st Quarter): 59–85.

Hendy, Peter (1996). 'Intergovernmental Relations: Ensuring Informed Cooperation in Strategic Policy Development.' *Australian Journal of Public Administration*, 55(1), 111–17.

Hilmer, Fred (1993). *National Competition Policy. Report by the Independent Committee of Inquiry* (Hilmer Report). Canberra: AGPS.

Howard, C., C. A. Saunders and B. M. L. Crommelin (eds) (1982). *The Co-operative Companies and Securities Scheme.* Information Paper No. 4, Intergovernmental Relations in Victoria Program. Melbourne: Law School, University of Melbourne.

Hurlstone, John (1995). 'Road Transport Law Reform.' Address to the Institute of Transport Studies, 2 May. Sydney: University of Sydney Graduate School of Business.

Industry Commission (1993). *Public Housing*, vol. 1. Canberra: AGPS.

——(1994). *Annual Report 1993–4.* Canberra: AGPS.

——(1995). *The Growth and Revenue Implications of Hilmer and Related Reforms: A Report by the Industry Commission to the Council of Australian Governments.* Canberra: Industry Commission.

——(1996). *State, Territory and Local Government Assistance to Industry. Draft Report.* Canberra: Industry Commission.

Interstate Commission (ISC) (1988). *Harmonisation of Road Vehicle Regulation in Australia.* 2 vols. Canberra: AGPS.

——(1990). *Road Use Charges and Vehicle Registration: A National Scheme.* Canberra: AGPS.

Joint Committee on Public Accounts, *see* Commonwealth of the Parliament of Australia.

Kasper, Wolfgang (1993). 'Making Federalism Flourish.' In *Upholding the Australian Constitution: Proceedings of the Samuel Griffith Society, Second Conference, July 1993.* Melbourne: Samuel Griffith Society.

Kellow, Aynsley (1992). *Saline Solutions: Policy Dynamics in the Murray–Darling Basin.* Deakin Series in Public Policy and Administration No. 2. Geelong: Deakin University.

——(1995). 'Federalism and Environmental Policy Reform: Past, Present and Future.' In Carroll and Painter (eds).

Kelly, Paul (1992). *The End of Certainty.* Sydney: Allen & Unwin.

Kincaid, John (1991). 'The Competitive Challenge to Cooperative Federalism: A Theory of Federal Democracy'. In Daphne A. Kenyon and John Kincaid (eds), *Competition Among States and Local Governments: Efficiency and Equity in American Federalism.* Washington, DC: The Urban Institute.

Laffin, Martin, and Martin Painter (eds) (1995). *Reform and Reversal: Lessons from the Coalition Government in New South Wales, 1988–1995.* Melbourne: Macmillan.

Leslie, Peter (1987). *Federal State, National Economy.* Toronto: Toronto University Press.

Liberal Party of Australia (1995). *Pathways to Real Jobs. The Coalition's Employment and Training Policy.*

Lindblom, C. E. (1965). *The Intelligence of Democracy.* New York: Free Press.

Lindsay, Mary (1996). *Can Good Intentions Ensure Good Outcomes? Commonwealth Disability Policy, 1983–1995.* Parliamentary Research Service Background Paper No. 6. Canberra: Department of the Parliamentary Library.

REFERENCES

Lundberg, David (1995). *A Fair Chance: Post-Compulsory Education Structures and Networks.* Canberra: AGPS.

March, James G., and Johan P. Olsen (1989). *Rediscovering Institutions.* New York: Free Press.

Martin, Lisa L. (1994). 'Heterogeneity, Linkage and Commons Problems.' *Journal of Theoretical Politics*, 6(4), 473–93.

Mathews, R. L. (1977). 'Innovations and Developments in Australian Federalism.' *Publius: The Journal of Federalism*, 7(3), 9–19.

Moon, Jeremy (1995). 'Minority Government in the Australian States: From Ersatz Majoritarianism to Minoritarianism?' *Australian Journal of Political Science*, 30, Special Issue, 142–63.

Nahan, Michael (1995). 'Competitive and Uncompetitive Approaches to Competition Policy and Microeconomic Reform.' In Carroll and Painter (1995).

National Association of Australian State Road Authorities (NAASRA) (1975). *A Study of the Economics of Road Vehicle Limits—Summary and Recommendations.* Sydney: NAASRA.

——(1985). *Review of Road Vehicle Limits for Vehicles Using Australian Roads.* Sydney: NAASRA.

National Centre for Vocational Education Research Ltd (NCVER) (1997). *Australian Vocational Education and Training Statistics, 1996.* Brisbane: Australian National Training Authority.

National Commission of Audit (NCOA) (1996). *Report to the Commonwealth Government.* Canberra: AGPS.

National Companies and Securities Commission (NCSC) (1986). *The Parliament and the National Companies and Securities Scheme.* Submission to the Senate Standing Committee on Constitutional and Legal Affairs (Reference: The Role of Parliament and the National Companies Scheme). Canberra: Official Hansard Report, 4–20.

National Crimes Commission (NCC) (1983). *Conference: Record of Proceedings.* Canberra: AGPS.

National Road Transport Commission (NRTC) (1992a). *The Economic Benefits of Improved Road Pricing.* Melbourne: NRTC.

——(1992b). *Discussion Paper on Heavy Vehicle Charges.* Melbourne: NRTC.

——(1996). *Benefits of National Road Transport Regulatory Reforms.* Melbourne: NRTC.

Nelson, Helen (1992). 'Recipes for Uniformity: The Case of Food Standards.' *Australian Journal of Political Science*, 27 (Special Issue), 78–90.

Ostrom, Elinor (1986). 'A Method of Institutional Analysis.' In F. X. Kaufmann *et al.* (eds), *Guidance Control and Evaluation in the Public Sector.* New York: Walter de Gruyter.

——(1990). *Governing the Commons: The Evolution of Institutions of Collective Action.* Cambridge: Cambridge University Press.

Overarching Group, *see* Commonwealth–State Overarching Group on Land Transport.

Painter, Martin (1987). *Steering the Modern State: Changes in Central Coordination in Three Australian State Governments.* Sydney: Sydney University Press.

——(1991a). 'Policy Diversity and Policy Learning in a Federation: The Case of Australian State Betting Laws.' *Publius: The Journal of Federalism*, 21(1), 143–58.

——(1991b). 'Intergovernmental Relations in Canada: An Institutional Analysis.' *Canadian Journal of Political Science*, 24(2), 269–88.

196 REFERENCES

——(1992). '"New Federalism" and Road Transport Regulation.' *Australian Journal of Political Science*, 27, Special Issue, 63–77.

——(1995). 'Microeconomic Reform and the Public Sector.' In Laffin and Painter (eds).

——(1996). 'Federal Theory and Modern Australian Executive Federalism.' In John Halligan and Ian Thynne (eds), *Public Administration Under Scrutiny: Essays in Honour of Roger Wettenhall*. Canberra: Centre for Research in Public Sector Management, University of Canberra, and Institute of Public Administration Australia.

——(1997). 'Reshaping the Public Sector.' In Brian Galligan, Ian McAllister and John Ravenhill (eds), *New Developments in Australian Politics*. Melbourne: Macmillan

—— and Kathy Dempsey (1992). 'Road Grants, Intergovernmental Competition and the Benefits of Duplication.' *Australian Journal of Public Administration*, 52(1), 54–65.

Parliament of the Commonwealth of Australia (1991). *National Road Transport Commission Bill 1991*, including as a *Schedule* the Intergovernmental Agreement signed on 30 July 1991.

——Joint Committee on Public Accounts (1995). *Report 342. The Administration of Specific Purpose Payments*. Canberra: AGPS.

Parkin, Andrew (1991). 'Housing Policy.' In Brian Galligan, Owen Hughes and Cliff Walsh (eds), *Intergovernmental Relations and Public Policy*. Sydney: Allen & Unwin.

Productivity Commission (1996). *Stocktake of Progress in Microeconomic Reform*. Canberra: Productivity Commission.

Saunders, Cheryl (1984). *Accountability and Access in Intergovernmental Affairs: A Legal Perspective*. Intergovernmental Relations in Victoria Program, Papers on Federalism No 2. Melbourne: Law School, University of Melbourne.

——(1990). 'Government Borrowing in Australia.' *Publius: The Journal of Federalism*, 20(4), 35–52

Sawer, Geoffrey (1977). *Federation Under Strain*. Melbourne: Melbourne University Press.

Senate Employment Education and Training References Committee (1995). *Report of the Inquiry into the Australian National Training Authority*. Canberra: Parliament of Australia.

Senate Select Committee on the Functions, Powers and Operation of the Australian Loan Council (1993). *Third Report*. Canberra: Parliament of the Commonwealth of Australia.

Senate Standing Committee on Constitutional and Legal Affairs (SSCCLA) (1986). *The Role of Parliament and the National Companies Scheme*. Canberra: Official Hansard Report.

Sharman, Campbell (1977). *The Premiers' Conference: An Essay in Federal State Interaction*. Canberra: Department of Political Science, Research School of Social Sciences, Australian National University.

——(1985). 'The Commonwealth, the States and Federalism.' In J. Woodward *et al.* (eds), *Government, Politics and Power in Australia*, 3rd edn. Melbourne: Longman Cheshire.

——(1990). 'Australia as a Compound Republic.' *Politics*, 25 (1), 1–5.

——(1991). 'Executive Federalism.' In Brian Galligan, Owen Hughes and Cliff Walsh (eds), *Intergovernmental Relations and Public Policy*. Sydney: Allen & Unwin.

REFERENCES

Simeon, Richard (1972). *Federal–Provincial Diplomacy.* Toronto: University of Toronto Press.

Simmonds, R. L. (1990). 'The Commonwealth Cannot Incorporate under the Corporations Power: *New South Wales v the Commonwealth.*' *Western Australia Law Review,* 20, 641–55.

Spann, R. N. (1979). *Government Administration in Australia.* Sydney: Allen & Unwin.

Spaull, Andrew (1987). *A History of the Australian Education Council, 1936–1986.* Sydney: Allen & Unwin.

Sproule-Jones M. H. (1975). *Public Choice and Federalism in Australia and Canada.* Canberra: Centre for Research on Federal Financial Relations, Australian National University.

Sturgess, Garry (1990). 'The Obstacles to Micro-Economic Reform by the Australian States.' Address to the Australian Institute of Management, Sydney, 23 April.

——(1993). 'An Overview of Mutual Recognition.' in Carroll (1993).

Taplin, John (1993). 'The National Road Transport Commission: A Fresh Attempt to Solve Road Problems.' *Australian Journal of Public Administration,* 52(3), 311–19.

Taylor, R. M. (1996). *Report of the Review of the ANTA Agreement* (Taylor Review). Canberra: AGPS.

Training Cost Review Committee (1990). *Training Costs of Award Restructuring.* Canberra: AGPS.

Walsh, Cliff (1992). 'Federal Reform and the Politics of Vertical Fiscal Imbalance.' *Australian Journal of Political Science,* 27 (Special Issue), 19–38.

—— and Norm Thomson (1993). *Federal Fiscal Arrangements in Australia: Their Potential Impact on Urban Settlement.* Canberra: Federalism Research Centre, Australian National University.

Warden, James (1992). 'Federalism and the Design of the Australian Constitution.' *Australian Journal of Political Science,* 27 (Special Issue), 143–58.

Warhurst, John (1982). *Jobs or Dogma? The Industries Assistance Commission and Australian Politics.* St Lucia: University of Queensland Press.

——(1983). *Central Agencies, Intergovernmental Managers, and Australian Federal–State Relations.* Canberra: Centre for Research on Federal Financial Relations, Australian National University.

——(1987). 'Managing Intergovernmental Relations.' In Herman Bakvis and William N. Chandler (eds), *Federalism and the Role of the State.* Toronto: University of Toronto Press.

Waterhouse, Michael (1994). *Credit Unions and the Financial Institutions Scheme.* Sydney: Credit Union Services Corporation.

Weller, Patrick (1995). *Commonwealth–State Reform Processes; A Policy Management Review.* Canberra: Department of Prime Minister and Cabinet.

Western Australia Legislative Assembly (1994). *Mutual Recognition. A Consideration of the Mutual Recognition Scheme.* Sixth Report of the Standing Committee on Uniform Legislation and Intergovernmental Agreements.

——(1996). *Review of the National Environment Protection Council (Western Australia) Bill 1996.* Fifteenth Report of the Standing Committee on Uniform Legislation and Intergovernmental Agreements.

Wettenhall, Roger (1985). 'Intergovernmental Agencies: Lubricating a Federal System.' *Current Affairs Bulletin,* 61(11), 28–35.

Wheare, K. C. (1946). *Federal Government.* Oxford: Oxford University Press.

REFERENCES

Wiltshire, Ken (1977). 'Introduction.' In *Administrative Federalism: Selected Documents in Australian Intergovernmental Relations.* St Lucia: University of Queensland Press.

——(1990). 'Barriers to Rationalising Commonwealth/State Overlap.' In *Towards a More Cooperative Federalism?* Economic Planning Advisory Council Discussion Paper 90/04. Canberra: AGPS.

Yeatman, Anna (1996). *Getting Real: The Final Report of the Review of the Commonwealth–State Disability Agreement.* Canberra: AGPS.

Zines, Leslie (1989). 'A Legal Perspective.' Galligan (1989).

Index

Aboriginal land rights, 48, 86, 121–2
Aboriginal training programs, 161
accountability, 7, 11, 18, 25, 27, 43, 54, 69, 99, 108, 118, 155, 158, 162, 165, 174
administrative federalism, 22
adoptive legislation, 113, 117, 125, 128–9, 141, 143, 149–50, 152, 156
adversarialism, 32, 104, 118, 121, 132, 154, 172–3, 182, 184, 186–7, 190
Advisory Council for Intergovernmental Relations, 105, 107
agreements, *see* intergovernmental agreements
agriculture, *see* Australian Agricultural Council; Murray–Darling River system
airline policy, 32
application of laws, *see* adoptive federalism
arm's-length federalism, 1–2, 7–9, 12–13, 22, 25–7, 29–31, 60, 62, 121–3, 132, 140, 147, 151–4, 159, 172; ministerial councils, 106, 109, 119; persistence, 23, 55, 184, **186–9**; *see also* competitive federalism
Arnold, Lyn, *see* Bannon–Arnold ALP governments
Asian Language Development Program, 46
Australia New Zealand Food Authority, 126
Australian Agricultural Council, 105–8
Australian Capital Territory, 113, 117, 141, 143
Australian Committee for Training Curriculum, 160, 166
Australian Competition and Consumer Commission, 82, 129
Australian Council of the Federation, 41–4
Australian Council of Social Service, 72

Australian Council of Trade Unions (ACTU), 133–4, 160
Australian Design Rules, 77, 145
Australian Education Council, 105–6, 159
Australian Financial Institutions Commission (AFIC), 125
Australian Labor Party (ALP)
 federal, 16–18, 57, 88, 108; *see also* Hawke ALP government; Keating ALP government; Whitlam ALP government
 New South Wales, 46, 71; *see also* Carr ALP government; Wran–Unsworth ALP governments
 Queensland, *see* Goss ALP government
 South Australia, *see* Bannon–Arnold ALP governments
 Tasmania, 37, 43, 45–6, 63
 Victoria, 33, 37, 43, 45–6, 48, 73, 77, 136
 Western Australia, *see* Lawrence ALP government
Australian Motor Vehicle Certification Board, 77
Australian Nation principle, 42
Australian National, 136, 139
Australian National Training Authority (ANTA), 45, 55, 74, 154, **158–73**, 178–9, 188, 190
Australian Qualifications Framework, 170–1
Australian Securities Commission (ASC), 116–18
Australian Standards Framework, 160
Australian Taxation Office, 115
Australian Transport Advisory Council (ATAC), 77–8, 133, 136, 148

INDEX

Australian Transport Council, 144, 148, 150
Austroads, 145
authority rules, *see* protocols
aviation law, 113

banks, 33
Bannon–Arnold ALP governments (SA), 33, 36–7, 41, 43, 45–9, 63–4, 78, 81, 127, 133–6
Barrie, Doreen, 94
Baxter, Ken, 47
Better Cities Program, 163
Borbidge Nat.–Lib. government (Qld), 46, 58
Bosch, Henry, 115
Bowen, Nigel, 116
Brown–Olsen Lib. governments (SA), 33, 46, 49, 83, 87, 143–4, 162–3, 171
Bryce, J., 12
bureaucrats, *see* officials
Business Council of Australia, 3, 49, 52, 71, 79, 87, 114, 137

Cabinet Offices (states), 67
Cabinets, 41, 65–6, 79–80, 107, 109, 136
Cain–Kirner ALP governments (Vic.), 33, 37, 43, 45–6, 48, 73, 77, 136
Canada, 13, 23–4
Carmichael Report (1992), 159
Carr ALP government (NSW), 30, 33–4, 46, 54, 144, 169–72
centenary of the federation, 68
central agencies, *see* officials
centralism, 2–3, 5, 17, 19–21, 26, 30–1, 37, 44, 65–6, 85, 113–16, 118–19, 181, 184, **185–6**
Chief Ministers, *see* political leaders
child care, 68, 155, 174
coalition governments, *see* non-Labor governments
Codd, Mike, 37, 65, 67, 69, 86
collaborative agreements, *see* intergovernmental agreements
collaborative federalism: case studies, **72–89**; context, **132–3**; definition, 8, **22–4**, 123, 181, 184; future, 2, 9, 31, **181–90**; means of achieving cooperation, **61–91**; offices, **65–7**; people, **63–5**; politics, **32–60**; protocols, **69–70**; theory and practice, **10–31**
commercialisation, 32–4, 39, 130, 133, 139
commissions, *see* inter-jurisdictional agencies

committees: NRTC, 145, 147; SPC/COAG, 37–40, 46–7, **67–9**, 70, 75, 81, 90, 127, 154, 174–6, 178; *see also* officials' committees
Commonwealth Aid to Roads Agreements, 98–9, 101
Commonwealth Employment Service, 156
Commonwealth government, *see* Hawke ALP government; Howard Lib.–NP government; Keating ALP government; Whitlam ALP government
Commonwealth grants, *see* financial relations
Commonwealth–State Disability Agreement (CSDA), **156–8**, 173
Commonwealth–State Housing Agreement, 101
Commonwealth–State Relations Division/Secretariat, 37, 57, 65, 67, 69
Commonwealth–State Steering Committee, 67–9, 78, 80, 83, 174
community services, *see* health and community services
companies and securities law, 22, 87, 108–9, **112–19**
compensation, *see under* corporatisation; National Competition Policy; privatisation; road transport reform
competition policy, *see* National Competition Policy
competitive federalism, 7, 9, 12, **25–31**, 61, 121, 153, **189–90**; *see also* arm's-length federalism
conflict, 1, 61–2, 88, 98, 122, 132, 164, 186–7, 189; road transport reform, **74–81**
Constitution: external affairs power, 45–6, 53, 131; federalism, 3–4, 6–7, 12–13, 16–17, 22–3, 28, 35, 62, 82, 96, 116, 119, 123, 126, 151–2, 186–7; financial relations, 20, 58, 97–8, 103, 184; interstate trade, 76–7, 134; reform, 37, 180, 189
consultants, 158
consultation: industry, 126, 133, 166; intergovernmental, 122–3, 127, 129, 131, 145–6, 155; ministerial councils, 105–7, 109, 169; public, **70–2**
consumer credit, 124, **128–9**
consumer protection, 127
consumers' movement, 71
contracting out, 33, 130
cooperative federalism, *see* collaborative federalism

INDEX

Cooperative National Companies and Securities Scheme (1981–82), 108, 113
coordinate federalism, *see* arm's-length federalism
coordination, 3, 5–6, 10, 16, **20–2**, 31, 35, 61, 66, 69, 76, 92–5, 97, 104, 166–7, 183, 187
Corporate Affairs Commissions, 115–16
corporatisation, 33–5, 38, 111, 130, 134–8, 159–61, 173; compensation, 134–6
Costello, Peter, 53, 55–7
Council of Australian Governments (COAG)
  duplication and overlap, 154, 158, 162, **173–9**
  establishment (May 1992), 43–4, 61, 74, 126, 174
  future, 181–6, 189
  history and character, 1, 4, 7–9, 11, 14, 23, 25–7, 29–32, 40–1
  machinery and processes, 63, 65–72, 74–5, 81–91, 93, 105–6, 109, 120–2, 124, 127–8, 130–2, 140, 148
  meetings, **45–60**; 1st (December 1992), 45–6; 2nd, Melbourne (June 1993), 47–8, 82–3, 86, 121, 174; 3rd, Hobart (February 1994), 49–51, 83–4, 174; 4th, Darwin (August 1994), 51–2, 84–6, 174; 5th (April 1995), 53, 85, 87–8, 178; (November 1995, cancelled), 53; 6th (June 1996), 55–6, 131, 178–9; (November 1996, cancelled), 57; (November 1997), 59
  see also committees
Council of Ministers, *see* Ministerial Councils
Council of the Federation, 41–4
Country Liberal Party (NT), 46, 49, 78–80, 117, 140–3, 149–50
Court Lib. government (WA), 33, 46, 48–50, 53, 57, 84, 86–7, 127–8, 137–9, 143–4, 149–50, 162–3, 165, 169, 172, 183, 185
credit laws, 124, 128–9
crime, 108, 131

Davis, Glynn, 65
Davis, Rufus, 2–3, 6
Dawkins, John, 48–9
decentralisation, 26, 28
decision-making, *see* joint decision-making
decision rules, *see* protocols
Department of Employment, Education and Training (and Youth Affairs) (DEET[YA]), 165–6, 168

Department of Prime Minister and Cabinet, *see* Prime Minister's Department
deregulation, 32–3, 48
Deveson Report (1990), 159
disability services, 15, 155, **156–8**, 173, 175–6
diversity, 26, 29, 54, 126, 128, 171, 182
division of powers, 6, 11–13, 16–18, 23, 27–8, 42, 107, 119, 155, 169, 185

Economic Planning Advisory Council, 12
economic reform, ix, 2–4; Commonwealth–state interdependencies, **35–6**, 37; competition policy, 82; competitive federalism, 25, 29–31; cooperative federalism, 10–11, 15, 18–20, 32–4, 38–9, 42–5, 47, 49, 57, 61, 63, 68, 71, 78–9, 124, 139, 152, 179–83, 187–9
education, 153; *see also* Australian Education Council; higher education; school education; vocational education and training
Edwards, Meredith, 69, 104, 177
efficiency, 14, 27, 29, 32, 42, 44, 61, 134–5, 154, 163–4, 167–8, 172
electricity supply, 39–40, 43–4, 46–7, 52, 68, 72, 82–3, 88, 130, 132, 183
employment, *see* labour market programs
Employment and Skills Formation Council (Carmichael Report, 1992), 159
energy policy, 49, 188; *see also* electricity supply; gas; Joint Coal Board
environmental policy, 37–9, 59, 68, 122, **127–8**, 131
European Community, 3
Evans, Gareth, 108–9
executive action, 92, 102–3, 107, 109, 111, 119, 128, 148, 152
executive federalism, 7, 25, 93, 183, 186–8
external relations power, 45–6, 53, 131

Fahey Lib.–NP government (NSW), 33, 45–7, 49–50, 82–3, 144
federal government, *see* Hawke ALP government; Howard Lib.–NP government; Keating ALP government; Whitlam ALP government
Federal Interstate Registration Scheme, 78
federal–state finances, *see* fiscal relations
federal system, 1–4

202 INDEX

federalism, **5–9**; models, *see* arm's-length federalism; collaborative federalism; competitive federalism; executive federalism; parliamentary federalism

Field ALP government (Tas.), 37, 43, 45–6, 63

Financial Agreement (1927), 102–5

financial assistance grants, *see* financial relations

financial institutions, *see* banks; Non-Bank Financial Institutions Scheme

financial markets, 32, 34, 104

Financial Premiers' Conferences, 23, 26, 44, 85, 104; (1990) 36, (1991) 39, 73, (1992) 44, 75, (1993) 48, (1994) 51, (1995) 53, 88, (1996) 55, 57

financial relations: Commonwealth–state institutions, 2, 11, **16–20**, 33, 96–102, 104–6, 123–4, 152–5, 179–81, 184–9; companies and securities law, 117–18; competition policy, 84–5, 87–8, 129–32; disability services, 156–8; fiscal reform, 4, 26–30, 35, 44, 89, 121; rail transport reform, 134–5, 137–8; road transport reform, 76, 140, 142–3; SPC/COAG, 14–15, 27–30, 36–42, 44, 48–59, 178–9, 184; vocational education and training, 74, 158–64, 167–8, 170, 172–4; *see also* growth funds; special-purpose grants; vertical fiscal imbalance

Finn Report (1991), 159

fiscal reform, *see* financial relations

fisheries, 22, 101

Fitzgerald, Vince, 159, 168–9

food standards, 38, 124, **125–6**

forest policy, 46

Forgan Smith, W., 65

funding, *see* fiscal relations

Galligan, Brian, 2, 12

game theory, 5–6, 62–3, 93–5, 111

gas, 46–7, 59, 68, 72, 82, 88, 124, 130, 132

GATT agreements, 97

Germany, 23, 25

Goss ALP government (Qld); companies and securities law, 116–17; competition policy, 50, 86, 88; consumer credit, 128; economic reform, 33–4; federalism, 28–30, 64; financial relations, 105; mutual recognition, 126; non-bank financial institutions, 72–3, 125; rail transport reform, 133, 135–7; road transport reform, 143, 148–9; SPC/COAG, 46, 49–50, 64–5,

72–3, 148; vocational education and training, 75, 162

government business enterprises, *see* public enterprises

government failure, 3, 18

grants, *see* financial relations

Grants Commission, 117

Greiner Lib.–NP government (NSW), 4, 12, 18–19, 21, 27, 33, 35–41, 45–6, 63–4, 71, 73–5, 80

Grogan, F. O., 106

Groom–Rundle Lib. governments (Tas.), 45–6, 56, 82, 87, 126, 143–4, 162

growth funds, 55, 156–7, 161, 163–4, 167, 187–8

gun laws, 1, 56–7, 190

Harman, Elizabeth, 71

harmonisation, *see* uniformity and harmonisation

Hawke ALP government, 1–5, 7, 10, 17, 19–22, 30–2, 35–4, 46, 59, 63–5, 67, 69, 71, 74, 77, 86, 96–7, 114, 120, 181; *see also* New Federalism

health and community services, 14–15, 53, 55–7, 59, 68, 72, 153, 155–8, 173–8

Health Ministers Conference, 125

Henderson, Alan, 69, 104, 177

High Court, 16–17, 35, 57–8, 98, 102, 112, 116, 118, 184; *Mabo* judgement, 126, 133, 166

higher education, 160, 169

Hilmer Committee, 45, 47, 51, 53, 60, 82–5, 88

Home and Community Care Program (HACC), 99, 155, 157, 174–5

hospitals, *see* health and community services

housing policy, 53, 55–7, 59, 70, 72, 153–4, 174, 179

Howard Lib.–NP government, 19, 29, 46, 53–7, 59, 139, 167–9, 190

industrial relations, 12, 37, 45, 49, 121, 131, 134, 167, 169, 183

industry: consultation, 126, 133, 166; vocational education and training, 161, 165–70, 173, 188

Industry Commission, 34, 52, 68, 70, 85–6

Industry Training Advisory Boards, 167

Institute of Directors, 114

institutional analysis, 8–9, **93–7**, 122

institutions
  intergovernmental relations, 6–7, 24, 62–3, 67, **92–120**; *see also* intergovernmental agreements;

INDEX

inter-jurisdictional agencies; joint action; Ministerial Councils; special-purpose payments
collaborative federalism, 1–2, 4, 8, 25, 31–2, 60, 75–6, 80, 89–91, **121–52**, 154, 181–90
interdependencies, 24, **35–6**, 90, 154, 185–7
intergovernmental action, *see* joint action
intergovernmental agreements; community services, 176–9; companies and securities law, 113; competition policy, 81–2, 84–5, 88, 129–31, 185, 188; consumer credit, 128–9; context, **132–3**; environment, 122, 124, **127–8**; food standards, 125–6; institutions, 92–4, 96–9, **100–3**, 105–6, 119, 122–3, 151, 181–2, 187–8; memoranda of understanding, 101, 145; Murray–Darling river system, 109–11; mutual recognition, 126–7; non-bank financial institutions, 42, 125; rail transport reform, 135–9; road transport reform, 39–40, 77–9, 81, 99, 140–3, 145, 148–50, 187; SPC/COAG, 4, 14, 25, 39–40, 42, 61, 67–8, 89–90, 99, **124**, 155; treaties, 131; vocational education and training, 74–5, **158–61**, 166, 172
intergovernmental relations: history and character, 11–12, 24; machinery, *see* institutions
inter-jurisdictional agencies, 92–3, **109–12**, 123, 159, 161, 165, 183, 188–9
international competitiveness, 3, 29
international treaties, *see* treaties
Inter-State Commission, 77–8
Interstate Corporate Affairs Commission, 112
interstate trade barriers, *see* trade barriers
investment, attracting, 28, 30, 34
ITABs, 167

joint action: cooperative federalism, 1, 8, 22–3, 25, 92–3, 95–7, 99, **100–3**, 109, 111, 119, 123–4, 132–3, 183, 186, 189; SPC/COAG, 4, 11, 38, 59–61, 70, 89–90, 120–2; *see also* road transport reform
joint agencies, *see* inter-jurisdictional agencies
Joint Coal Board, 109
joint decision-making, 104, 131, 154, 156, 161, 165, 184, 187

Kasper, Wolfgang, 28

Keating, Mike, 69, 86
Keating ALP government, 2, 17–19, 36–50, 52–3, 55, 69, 74–5, 81–6, 88, 97, 134, 136, 168
Kellow, Aynsley, 64, 94, 111
Kemp, David, 169, 172
Kennett Lib. government (Vic.), 30, 33, 45–7, 49–51, 57, 68, 82–3, 85–8, 147, 149, 162–3, 169, 183
Kerin, John, 41
Kirner, Joan, *see* Cain–Kirner ALP governments

Labor Party, *see* Australian Labor Party
labour laws, *see* industrial relations
labour market programs, 155–7, 159, 161, 165–6, 168–9, 174, 183
land rights, 48, 86, 121–2
Lawrence ALP government (WA), 33, 37, 41, 43, 46, 63–4, 80, 133–9, 142–3
leaders, *see* political leaders
Leaders' Forums, 26, 54, 90; preliminary meeting, Adelaide (November 1991), 26–7, 29, 43, 54, 73; Sydney (July 1994), 51, 54, 84–5; Adelaide (February 1995), 52, 87; Brisbane (November 1995), 54; (1996–97), 54, 57, 58
legal profession reform, 68, 85
Liberal Party, *see* non-Labor governments
Lindblom, C. E., 24
Loan Council, 34–5, 39, 48, 103–5

Mabo judgement, 48, 86, 121–2
majority voting rules, *see* protocols
managerialism, 14–15, 25, 63, 93, 99; *see also* public sector managerial reform
market policies, *see* economic reform; national market
Mathews, R. L., 12
Medicare, 59, 177
memoranda of understanding, 101, 145
microeconomic reform, *see* economic reform
Microeconomic Reform Working Group (COAG), 82–3, 88
Ministerial Councils, 11, 25, 44–6, 50, 66, 68, 70, 74, 80–1, 92–3, **103–9**, 119, 123, 127–8, 155, 183, 190; agriculture, 105–8; attorneys-general, 112; consumer credit, 128–9; education, 105–6, 159; environment, 128; financial institutions, 125; food standards, 126; health and community services, 125, 178; Murray–Darling Basin, 110–11; National Companies

INDEX

Ministerial Councils *cont'd*
and Securities Commission/
Australian Securities Commission,
113–17; police and justice, 56;
restructuring, 148, 162; road
transport, 141–3, 145–50, 188; social
welfare, 156; vocational education and
training, 159–66, 169–71, 173, 175,
190; *see also* Loan Council; Premiers'
Conferences
models of collective action, *see* game
theory
Modern Apprenticeship and Training
System, 169–70
Murray–Darling river system, 94, 100,
109–12
Mutual Recognition Scheme, 1, 40, 42, 44,
55, 71, 124, **126–7**, 148, 171

national agencies, *see* inter-jurisdictional
agencies
National Association of Australian State
Road Authorities (NAASRA), 77
National Commission of Audit (NCOA),
29–30, 54–5, 57, 168–9
National Companies and Securities
Commission (NCSC), 109, **113–16**
national companies legislation, 22, 87,
108–9, **112–19**
National Competition Council, 51, 82, 84,
129, 188
National Competition Policy (NCP), 1,
4, 33, 40, 42, 45, 47, 49–55, 70–2,
81–9, 90, 101, 139, 171, 185, 187–8;
Agreement, 55, 124, **129–31**,
132–3, 144, 151–52; compensation,
83, 85–7; training market, 168,
171
National Crime Authority, 108
National Environment Protection
Authority/Council, 127–8
National Farmers' Federation, 79
National Fiscal Outlook, 49
National Food Authority, 38, 124, **125–6**
National Forest Policy, 46
National Framework for the Recognition
of Training, 160, 169–71
National Grid Management Council, 40,
44
national interest, 26, 42, 61–2, 89, 96, 99,
131, 185
national market, 39, 43–4, 47, 61, 72, 87
National Office of Overseas Skills
Recognition, 159
National Party, *see* non-Labor
governments

National Press Club speeches: Greiner
(1990), 27, 37, 40; Hawke (1990), 3, 5,
20, 37, 40, 63, 67; Keating (1991), 18,
40
National Rail Corporation, 40, 43–4, 47,
124–5, **133–9**, 140
National Road Freight Industry Inquiry
(1983–84), 77
National Road Transport Commission
(NRTC), 1, 39, 44, 80–1, 124–5, 133,
140–50, 151–2, 187–8
National Staff Development Committee,
166
national standards, *see* uniformity
National Task Force on Employment and
Training (NETTFORCE), 165
National Training Authority, *see* Australian
National Training Authority
National Vocational Education and
Training Agreement, 124–5, 154, 161,
166–73
native title, 48, 86, 121–2
NCOA, *see* National Commission of Audit
NCP, *see* National Competition Policy
neo-liberalism, 28–9; *see also* economic
reform; public sector managerial
reform
NETTFORCE (National Task Force on
Employment and Training), 165
New Apprenticeships, 170
New Federalism, 1, 7, 10–12, 31, 40–3, 59,
100, 181, 183; launch (1990), 3–4,
19–20, **36–7**, 64, 120
New South Wales: Cabinet Office, 36, 64,
71; companies and securities law,
115–18; competition policy, 83, 86,
144; Murray–Darling river system, 100,
109–12; mutual recognition scheme,
126; Premier's Department, 38; rail
transport reform, 133–6, 138; road
transport reform, 77–80, 140–4, 146,
149; SPC/COAG process, 4, 19, 21,
35–41, 45–7, 49–50, 54, 63–4, 68, 71,
73–5; Treasury, 86; vocational
education and training, 162, 169–72;
see also Carr ALP government; Fahey
Lib.–NP government; Greiner
Lib.–NP government; Wran–Unsworth
ALP governments
New Zealand, 34, 55, 126
Non-Bank Financial Institutions Scheme,
39, 42, 68, **72–4**, 124, **125**
non-Labor governments: federal, *see*
Howard Lib.–NP government; New
South Wales, *see* Fahey Lib.–NP
government, Greiner Lib.–NP

INDEX

government; Northern Territory, 46, 49, 78–80, 117, 140–3, 149–50; Queensland, 46, 58; South Australia, 33, 36–7, 41, 43, 45–9, 63–4, 78, 81, 127, 133–6; Tasmania, 45–6, 56, 82, 87, 126, 143–4, 162; Victoria, *see* Kennett Lib. government; Western Australia, *see* Court Lib. government

Northern Territory CLP governments, 46, 49, 78–80, 117, 140–3, 149–50

Northern Territory statehood, 68

Office of Road Safety, 77, 145

officials, 8, 11, 22, 27, 38, 40, 55, 62, 64–9, 71–5, 89, 93, 97–8, 107, 115, 154, 165, 167–8, 173, 184–6

officials' committees, 25, 37, 66, **67–9**, 74–5, 78–80, 82–8, 92, 106–8, 110, 115, 124, 126, 133, 145, 155–6, 175

Olsen, John, *see* Brown–Olsen Lib. governments

One Nation (economic statement), 43, 47, 134

operating procedures, *see* protocols

Ostrom, Elinor, 95

Overarching Group on Transport, 78–80, 142

overlap and duplication: intergovernmental relations, 119, 127; New Federalism, 9–11, 20, 22, 26, 29, 31, 37–9, 50–6, 59, 68, 72, 100, **153–80**, 185, 188–9; theory of federalism, 5–7, **12–16**

Parkin, Andrew, 101

parliamentary federalism, 7

Parliaments, 27, 41, 54, 62, 97, 100–3, 110–14, 116–19, 123, 128, 131–2, 137–9, 146, 149, 152, 162, 168, 186–7

party politics, *see* politics

performance criteria and standards, 15, 99, 167, 169, 173

Perron, Marshall, *see* Northern Territory CLP governments

political leaders, 8, 22, 27, 37, 40–3, 62–6, 81, 86, 89, 175, 190; *see also* Leaders' Forums

politics: competition policy, 82; cooperative federalism, 24, 62, 102–5, 107, 109, 118–19, 121, 131–3, 139–40, 150–3, 180–90; SPC/COAG, 32, 36, 38, 40, 45–6, 59–60, 64–5, 67, 69, 89–90; vocational education and training, 74–5, 158, 172

Premiers, *see* political leaders

Premiers' Conferences, 19, 92, 103–4, 106; *see also* Financial Premiers' Conferences; Special Premiers' Conferences

Premiers' Departments, 66–7

Prime Minister's Department, 38, 65, 67–9, 80, 86; Commonwealth–State Relations Division/Secretariat, 37, 57, 65, 67, 69

privatisation, 32–3, 35, 38, 83, 130, 134, 139, 180; compensation, 48, 83

procedures, *see* protocols

protocols: agreements, 119; corporatisation, 137–9; institutional analysis, 95–7, 122–3; inter-jurisdictional agencies, 109–11, 129; ministerial councils, 103–4, 107–9, 113, 115, 117, 125–9, 141–3, 147–8, 161–3, 183; road transport reform, 76, 132–3, 140, 151–2; SPC/COAG, 25, **69–70**, 72–90, 132–3, 140, 182, 186–8; treaties, 131

public consultation, *see* consultation

public enterprises, 32–5, 39, 71, 81–4, 129; *see also* commercialisation; corporatisation; National Competition Policy; privatisation

public sector managerial reform, ix, 4, 9, 18, 33, 63, 71, 129, 158, 177

public servants, *see* officials

public utilities, *see* public enterprises

Pyramid Building Society, 73

quality assurance, 99

Queensland: companies and securities law, 112, 115–17; intergovernmental agreements, 103, 125, 128; Murray–Darling river system, 109–10; Office of the Cabinet, 65; Premier's Department, 79; rail transport reform, 133, 135–7; road transport reform, 140, 143, 148–9; Torres Strait Fisheries Agreement, 101; Treasury, 73; vocational education and training, 162, 165; *see also* Borbidge Nat.–Lib. government; Goss ALP government

Rae Committee (1974), 112–13

rail transport reform, 3, 35, 38–40, 43, 47, 79, 82, 86, 102, **133–9**, 140; *see also* National Rail Corporation

recession (early 1990s), 36, 43, 90

regional differences, 128, 171

INDEX

regulatory reform, 68, 129, 188; *see also* Mutual Recognition Scheme; road transport reform; uniformity and harmonisation

Reserve Bank, 73

responsibilities, *see* overlap and duplication

revenues, *see* financial relations; tax revenues

road-funding arrangements, 98–101

road transport reform, 1, 6, 14, 35, 44, 62, 68, **75–81**, 124–5, 130, 132–3, 151–2, 155–6, 187–8; compensation, 143; joint schemes, 38–40, 42, 76, 78–81, **140–50**; uniform charges, 38–40, 42, 76, 78–9, 140–1, **142–4**, 145–6, 148–50; uniform regulations, 94, 140–1, 143, **144–50**

Rocla Concrete Pipes case (1971), 112

roles, *see* overlap and duplication

Rudd, Kevin, 65, 75

rules, *see* protocols

Rundle government, *see* Groom–Rundle Lib. governments

Russell, Don, 75

Sawer, Geoffrey, 23

school education, 12–14, 55

securities law, *see* companies and securities law

Sharman, Campbell, 97, 104, 186

Simeon, Richard, 24

Snowy Mountains Commission, 109

Social Welfare Ministers' Conference, 156

South Australia: companies and securities law, 115–16; Ministerial Councils, 109; Murray–Darling river system, 100, 109–11; mutual recognition scheme, 127; rail transport reform, 102, 133–6, 139; road transport reform, 78, 81, 143–4; SPC/COAG process, 47–9; State Bank, 45, 48; *see also* Bannon–Arnold ALP governments; Brown–Olsen Lib. governments

Special Conference of Ministers for Training (1989–90), 159–60

Special Premiers' Conferences (SPC) duplication and overlap, 154–7, 173–4 history and character, x, 1, 4, 7–8, 11, 23, 25–6, 29–32, 35, **36–44**, 46, 49, 53, 59–60 machinery and processes, 63, 65–76, 81, 86, 89–91, 93, 99, 104, 109, 120–2, 124, 132, 140, 151 meetings: Brisbane (October 1990), 4, 14, 36, **36–9**, 40, 64, 67–8, 72–3, 76, 78–9, 125, 133, 155, 157, 174; Sydney (July 1991), **39–40**, 68, 71, 79–81, 125, 133, 138, 141–2, 156; Adelaide (November 1991), 39, **40–4**, 64, 68, 126, 174

reform record, 181–6

special-purpose payments: companies and securities law, 117; competition policy, 50–2, 129; disability services, 156–7; history and machinery, 17, 37, 92, **97–100**, 101–2, 107; reform, 14, 16, 20, 27, 29, 36–40, 50–2, 54, 93, 153, 155–6, 179; road transport, 40, 156; roads, 141, 143–4; vocational education and training, 160, 163–4, 172–3

standards, *see* Mutual Recognition Scheme; uniformity

Standards and Curriculum Council, 166

Standing Committee of Attorneys-General, 112

state enterprises, *see* public enterprises

Steering Committee, *see* Commonwealth–State Steering Committee

Stone, Shane, *see* Northern Territory CLP governments

structural efficiency principle, 42

structural reform, *see* economic reform

Sturgess, Garry, 36, 64–5, 71, 75

subsidiarity principle, 26, 42

Sumner, Christopher, 109

Supported Accommodation Assistance Program, 155, 175

TAFE systems, 43–4, 74–5, 159–60, 163–4, 167, 169–73

Taplin, John, 94

tariffs, 32

Tasmania: companies and securities law, 112; dairy industry assistance, 108; rail system, 136, 139; road transport reform, 141, 143–4; *see also* Field ALP government; Groom–Rundle Lib. governments

tax revenues, 16–17, 19, 27, 30, 35, 37, 41, 44, 48, 51–5, 57–9, 62, 76, 87–8, 141–5

Taxation Task Force, 58

Taylor Review (ANTA Agreement), 166–8

technical and further education, *see* TAFE systems

technological change, 6, 112

template legislation, *see* adoptive legislation

tied grants, *see* special-purpose payments

INDEX

207

Torres Strait Fisheries Agreement (1984), 100–1

trade barriers (interstate), 1, 3, 32, 46–8, 76, 130, 185, 189

trade practices, 42, 81–4, 88, 129

trade unions, 71, 74, 97, 160, 167–8

training, *see* vocational education and training

Training Cost Review Committee (Deveson Report, 1990), 159

transition funds, *see* growth funds

transport policy, 77, 133, 153, 183, 185, 188; *see also* rail transport reform; road transport reform

Transport Workers Union, 97

Treasury (Commonwealth), 49, 55, 73

Treasury Departments (states), 52, 66, 73, 75, 98, 165

treaties, 44, 53, 55, 68, 124, 126–7, **131**

unemployment, *see* labour market programs

Uniform Companies Acts (1961–62), 112

Uniform Credit Laws Agreement, 124, **128–9**

uniformity and harmonisation, 4, 7, 11, **20–2**, 31, 35, 38, 41, 77–8, 92–4, 103, 119, 182–3; companies and securities law, 112–19; competition policy, 132; competitive federalism, 29; cooperative federalism, 10–11, 15–16, 25, 38, 42, 73, 87, 89; environmental policy, 128; food standards, 125–6; gun laws, 1, 56–7, 190; non-bank financial institutions, 125; road transport charges, 141, **142–4**, 152; road transport regulations, 77, 81, 94, **144–50**, 187; standards and regulations, 126–7; vocational education and training, 160

unilateralism, 96, 118, 127, 131, 163, 166, 172, 183, 186

unions, 71, 74, 97, 160, 167–8

United Nations Draft Declarations, 131

United States, 97, 118

utilities, *see* public enterprises

Vehicle Standards Advisory Committee, 77

vertical fiscal imbalance, 11, **16–20**, 25, 27, 38–9, 41, 43, 53–6, 58–9, 154, 185

vetos, *see* protocols

Victoria: companies and securities law, 115–18; financial institutions, 33, 73; Murray–Darling river system, 100, 108–11; mutual recognition scheme, 126–7; rail transport reform, 133–6, 138; road transport reform, 62, 77, 79, 140–1, 143, 147, 149; SPC/COAG process, 68, 183; vocational education and training, 74, 162–4, 169, 172; *see also* Cain–Kirner ALP governments; Kennett Lib. government

vocational education and training, 15, 43–5, 55, 74, 100, 124–5, 154–5, **158–73**, 177–9, 183, 185, 188, 190

voting rules, *see* protocols

Warhurst, John, 66, 92

water resources, 68, 82, 94, 100, 109–12, 124, 130–2, 183

welfare services, 53, 72, 156

Weller, Patrick, 67, 70, 89

Western Australia: COAG process, 185; companies and securities law, 112, 115–18; competition policy, 86–7; Parliament, 127, 137–9; rail transport reform, 133–6; road transport reform, 62, 79–80, 140, 142–4, 149–50; WA Inc., 137; *see also* Court Lib. government; Lawrence ALP government

Westminster system, 92, 186

Wheare, K.C., 12

Whitlam ALP government (1972–75), 97, 112

whole-of-government capacity, 65–6, 69–70, 78

Willis, Ralph, 84

Wiltshire, Ken, 13, 22

Working Group on Commonwealth–State Roles and Responsibilities, 50, 174

working groups, *see* committees

working rules, *see* protocols

Wran, Neville, 71

Wran–Unsworth ALP governments (1980s), 33, 37

Yeatman, Anna, 158

For EU product safety concerns, contact us at Calle de José Abascal, 56–1°, 28003 Madrid, Spain or eugpsr@cambridge.org.